The social face of the regulatory state

MANCHESTER
1824
Manchester University Press

The social face of the regulatory state

Reforming public services in Europe

Sandra Eckert

Manchester University Press

Published by Manchester University Press
Altrincham Street, Manchester M1 7JA

www.manchesteruniversitypress.co.uk

British Library Cataloguing-in-Publication Data
A catalogue record for this book is available from the British Library

Library of Congress Cataloging-in-Publication Data applied for

ISBN 978 0 7190 9031 8 hardback

First published 2015

Typeset
by Carnegie Book Production, Lancaster
Printed in Great Britain
by CPI Group (UK) Ltd, Croydon, CR0 4YY

To my parents

Contents

Figures and tables

Figures

Tables

Acknowledgements

More than ten years ago I came to the European University Institute in Florence to join a research project led by Adrienne Héritier, with some vague ideas for the PhD project I was embarking on. Influenced by an emerging literature on governance in the European Union, I had thought of studying coordination processes in the area of European social or macroeconomic policy. Adrienne diverted my interest to an area of study I had not thought of previously, that is public service reforms in the European multi-level context. She suggested that it would be worthwhile covering postal reforms because there was a lot of political resistance to change in this area, and because few political scientists had so far paid special attention to this sector. This suggestion was the starting point of an intellectual journey which oscillated between the peculiarities of postal reform in Europe and beyond, and more general trends in regulation and capitalism. Many people have accompanied and supported me during this journey, which resulted in a PhD dissertation defended at the Free University Berlin, several journal articles and this book. Adrienne gave the decisive impulse for the selection of the topic as well as an enduring interest in comparative public policy. She accompanied the project with thoughtful input and comments, notably in her function as the second reader of my PhD thesis. My PhD supervisor Tanja A. Börzel taught me to design a research project, and to bring it to completion within a reasonable period of time. I am highly grateful for Tanja's support in my research and my academic development, and the role model she gives in sticking things through. Without the encouragement of Waltraud Schelkle, whom I encountered during my graduate studies at the London School of Economics and Political Science, I would not have embarked on writing a PhD thesis in the first place. For this as well as her continued interest in my projects she deserves a special line of gratitude.

Throughout the process of writing my PhD thesis and this book I have presented my work on many occasions and received insightful comments and suggestions for improvement. In particular, I would like to thank the participants of the following events: the workshop on 'The determinants of policy change' during the 2007 Joint Sessions of Workshops in Helsinki; the conferences organised in 2007 and 2009 by the Global Postal Research and Educational Network at the École Polytechnique Fédérale de Lausanne; the conference on 'The role of the state in public service delivery' at the Lee Kuan Yew School of Public Policy in Singapore in 2007; the workshop on 'Rethinking capitalist governance after the crises' organised in cooperation with the Social Science Research Center Berlin and the Free University Berlin by Dieter Plehwe and David Levi Faur; the workshops organised during the conferences of the European Consortium of Political Science Standing Group on Regulatory Governance in 2010 and 2012; the workshops organised by the research network on Regulation & Governance during the Society for the Advancement of Socio-Economics annual conference in 2013 in Milan; the workshop on 'The future of the regulatory state: adaptation, transformation or demise?' organised by Nick Sitter and Martin Lodge in cooperation with the IPSA Structure & Organization of Government group at the BI School of Management in Oslo in 2011; and the 'Third Florence conference on the regulation of infrastructures: taking stock of current challenges' organised by the Florence School of Regulation at the European University Institute in 2014. I also owe much to my fellow researchers who have discussed my work during the PhD colloquia led by Adrienne Héritier at the European University Institute, and by Tanja Börzel at the Free University Berlin. Helpful input has furthermore been provided during presentations of the book project to the participants of the research college 'The Transformative Power of Europe' in Berlin and to my colleagues at the department of social science at the University of Osnabrueck. I would like to particularly thank Nicole Bolleyer, Amber Davis, Burkard Eberlein, Hanan Haber, Lisbeth Hooghe, Andrea Lenschow, David Levi-Faur, Diana Panke, Waltraud Schelkle, Vivien Schmidt, Carina Sprungk, Mark Thatcher and Ingeborg Tömmel for providing comments at various stages during the project, or reading drafts and parts of the manuscript. Two anonymous reviewers for Manchester University Press provided insightful and constructive comments which helped me improve the manuscript.

Financial support to conduct this research is gratefully acknowledged. Funding has been received from the European Union in the framework of the FP 7 project on 'New Modes of Governance' (NEWGOV) coordinated at the European University Institute, and the German Research Council in the context of the Research College 'The Transformative Power of Europe' at the Free University Berlin. I am also grateful for financial support received to cover travel expenses when holding positions at the Center for European Integration of the Free University Berlin, the Chair for European

Integration at the University of Osnabrueck, and the Chair for Political Science and Contemporary History at the University of Mannheim. Helpful research assistance has been provided by Anja Durovic, Philipp Schinz, Jenna Schulte and Tanja Tanita Stamm. Many policy practitioners have shared their valuable insights on reform and regulation in the public utilities during various rounds of interviews conducted in Berlin, Bonn, Brussels, Paris, London and Singapore between 2007 and 2013. Without their experience on the ground I would not have been in a position to write this book. Finally, I would like to thank the staff at Manchester University Press for their editorial advice and guidance throughout the project.

On a more personal note I would like to express my gratitude to my colleagues, friends and family members. Beate Reifenberger has been more than an invaluable colleague to me, providing advice on many occasions. Nicole Bolleyer, Tanja Börzel, Jana Costas, Andrea Herrmann, Isabel Kusche, Andrea Lenschow, Diana Panke, Ingeborg Tömmel and Vera van Hüllen have not only been intellectual companions, but have become close friends over the years. Without Nicole urging me to submit my book proposal and the hands-on advice provided by Diana I would probably never have managed to realise the project and, in any case, things would have been much more difficult without the incessant encouragement from my colleagues and friends. During the years of completing this project and luckily much before, Daniel Panajotow offered the wonderful combination of optimism, support and a sense of perspective. As Daniel became a part of my life, his parents Imke and Lüdmil have supported me in my endeavours, and I am indebted to all three of them. My brother Ralf Eckert has accompanied my path from the outset, and I know I can always count on him and his family. Last and most important, I thank my parents, Doris and Siegfried Eckert, for their unconditional and loving support. It is amazing how they have had confidence in me no matter what I chose to do in life. It is to them that I dedicate this book.

Abbreviations

AE *Agence Europe*
AGV *Arbeitgeberverband Postdienste* (Employers' Association of Postal Services)
ARCEP *Autorité de Régulation des Communications Électroniques et des Postes* (Authority for the Regulation of Electronic Communications and Postal Services)
ART *Autorité de Régulation des Télécommunications* (Authority for the Regulation of Telecommunications)
BKartA *Bundeskartellamt* (Federal Competition Authority)
BNetzA *Bundesnetzagentur für Elektrizität, Gas, Telekommunikation, Post und Eisenbahnen* (Federal Network Agency for Electricity, Gas, Telecommunications, Post and Railway)
BT British Telecoms
CDU *Christliche Demokratische Union* (Christian Democratic Union)
CEPT *Conférence Européenne des Administrations des Postes et des Télécommunications* (European Conference of Postal and Telecommunications Administrations)
CERP *Comité Européen de Réglementation Postale* (European Committee for Postal Regulation)
CFDT *Confédération Française Démocratique du Travail* (French Democratic Confederation of Labour)
CFE-CGC *Confédération française de l'encadrement-Confédération Générale des Cadres* (The French Confederation of Management-General Confederation of Executives)
CFTC *Confédération Française des Travailleurs Chrétiens* (French Confederation of Christian Workers)
CGPT *Christliche Gewerkschaft Postservice und Telekommunikation* (Christian Union Postal Services and Telecommunications)

CGT	*Confédération Général du Travail* (General Confederation of Labour)
CMA	Communications Managers Association
CME	coordinated market economy
COM	European Commission
CSSPpt	*Commission Supérieure du Service Public des Postes et Télécommunications* (Higher Commission on Public Services in Telecoms and the Postal Sector)
CSU	*Christlich-Soziale Union in Bayern* (Christian Social Union in Bavaria)
CWU	Communication Workers Union
DG	Directorate General (European Commission)
DPAG	*Deutsche Post Aktiengesellschaft* (German Post Stock Corporation)
DPG	*Deutsche Postgewerkschaft* (German Postal Workers' Union)
DPVKOM	*Deutsche Kommunikationsgewerkschaft* (German Postal Association Communication Workers' Union)
DPWN	*Deutsche Post* World Net
EC	European Communities
ECJ	European Court of Justice
EP	European Parliament
EU	European Union
FDP	*Freie Demokratische Partei* (Free Democratic Party)
FO	*Confédération Général du Travail-Force Ouvrière* (General Confederation of Labour-Workers' Force)
GDR	German Democratic Republic
GNBZ	*Gewerkschaft der Neuen Brief- und Zustelldienste* (Union of New Mail and Delivery Services)
HL	House of Lords
IP	press releases published by the European Commission
IPO	initial public offer
KfW	*Kreditanstalt für Wiederaufbau* (Development Bank)
LME	liberal market economy
MEP	Member of European Parliament
MP	Member of Parliament
NAO	National Audit Office
NCC	National Competition Council
NCU	National Communications Union
ÖTV	*Gewerkschaft Öffentliche Dienste, Transport und Verkehr* (Public Services and Transport Union)
POEU	Post Office Engineering Union
Postcomm	Postal Services Commission

PTT	*Postes, Télégraphes et Téléphones* (Post, Telegraph and Telephone)
PUDLV	*Post-Universaldienstleistungsverordnung* (Ordinance on the postal universal service)
RegTP	*Regulierungsbehörde für Telekommunikation und Post* (Regulatory Agency for Telecommunications and Postal Services)
SEC	documents of the European Commission which cannot be classified in any of the other series
SGEIs	services of general economic interest
SGIs	services of general interest
SHEX	Shareholder Executive
SME	state-led market economy
SOP	*Syndicat des Opérateurs Postaux* (Association of Postal Operators)
SPD	*Sozialdemokratische Partei Deutschlands* (Social Democratic Party of Germany)
SUD	*Solidaire, Unitaire, Démocratique* (Trade Union Solidary, Unitary, Democratic)
TEC	Treaty establishing the European Communities
TFEU	Treaty on the Functioning of the European Union
UCW	Union of Communication Workers
UNSA	*Union nationale des syndicats autonomes* (National Union of the Autonomous Labour Unions)
UPU	Universal Postal Union
UPW	Union of Post Office Workers
USO	universal service obligation
USP	universal service provider
USPS	United States Postal Services
VAT	value added tax
ver.di	*Vereinte Dienstleistungsgewerkschaft* (German Trade Union for the Public and Private Services Sectors)
VoC	varieties of capitalism

1

Introduction

Capitalism in Europe is transformed as a result of liberalisation, privatisation and regulatory reform in the public utilities. European law has required market opening and institutional change in key sectors such as telecoms, energy and transport, which has often had an additional indirect effect taking the form of corporatisation and privatisation of public operators. How individual countries go about the policy challenges posed by such change is a fascinating question from a comparative capitalism perspective. Do varieties of capitalism translate into varieties of public service reform? The obvious answer would be yes, since liberal market economies such as Britain or the United States have formed the vanguard of an international reform movement. Change in the liberal model is supposed to be driven by market dynamics, which is why public monopolies and state intervention are at odds with this type of capitalism. Surprisingly, liberal market economies have long maintained such structures in a key sector of their national economies: Countries that have been the first movers in telecoms and energy reform, such as Britain, have not been leaders in postal reform. Tackling the privatisation of many public utilities and dismantling trade unions across the board, Margaret Thatcher shied away from engaging in postal reform, and subsequent governments followed her example.

The initial public offer (IPO) of Royal Mail in 2013 thus constituted a landmark change. In a first phase of postal reform opposition in Britain resembled the degree of resistance change had met in all public sectors in France and most of the southern European countries. By contrast, Germany and the Scandinavian countries, which had followed the British example in other sectors, formed the vanguard of the European postal reform movement. Germany, for instance, engaged in meaningful domestic reform from the 1980s onwards, corporatising and privatising its telecoms and postal incumbents at about the same time, and roughly three decades before the British dared to tackle Royal Mail's privatisation. From a comparative capitalism perspective the question arises why national economies adopt different reform approaches across sectors and over time.

This leads me to the second research topic of this book, which asks how the emerging regulatory state protects consumers and employees. Unravelling the state as service provider and employer poses significant social policy challenges to the emerging regulatory state, though to a different degree, and relating to different aspects across sectors. In the telecoms sector the social impact of reform has been framed predominantly in a positive way by policy makers, who have been emphasising the benefits of liberalisation policies for consumers in terms of a wider range of choices and lower prices. The employment effects have mostly been sidelined by consumer-related issues, which take on new forms in the digital age, such as data protection and network equality. European policy makers have been consistently keen on developing and expanding the supranational regulatory framework in the area of electronic communications, seeking to sell the consumer benefits as achievements of the Single European Market. The situation has been completely different in the low-tech and labour intense postal sector. The benefits for private consumers – leaving big business customers aside – are not as obvious as in telecoms, and postal reform has more often than not made headlines in relation to service cut-backs in mail delivery and the closure of local post offices. What is more, the so-called last mile, which is the delivery of postal items to individual households, involves human manpower that cannot be substituted. Postal delivery is a proximity service in a classical sense – it is about people serving other people. The postwomen and postmen, visibly delivering their service to our doorstep, enjoy quite some sympathy among their fellow citizens, and slogans such as 'hands off our postman' are unheard of in other sectors.

Social challenges are also prominent in another public utility – that is the energy sector, with its heavy and costly infrastructure and the increasingly scarce resources it draws upon. Here the benefits of liberalisation for the end consumer are most disputable in the face of rising energy prices and persisting shortcomings in security of supply. Compared to the telecoms sector the European liberalisation agenda has been a relative failure, not only with respect to the initial promise to provide cheaper energy across member states, but also with regards to the creation of a truly integrated energy market. Employment related issues have become a topical issue especially in the context of the economic and financial crisis, although not with respect to the social effects of liberalisation for employees in the sector, but instead with regards to the detrimental effect of rising energy prices on job creation and growth in the wider economy. In that context, socioeconomic rationales currently tend to outperform environmental goals of policymaking, where competitiveness and affordability issues dominate many policy debates, including those on clean energy. In view of these topical issues, it is high time to reconsider the social face of the regulatory state.

Adopting a comparative capitalism approach

The starting point to adopt a comparative capitalism approach is the double observation that the wider socioeconomic context will influence the reform choices adopted by distinct varieties of capitalism, while change in the public sectors is likely to have broader consequences for pre-existing capitalist regimes. Once the state stops providing and financing services of general interest such as letter mail, telecoms or energy directly, this alters the public-private divide where the state embraces a new role as a hands-off regulator who steers at a distance. The way in which this new setting materialises is, however, expected to vary in line with the role of the state in the national economy prior to reform as well as with established practices of interaction with business and organised labour. A highly interventionist state will not cease its powers in shaping industrial policy from one day to another, while a very weak state with limited capacity may find it hard to effectively steer policies from a distance. The upshot is to say that varieties of capitalism are expected to translate into varieties of reform.

This book therefore adds to a comprehensive body of literature studying newly emerging regulatory regimes in various sectors and countries, yet it complements existing research with a shift in perspective. Regulatory reform has been studied by political scientists from a comparative administrative perspective seeking to identify converging trends in the institutional design of emerging regimes (Héritier and Coen, 2005). Or different forms of internationalisation have been analysed as to their impact on domestic reform (Thatcher, 2007a), with a specific focus on European market making policies (Smith, 2005b). Although differences between regulatory regimes have attracted considerable attention in this literature (Héritier and Coen, 2005), a conceptual framework general enough to systematically capture variation across time and space has not been developed. Rather than inducing such an explanatory account from a limited set of empirical evidence, the book builds on the varieties of capitalism framework (Hall and Soskice, 2001a). Drawing on various efforts to bridge research on regulation and capitalism (Eckert, 2010; Schmidt, 2002; Thatcher, 2007c), the book adds to discussions about the explanatory power of country typologies in comparative capitalist research (Hancké, 2009; Hancké et al., 2007a), and broadens their scope into the realm of public service reform. In particular, the analysis of public service reforms relates to the question of change and the explanatory challenge this poses for the historical institutionalist typology (Streeck and Thelen, 2005a), which assumes that countries will follow their distinct paths due to the comparative advantages entailed. The different reform patterns we find across sectors furthermore point to variation within national capitalism (Atkinson and Coleman, 1989: 49; Freeman, 1986; Hollingsworth et al., 1994a: 8–9, 273–9; Levi-Faur, 2006a: 367–9), which poses another challenge to the typological approach.

The book claims that distinct patterns of interest intermediation and state-economy relations determine the politics of reform, but that these vary significantly across time and sectors. Here the book builds on conceptual innovations in the literature. Hancké et al. (2009: 290–3) have suggested situating countries with respect to state-economy relations and the density of interest organisation into different categories as the two key dimensions of capitalism. Along this line of argumentation, liberal market economies (LMEs) and coordinated market economies (CMEs) are situated in the same category of arm's length state-economy relations, yet combine with fragmented (LME) versus dense (CME) interest organisation. I furthermore take on board Schmidt's (Schmidt, 2002, 2008) suggestion to add a third variety, that is, a state-led market economy (SME), to the dichotomy. SMEs share fragmented interest organisation with LMEs, but differ from the other variants in cultivating close state-economy relations. It is expected that these capitalist types translate into variation in terms of timing, scope and dynamics of reform: SMEs are expected to be reform laggards, where reform dynamics and outcomes are controlled by the state; CMEs are expected to take a middle position, where change is interest-driven and moderate; LMEs are expected to be reform leaders, engaging in market-driven and comprehensive change. The book furthermore expands this conceptual framework to the analysis of policymaking in the public service sectors, and in so doing adopts a governance perspective. In line with close state-economy relations political regulation constitutes the best match with SMEs; dense interest organisation privileges corporatism in CMEs; fragmented interest organisation, as well as a hands-off approach, leave ample leeway to independent regulation in LMEs.

These patterns are, however, not expected to hold in each and every case. Rather, empirical evidence has taught us that national economies constitute 'complex amalgams' characterised by discontinuities and variation across policy fields (Crouch, 2009: 90). This observation is particularly relevant for postal policies in LMEs, which continued to be characterised by relatively close state-economy relations and dense patterns of interest organisation for a considerable period of time, while other parts of the economy changed drastically. Such policy stability in the postal sector may appear as an anachronism in the overall LME context, and may even be seen as a legitimate reason to refute the typological approach as such. At a closer look, however, it can be seen that the reasons behind this pattern reside in the very nature of the liberal regime. The LME-type lacks the transmission belts to effectively seek support for socially costly change, very much like SMEs do in the absence of strongly organised interests. Rather than pushing through unwanted change, governments have thus chosen to abstain from reform. Ultimately, the limited policy capacity of liberal capitalism in addressing social concerns has caused postal reform deadlock for significant periods of time.

Tackling the social dimension of the regulatory state

Public service reform has become a dominant phenomenon in Europe and internationally, and has attracted considerable attention in academic research. It has been widely acknowledged that liberalisation and privatisation have triggered an ongoing process of reregulation, specifically in terms of regulation for competition. Compared to the mid-1990s, when Majone first coined the term of the 'regulatory state' (Majone, 1994), regulatory capitalism has diffused globally (Levi-Faur, 2005) and regulation has become a major subject of interdisciplinary research (Lodge, 2008; Lodge et al., 2012). Regulation scholars have very much focused on the rationale behind economic regulation, while social regulation has attracted far less attention. Yet reforms have unravelled the state as a service provider and employer, an evolution which combines with a widespread trend of welfare state retrenchment. Consequences of reform on employment and service provision have been addressed (Héritier and Schmidt, 2000), but these issues have not taken centre stage in the political science literature.

This lacuna is astonishing, given that legal scholars in particular have acknowledged that regulation in practice may be a suitable means to further social solidarity (Prosser, 2006) and realise public interest goals (Croley, 2008). Yet the regulatory governance literature frequently draws a general line between those sectors and institutions mainly involving economic regulation and others that mainly involve social regulation. Findings of quantitative cross-sector analysis suggest that social regulators have less institutional independence in comparison to economic regulators and that the realm of social regulation is more politicised (Gilardi, 2005: 141, 151–3; Wonka and Rittberger, 2010: 745). This qualitative study shifts the focus towards the dynamics between economic and social regulation within sectors. Adopting a governance perspective, it furthermore seeks to capture the complexity of policymaking in institutional and procedural terms. The role of regulation in realising social policy goals has more recently attracted the interest of political scientists (Levi-Faur, 2013). For instance, the regulatory underpinning of the welfare state has been researched in the area of old-age security, drawing on analogies from reform experience in the utilities (Leisering and Mabbett, 2011). This book takes a closer look at the flipside of the coin, which is the redistributive underpinning of the regulatory state.

A key claim is that the emerging regulatory state does not simply replace the positive state as claimed by Giandomenico Majone (Majone, 1997), but rather coexists with more traditional forms of statism. I argue that the regulatory state is underpinned by redistribution, and that redistributive policies will therefore not disappear with the transition towards the regulatory state. Rather, redistributive policies constitute a fall-back option where regulation does not address social concerns, very much along the lines of the Polanyian double movement (Polanyi, 1957: 130). Another set of claims is about the role of distinct modes of regulation in addressing policy issues. The literature on regulatory economics highlighted the efficiency gains for economic regulation in depoliticised, delegated settings, while pointing to accountability risks involved where independent agencies engage in social regulation. Examining the role of independent regulation in the area of postal policy, I find that regulatory agencies are indeed reluctant to realise broader social goals particularly in the area of employment policy, while they consider regulation for competition as their core business. Employment related policy concerns do indeed form an unhappy marriage with the regulatory state, at least where the activities of independent regulatory agencies are concerned. This has important repercussions for the role of organised interests in the regulatory era. Here I argue that organised labour is in decline, while organised consumer interests are on the rise. The regulatory state forms a happy marriage with a market ideology that promotes consumer interests in an era of 'consumer capitalism' (Trumbull, 2006).

Postal reform in a comparative perspective

The empirical focus of this book is on change in the postal sector, but it puts such evidence into a broader perspective. Postal reform is a particularly insightful case for several reasons: it is a hard case for change due to its high degree of politicisation and social salience. Postal operators figure among the oldest institutions on a nation state's territory, they are historically among the biggest domestic employers with high levels of unionisation, and they have often provided critical social services. At the same time the letter mail business is not subject to technological innovation and internationalisation, and thus is rather insulated from commonly known exogenous pressures for change. One would therefore not expect sudden and massive change in this sector but, if at all, incremental reforms and path dependent developments. In addition, postal reform is puzzling when it comes to variation across countries. Liberal market economies, known as reform leaders in other public sectors, have sought to resist internationally diffused change. The reform experience in the sector hence contradicts received wisdom that reform triggers change towards the liberal model of capitalism and therefore causes less adaptation pressure for liberal, in comparison to other, regimes.

Another reason why postal reform merits special attention is that this sector has so far not taken first priority in the political science literature on public service reform. The amount of political science research which has been conducted on other sectors such as energy, rail or telecommunications (Bartle, 2002, 2005; Eberlein, 2012; Eising, 2002; Héritier and Coen, 2005; Jabko, 2006; Levi-Faur, 1999; Schneider, 2007; Schneider et al., 1994; Thatcher, 1999; Héritier et al., 2001) appears out of proportion when compared to the few publications dedicated to the postal sector, usually taking the form of small book chapters or sections in journal articles (Smith, 2001, 2005a; S.K. Schmidt, 2005; Thatcher, 2007b). By contrast, the sector has attracted extensive research by economists and lawyers. The sector has been analysed intensely from a competition law perspective (e.g. Geradin, 2002), and in particular in the economic literature on regulation. The specialists in regulatory economics Crew and Kleindorfer have published a series of edited volumes since the 1990s gathering input from annual conferences on postal economics and regulation (Crew and Kleindorfer, 1991, 2012). Regulatory economists often adopt a rather narrow vision of regulation and have been criticised as being 'obsessed by economic regulation', and they thus 'tend to ignore social regulation' (Ogus, 2004: 31, 38). The book therefore fills not only a disciplinary gap in the literature, by adding analysis from a political science perspective, but also a substantial gap, by focusing on social goals of regulation.

The empirical focus is on three varieties of postal reform, namely in France, Germany and Britain. These countries have been selected as coming closest to the ideal-typical distinction between liberal, coordinated and state-led market economies (Hall and Soskice, 2001a; Schmidt, 2008). The comparison of change in the same sector, but in three different socioeconomic settings shows what is specific about postal reform, but also what is specific about individual varieties of capitalism, as these engage in different reform paths and policy choices. These case studies are situated in a wider comparison of postal reform in Europe and internationally, dedicating particular attention to the reform record across varieties of capitalism. And beyond the peculiarities of postal reform this book addresses emerging regulatory regimes at the supranational and national level in the telecoms and electricity sectors to draw a broader panorama of public service reforms in Europe.

The structure of the book

Chapters 2 and 3 develop the conceptual framework for the empirical analysis conducted in the book. They introduce the reader to the research questions, theoretical framework and key concepts. Chapter 2 approaches public service reform from the angle of comparative capitalism. It presents the three types of capitalism examined in the book, and extends the typological distinction to the analysis of change in the public utilities. To this end a first section revisits the dichotomy developed by Hall and Soskice (2001a), contrasting LMEs and CMEs, and broadening its scope to include SMEs as a third type of capitalism. It situates these types along two dimensions, the role of the state and interest organisation, and shows where they overlap and differ. The distinction between three types of capitalism underpins the selection of country cases. The book studies France (SME), Germany (CME) and Britain (LME) as the three prototypes which come closest to the ideal-typical distinction between SMEs, CMEs and LMEs. I then go on to formulate specified expectations about how these types of capitalism translate into varieties of public service reform, differentiating between the timing, dynamics and scope of change. The chapter furthermore discusses the limits of a typological approach in addressing such change, which in the public service sectors takes the form of privatisation, liberalisation and regulatory reform. The question whether we observe common trends or persisting divergence in national capitalism continues to be of key interest (Jackson and Deeg, 2012), and relates to the wider question of institutional change (Streeck and Thelen, 2005a). Referring back to earlier contributions in the literature that have highlighted variation at the level of sectors rather than countries (Hollingsworth and Schmitter et al., 1994a), a last section discusses sector varieties of capitalism. Here I explain why a comparative study on change in one sector is insightful from a comparative capitalist perspective, and why the focus on postal reform is particularly relevant.

Chapter 3 links the comparative study to the interdisciplinary literature on regulation. It shows why the realisation of social policy goals in the age of regulation should be a key focus of political science research – that is, why we should study the social face of the regulatory state. The chapter revisits Majone's seminal thesis about the transition from a 'positive' to a 'regulatory state' (Majone, 1997). It pays tribute to the implications his argument bears in terms of the type of policies that are expected to prevail in the regulatory state as well as the type of institutions that should play the most prominent role. Here I discuss the assumed shift from redistribution to social regulation on the one hand, and from political to independent regulation on the other hand. I argue that regulation does not actually replace redistributive policies, and illuminate the role independent regulatory agencies may assume in the fields of economic and social regulation. What the shifts in policymaking and institutional arrangements imply for organised interests is discussed in a separate section, paying particular attention to the interests of businesses, consumers and employees. The chapter concludes by developing a governance perspective on policymaking in the public service sectors that links the regulatory state hypothesis to varieties of capitalism. To that end expectations are being formulated about how various modes of policymaking may be used to realise social goals in the postal sector, and how their relevance may vary across varieties of capitalism.

Chapter 4 introduces the European context for policymaking in the public utilities. It questions whether a European model of public service regulation has emerged throughout the process of supranational reregulation accompanying liberalisation in various sectors. The chapter compares the evolution of an EU-wide regulatory regime in three sectors, namely telecoms, postal and electricity since the late 1980s. Three phases of reregulation can be distinguished, an initial phase launching market opening in the public utilities (1988–98), an intermediary phase of reregulation (1999–2003), and a last phase of consolidating the regulatory regimes (2004–9). A concluding section discusses to what extent there is a European dimension to social regulation in these sectors, referring to aspects related to service provision and employment.

In-depth comparison of postal reform in three countries is conducted in Chapters 5, 6 and 7. These chapters cover developments from the late 1980s until 2013, and provide for original empirical material gathered through interviewing of stakeholders in all three countries. Chapter 5 explains why reform in France has come with delay and how the state-led model has accommodated change. It analyses how a predominant *service public* doctrine has shaped the reregulation of service provision and what role the social partners have played in a context of low union density and organisational fragmentation. Chapter 6 examines the German reform path, which can best be described as negotiated change. It shows how dense patterns of interest organisation in the coordinated variant have influenced reform choices and outcomes. However, it also questions to what extent postal corporatism is under threat in a liberalised environment and what the regulatory responses were to address this challenge. Chapter 7 discusses postal reform in Britain, which constitutes an outlier in the context of the liberal market economies. Why were the British not among the liberalisation and privatisation pioneers in this sector, and how did they eventually catch up with a diffusing reform movement? These are the key questions addressed in the analysis. The chapter illustrates that the context for reform in Britain in many ways deviated from typical LME patterns.

Chapter 8 engages in systematic comparison of postal reform in France, Germany and Britain. A first section summarises the politics of postal reform in those three countries, scrutinising the expectations formulated in Chapter 2 in the light of the empirical findings. It then goes on to elaborate on the extent to which the postal reform record in these three countries differs from change in the telecoms and electricity sectors, in order to delineate country-specificities from sector-specificities. The remainder of the chapter discusses the regimes of postal regulation that have emerged in the three countries, comparing them to postal policy and regulation in other EU member states. Chapter 9 broadens the scope of country comparison beyond the EU context and engages in international comparison of postal reform. Here particular emphasis is put on the varying reform record in liberal market economies, contrasting LME postal reform leaders and LME postal reform laggards. While New Zealand and Australia have taken the lead of the international postal reform movement, the situation in the United States and Canada has for a considerable time been characterised by reform deadlock. Interesting insights can furthermore be drawn from the contrasting reform experience in Asia, comparing change in the Japanese CME and the SME in Singapore. Under Koizumi Japan had engaged in a bold move towards privatisation, only to reverse reform some decades later. And in Singapore the postal market has been fully liberalised de jure, yet without meaningful policy change de facto. The chapter rounds up with a section on postal reform in emerging market economies in the Latin American context, which illustrates that the reform recipes developed in mature market economies may not apply in a different context.

Chapter 10 concludes on how the book contributes to research on comparative capitalism and regulation. It brings together the insights from the in-depth analysis of the politics of postal reform in three countries, and wider comparison conducted in Chapter 9, and positions them in the context of the research debates on varieties of capitalism. It also summarises the findings on social regulation in the public service sectors at the European and national level, and situates them with respect to the questions raised in the interdisciplinary literature on regulation. The chapter ends with the challenges ahead in public service regulation, such as declining mail volumes, the Internet society or energy poverty.

2

Public service reforms and comparative capitalism

Liberalisation and privatisation reforms have fundamentally changed the public service sectors in Europe and internationally. This transformation in key sectors of national economies has not left the wider socioeconomic architecture of capitalism untouched. The state no longer acts as a service provider and employer, it ceases to intervene directly into the economy, and instead adopts a hands-off approach in steering economic actors and markets. Yet the comparative literature teaches us that divergence persists despite such common trends. Adopting a comparative capitalism perspective raises the question whether varieties of capitalism translate into varieties of public service reform. In line with arguments about path dependence, the type and timing of reform, as well as reform outcomes, are expected to vary across capitalist regimes. In what follows, I develop a conceptual framework for the comparative analysis of reform processes across countries based on the varieties of capitalism typology, but also address the limits of a typological approach.

The role of the state and organised interests

Variation between regulatory regimes across countries and sectors has attracted considerable attention in political science research on public service reform (Héritier and Coen, 2005; Thatcher, 1999, 2007a; Héritier et al., 2001). When identifying explanatory variables to account for diverging outcomes, the literature has drawn on established concepts and theories from various subfields of political science such as comparative politics, policy analysis or administrative studies. The analysis conducted in this book bridges the rather separate literatures on regulation and comparative political economy (Eckert, 2010; Thatcher, 2007c). Comparative political economy as an academic discipline studies national political economies and seeks to explain variation systematically (Amable, 2003; Hall and Soskice, 2001a: 1; Lijphart and Crepaz, 1991;

Traxler et al., 2001). Typology formation has been a popular conceptual and methodological device in this endeavour, which seeks to strike the balance between the quest for parsimonious research designs and empirical complexity (Collier et al., 2012). If typologies bear explanatory power for national economies in their entireness, this should also apply to the area of public service reform. Types of capitalism should thus translate into types of reform. To date, the dichotomy developed by Hall and Soskice (Hall and Soskice, 2001a) has been most influential, with its catchy and simplistic distinction between liberal market economies (LMEs) and coordinated market economies (CMEs). The key argument is to say that distinct capitalist regimes continue to exist, and to function differently, in accordance with their underlying coordination mechanisms. LMEs are characterised by coordination through markets, as opposed to CMEs, which are characterised by extra-market coordination between public and private actors.

There has been a vivid debate around the varieties of capitalism approach (Crouch, 2009; Hancké et al., 2007a), questioning the adequacy of the initial dichotomy and discussing alternative typologies (Amable, 2003; Fioretos, 2011b; Schmidt, 2002). More precisely, the distinction between LMEs and CMEs has been criticised to result from an 'obsession with neoliberalism and a contrast between it and a model of "organised capitalism"' (Crouch, 2009: 89). In view of the research topic covered in this volume, the fact that the firm-centred approach developed by Hall and Soskice does not take into account the role of the state systematically, is of vital interest. The typology's 'relational view of the firm' (Hall and Soskice, 2001a: 6) aims to capture the strategic interactions among economic actors and does not attribute an architectonical role to the state (Hancké et al., 2007b: 15, 23–8; Hancké et al., 2009: 283, 293–9). This microlevel focus on the role of the firm stands in contrast, and potentially contradicts the ambition of the framework to account for 'the macrolevel picture of whole economies' (Crouch, 2009: 94). Such a narrow focus on the role of the firm in the capitalist architecture is at odds with the broader focus of the comparative capitalism literature, which predates the typology.

In the earlier literature the classic distinction was between three models of running an economy, namely statism, liberalism and corporatism (Katzenstein, 1978a; Shonfield, 1965). Integrating the state as a key actor into the conceptualisation is particularly relevant when researching public service reforms and regulation, where the latter can be understood as 'deliberate state influence' (Baldwin et al., 2012: 3). In order to account for the constitutive role of the state, concepts such as 'state-influenced capitalism' (Schmidt, 2008: 313) or 'etatism' (Hall, 1986: 164) have been discussed in the literature. In these capitalist regimes it is the state which steers economic activity in the absence of other coordinative mechanisms (Schmidt, 2008: 314). Complementing the initial dichotomy developed by Hall and Soskice, I thus take up Vivien Schmidt's (2008) suggestion to include state-led market economies (SMEs) as a third variety alongside LMEs and CMEs. I also build on the suggestion made by Hancké and others to situate country variation along two dimensions: variation with respect to the density of interest organisation on the one hand, and variation with respect to state-economy relations on the other hand (Hancké et al., 2009: 290–3). Integrating these two dimensions constitutes a link to the literature on corporatism and neo-corporatism (Berger, 1981; Crouch and Streeck, 2006; Goldthorpe, 1984; Schmitter, 1974; Schmitter and Lehmbruch, 1979), and to the role of the state as a classic theme in research on the political economy (Hayward, 1986; Levy, 2006; Sbragia, 2000; Smith, 1986; Weiss, 2003b). Figure 2.1 situates the three distinct varieties along these two dimensions, that is interest organisation, and the role of the state. While LMEs and SMEs are characterised by fragmented interest organisation, and thus overlap on this dimension, CMEs are characterised by dense interest organisation. By contrast, it is LMEs and CMEs that share a hands-off approach, which is why they overlap on the second dimension. Here SMEs stand apart with a stronger role attributed to state intervention compared to the other two varieties.

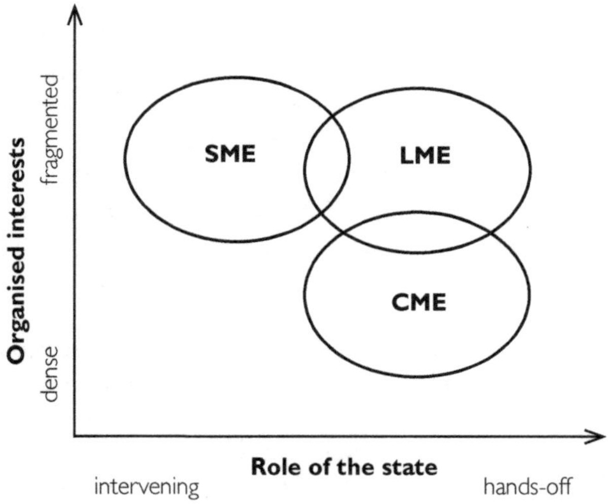

Figure 2.1: Three types of capitalism

The two dimensions not only allow us to systematically situate the three varieties with respect to commonalities and differences, but also relate to wider and classical debates in the political economy literature on the role of the state and organised interests. In a Musgravian sense, the state bears responsibility to further social welfare, namely through its allocative function by providing public goods, and through its stabilising function by correcting disequilibria, such as unemployment or precarious working conditions (Majone, 1993: 157; Musgrave and Musgrave, 1973).

From a comparative capitalism perspective, the role of the state is expected to vary. Such variation can be conceptualised along the four dimensions of statism which have been defined by Hall (1986: 164–5). Hall's notion of statism refers to the extent to which a state: a) operates as a cohesive unit; b) is insulated from societal demands; c) is capable to implement policy, if required imposing it on resistant social groups; and d) disposes of the political authority to speak for the public interest. According to Hall, the first dimension is about the extent to which a political and administrative apparatus of a state is unified. A greater degree of fragmentation will characterise political systems where the executive and the legislature are detached, or where sub-national units play an important role. Thus, distinct capitalist regimes could fall into the same category on this dimension, which strongly correlates with political system features. This also holds for the third dimension, as it relates to the governance capacity of the central political unit. The second dimension relates more directly to coordination mechanisms in national economies, which can attribute a more or less central role to societal interests. The absence of coordinative mechanisms also implies that non-coordinated economies will exhibit a greater need for detailed regulation and formalised contracts (Hall and Soskice, 2001a: 8).

While on the first three dimensions of statism LMEs and SMEs bear many similarities, there is a fundamental difference on the fourth dimension. The idea that the state disposes of the political authority to act in the public interest is at odds with liberalism from a normative point of view. Attributing such a central role to state intervention would undermine the allocative function of markets. In line with a hands-off approach privileged in liberal market economies, the state should thus only intervene in the case of market failure. The perception whether or not a government is acting in the public interest may also depend on its party affiliation. While in accordance with a left-right cleavage the expectation would be that a right-wing government will engage in more encompassing reform, a left-wing government may actually be in a better position to legitimise such change. Empirical research has indeed supported this 'party paradox' claim where government coalitions on the left have been pushing for more encompassing reforms compared to their conservative counterparts (Cioffi and Höpner, 2006). Such a capacity may be particularly relevant in LMEs and SMEs, as these varieties cannot rely to the same extent as CMEs on a transmission belt towards societal interests in order to legitimate change. And, vice versa, governments in the non-coordinated regimes do not rely to the same extent on organised interests – that is, a left-wing government would not to the same extent have to confront typical allies such as trade unions with unpopular change. By contrast, in CMEs parties would be expected to maintain strong links with organised interests – that is, a left-wing government would prove particularly responsive to the interests of trade unions. Such links may, however, also be used to engage in meaningful negotiations with the social partners, and thus be an asset for left-wing reform entrepreneurs.

Depending on their organisational capacity, private interests may play a central, at times even statutory, role in the national economy. Normatively speaking, a strong role for organised interests constitutes a mismatch with liberal regimes which consider private interest to be outside the public function (Crouch, 1986: 182). By contrast, they are at the core of corporatist, coordinated capitalist regimes. According to Hall and Soskice, CMEs are characterised by extra-market coordination (Hall and Soskice, 2001a: 8, 10). Such coordination presupposes dense patterns of interest organisation and limits the role of the state in the economy (Hancké et al., 2009: 291–2). The role that employer organisations and trade unions play in negotiating durable bargains on labour related issues has been analysed extensively by the neo-corporatist literature (Berger, 1981; Crouch and Streeck, 2006; Goldthorpe, 1984; Schmitter, 1974; Schmitter and Lehmbruch, 1979). Key economic interests are thus involved in shaping public policies, to the extent that they may complement, or even substitute, political action (Pierson, 2001: 7). In coordinated market economies, highly organised business actors are likely to engage in self-regulation (Hancké et al., 2009: 292). And in the industrial relations domain of national economies the social partners perform an important stabilising function by negotiating collective agreements. Coordinated regimes are characterised by industry-level bargains which require well organised unions and employers (Hall and Soskice, 2001a: 24–5).

It is undisputable that a typological distinction, which operates at the macrolevel of national economies, and differentiates between two rather broad dimensions, bears certain limitations. Other important dimensions may be overlooked or underrated, and the sketchy nature of conceptualisation may cause a bias towards overgeneralisation. On the other hand, this parsimonious conceptualisation constitutes a good starting point for more detailed empirical research. This may be an asset in view of the major setback of the rich literature on comparative capitalism, which has been that the various types of capitalism identified in the literature have often been derived inductively, rather than deductively, to match types and cases (Crouch, 2009). Since the empirical focus underlying such inductive concept development has been on mature capitalist regimes in the Western world, this poses important geographical limitations to the typology. With its empirical focus on change in France, Germany and Britain, the book does not overcome these limits. These countries have been considered as empirical prototypes for SMEs, CMEs and LMEs, and have very much underpinned concept formation, to the extent that the 'typical' features of the three variants tend to be overstated. While the core empirical analysis conducted here does not transgress the geographical limits of the typology, it does however point to the limits of the typological distinction to capture variation within national capitalism, where the sector studied deviates from expected patterns on several aspects. This being said, the consideration of international postal reform conducted in Chapter 9 does underpin the need to widen the conceptual framework beyond the remits of Western European and Northern American economies, considering change in Asian and Latin American emerging market economies. Here the book links to recent efforts to expand the geographical scope of the varieties of capitalism framework (Nölke and Claar, 2013; Nölke et al., 2014).

Types of capitalism and varieties of reform

In studying public service reform, the empirical focus of this book is on change, which constitutes a key challenge to research on comparative capitalism. The varieties of capitalism (VoC) framework has not been particularly helpful in overcoming this challenge, as it has contributed to a tendency to overemphasise stability, and to conceptualise feedback dynamics as being genuinely positive. Streeck and Thelen have argued that the VoC literature would therefore 'understate the magnitude and significance of current changes' (Streeck and Thelen, 2005b: 5). According to Pierson, the typology illuminates the distinct equilibria in different economies, but does not account for how these have emerged (Pierson, 2000: 264), a criticism shared by Crouch (Crouch, 1986). The typology does not clearly lean to one of the three neo-institutionalisms, although it owes much to the historical institutionalist idea of path dependence, which is a rather vague concept. A rationalist reading has been provided by Pierson (2000), who has established the notion of increasing returns as being central to explain continuity caused by self-reinforcing, positive feedback mechanisms. According to Thelen and Streeck, such equilibrium models can only incorporate change in the form of exogenous shocks into their line of reasoning (Streeck and Thelen, 2005b: 1). In her work on historical institutionalism, Thelen has sought to identify more sophisticated mechanisms to account for gradual institutional change beyond the dichotomy of path dependence and critical junctures (Mahoney and Thelen, 2010; Thelen, 1999). The varieties of capitalism framework is clearly more on the side of incremental change. It assumes that firms will engage in adaptation strategies through which they can sustain their comparative competitive advantages (Hall and Soskice, 2001a: 62–4). Hall and Soskice thus expect that 'institutional complementarities generate disincentives to radical change' (ibid.: 64).

Following this line of reasoning, the way in which distinct types of capitalism translate into types of public service reform should depend on the varying role of the state and organised interests throughout the reform process. Expectations for the timing, dynamics and scope of reform across these three types of capitalism are summarised in table 2.1: in SMEs the state will be the main actor in the process (i.e. where reform occurs, it will be state-driven). In CMEs organised interests are expected to play a key role given that the state rather adopts a hands-off approach (i.e. where reform occurs, it will be industry-driven). In CMEs reform processes will therefore be shaped by such organised interests, and the state will not be in position to simply impose change. Given the need to secure approval by powerful stakeholders, reform processes are likely to involve lengthy and comprehensive processes of negotiation, which is why coordinated economies are not expected to engage in fast-track reforms. In the absence of strongly organised interests and an intervening state, reform in the LME would be driven by market dynamics. Accordingly, the timing of reform would differ: privatisation and liberalisation reforms correspond to the market-driven logic in liberal regimes, which is why these countries should be reform leaders. By contrast, interventionism in state-led regimes constitutes the biggest mismatch with such change, which is why these countries should be reform laggards. CMEs would be situated in between, taking more time to agree on reform in the presence of strongly organised interests. Finally, the scope of change can be expected to vary across types, with encompassing and far-reaching change in LMEs (state-)controlled change in SMEs, and negotiated change in CMEs.

The validity of such country-specific expectations along the lines of national capitalist typologies is scrutinised on the basis of in-depth country comparison. The selection of country cases is an obvious choice according to the VoC typology. The book analyses postal reforms in Britain, Germany and France. The comparison therefore is about

Table 2.1: Three types of public service reform

	SMEs	CMEs	LMEs
Timing	laggard	hybrid	leader
Dynamics	state-driven	interest-driven	market-driven
Scope	controlled	moderate	comprehensive

countries which as prototypes empirically come closest to the ideal-typical distinction between liberal, coordinated and state-led market economies (Hall and Soskice, 2001a; Schmidt, 2008). Change in these countries will be operationalised with respect to three elements of reform which are discussed in the next section on privatisation, liberalisation and regulatory reform.

Privatisation, liberalisation and regulatory reform

The ways in which capitalism has transformed, and whether there are common trends or persisting divergence, remain topical questions in the literature. As discussed previously, the varieties of capitalism typology is better at explaining institutional continuity than at explaining change (Streeck and Thelen, 2005b: 6). What we should find if the VoC line of argumentation bears validity, however, is that common trends materialise differently across countries. This requires, first, that there is agreement on what these common trends in contemporary capitalism are. Streeck and Thelen have argued that liberalisation, understood as the 'secular expansion of market relations' (Streeck and Thelen, 2005b: 2) has been a prevailing trend in contemporary capitalism. Jackson and Deeg argue that 'growing *liberalization* in relation to the role of the state and a growing *segmentation* (dualization) in terms of employment conditions and social protection' (Jackson and Deeg, 2012: 1113) are the two common trends which can be observed in European capitalism. With respect to public service reform, it makes sense to differentiate among privatisation, relating to the ownership of service operators, liberalisation, which relates to the question whether services are provided under a monopoly or in a competitive situation, and regulatory reform as a third element, which relates to the allocation of policymaking powers.

Focusing on commonalities, rather than divergence, all three elements are expected to substantially change the role of the state. In the public service sectors the state used to play a central role across capitalist regimes. State intervention and public ownership were the predominant mode during the nineteenth and twentieth centuries for ideological, as well as strategic reasons (Milward, 2011). Prior to reform, the area of public services constituted a 'public space' (Crouch, 1986) for which political actors have claimed sole authority. Centralising the provision of public services such as telecommunications, post and rail has been a key element in the formation of nation states (Milward, 2011: 90–1). State involvement in the public utilities served various functions of geopolitical and social nature. In particular, it helped integrate citizens into the emerging national space, and was a means of engaging in national redistributive policies (Clifton et al., 2007: 661). The standard model of providing public services was through state monopolies, where regulation and operation of the sector were centralised within ministries. National incumbents providing postal and telecommunications services were among the biggest domestic employers and provided critical social services. Privatisation thus constitutes a major break with the past, where the state ceases to directly own and control critical infrastructure. Besides being a rollback of the state, privatisation also involves the expansion of the logic of financial markets once former public enterprises are traded on the stock market. More recent contributions have framed this trend as 'financialisation' (Epstein, 2005; Krippner, 2005). Researchers interested in this phenomenon analyse profitmaking through financial channels, the rising importance of shareholder value, the dominance of capital market financial systems, or the role played by financial trading and its new instruments.

Liberalisation also redraws the line between public and private tasks, ensuring the provision of public goods through competitive market mechanisms, rather than through central steering. As discussed in detail in Chapter 3, privatisation and liberalisation reforms have entailed the emergence of the regulatory state, where reregulation is required to steer the functioning of markets as well as the provision of public services. To make these new institutional settings work, regulatory reform reallocates policymaking competencies, which broadly speaking results in a hands-off approach of the state in steering these economic sectors.

Privatisation, liberalisation and regulatory reform will also alter the role of organised interests. When engaging in privatisation, states cease to be employers and thus also no longer directly interfere in employment conditions in these sectors. A major consequence is that the status of the workforce will change from civil servants to ordinary employees. The abolition of a public monopoly through privatisation and liberalisation clearly involves organisational segmentation on the side of the employer, which may also have repercussions for the organisational structure of employees' interests. Where de jure liberalisation results in de facto competition among various market players, this increases fragmentation among the social partners. Thus liberalisation clearly enhances trends of segmentation, that is, a changing role of organised capital and labour in modern political economies. Social partners have struggled hard to maintain sufficient levels of organisational capacity and density in order to keep their seat at the negotiation table, but often failed to do so. The decline of organised interests has been documented thoroughly in the literature (Iversen, 1999; Traxler et al., 2001; Visser, 2006), and various terms such as the 'end of organized capitalism' (Lash and Urry, 1987), the 'end of corporatism' (Lange et al., 1995) and the 'end of neo-corporatism' (Lash, 1985) have been used. The key observation is that extra-market coordination presupposes dense patterns of interest organisation. The destabilisation of established coordination mechanisms would thus come as a serious threat to coordinated capitalism. The question therefore arises whether coordination is stable over time, or can at least be replaced by functional equivalents, in order to maintain the complementarities which make up this type of capitalism.

The stability and longevity of interest organisation has become a classic in the literature on corporatism, and reoccurred in the discussions on neo-corporatism (Berger, 1981; Crouch and Streeck, 2006). The decline of both industry-wide collective bargaining and of the role of intermediary organisations which can be observed across Europe (Schmitter, 1991) puts the coordinated variant of capitalism under stress. Liberalisation and dualisation (Jackson and Deeg, 2012) are two interdependent trends enhancing the erosion of interest organisation. In the public service sectors trade unions traditionally played an important role relying on a strong organisational basis. In order to maintain organisational strength, there may be a merger of unions. Another corrective mechanism available in this context is to regulate wage levels and working conditions through political decisions rather than through collective bargaining. Such intervention may, however, additionally destabilise existing coordination, and goes against the principle of granting autonomy in wage bargaining, a highly esteemed principle in the coordinated variant.

Taken together, these trends could be seen as an evolution towards the liberal model at the cost of mechanisms prevalent in the coordinated and state-led regime, a shift which has been diagnosed in the literature (Lane, 2003). More specifically, liberalisation and privatisation would imply a rollback of the state; segmentation would lead to a decline of organisational capacity of business and employees, and thus undermine the role of organised interests. Liberalisation, privatisation and segmentation are processes which prevail in the public service sectors where former monopolies have been opened to competition, work patterns have changed and privatisation has led to new financing mechanisms and corporate logics. The diffusion of such change has been explained as a direct reaction to shortcomings of the nationalisation policies which dominated in the previous phase. New ideologies would have put into question existing policy assumptions, to the extent that reform enthusiasm from the 1970s onwards prevailed, and privileged radical reform over a more balanced approach (Clifton et al., 2007). Other explanations have emphasised the role of supranational and international institutions in this process. Supranational and international organisations such as the EU, the World Bank (e.g. Andres et al., 2007) or the Organisation for Economic Co-operation and Development (OECD, 2005) have promoted change, which can thus be conceptualised as Europeanisation, internationalisation and globalisation. The scope of such external influence does put into question the adequacy of comparative capitalist and welfare typologies which mainly distinguish between national types. While to some extent the policy areas studied by comparative capitalism scholars continue to be mainly shaped within national (welfare) states (Crouch, 2009: 91), the impact of the supranational and international level has been underplayed in this literature. The empirical delineation between Europeanisation and globalisation is tedious, yet it can be argued that Europeanisation as a process is more tangible (Schmidt, 2002: 41–2, 303–5). Thatcher, by contrast, conceptualised the European influence as a specific form of internationalisation (Thatcher, 2007a). A few authors have suggested transgressing the national level as the major unit of analysis by privileging a multi-level perspective. Fioretos, for instance, has sought to systematically integrate multilateralism into his comparative analysis of European capitalism (2011b); Whitley and colleagues consider national and international levels as being mutually constitutive (Morgan et al., 2005).

Contrasting with the convergence hypothesis, which is often underpinned by a diagnosed predominance of neoliberal ideas, a diverse community of scholars emphasises persisting divergence. The VoC literature contributes to this strand, as the typology points to the stability of non-liberal regimes. Proponents of 'regulatory capitalism' agree with VoC scholars on the absence of a common trend towards neoliberalism, which according to their interpretation turns out to be a 'fairytale' (Braithwaite, 2008a: 5). Rather, the transition towards regulatory capitalism would constitute an alternative choice to neoliberalism and deregulation (Braithwaite, 2008a: 4–12; Levi-Faur and Jordana, 2005). Although the emergence of regulation and regulatory capitalism is seen as a dominant and prevailing trend (discussed in further detail in Chapter 3), this strand of literature does point to a considerable degree of cross-country divergence. Such persisting divergence has also been acknowledged by political economists who have emphasised the role of internationalisation, arguing that rather than leading to convergence, it leads instead to the emergence of hybrids through processes of recombination (Deeg and Jackson, 2007; Fioretos, 2011b: 155–8). Similar conclusions have been drawn by the scholars studying Europeanisation. This research community has argued that cross-country divergence persists, despite the increasing importance of the European level (Börzel, 2005; Börzel and Risse, 2006; Héritier et al., 2001; Lütz, 2004; Risse et al., 2001). In view of the similar thrusts of these argumentations with respect to divergence, a few contributions have bridged the two rather distinct perspectives on Europeanisation and comparative capitalism (Menz, 2005; V. Schmidt, 2002, 2005).

Sector varieties of capitalism

Setting apart the problem that there may be significant variation over time, which undermines the accuracy of supposedly stable national types, the typological approach poses another problem, which is its macrolevel focus. The approach certainly has merits in terms of parsimonious explanations, and arguably the nation state also continues to be strongly influential on capitalist and regulatory governance (Hollingsworth and Streeck, 1994: 271–3; Weiss, 2003a). Yet the focus on country-specificities comes at the cost of postulating 'virtually hermetically sealed national institutions' (Crouch, 2009: 91), and of neglecting the complexity and heterogeneity of (country) cases. It is thus worthwhile to consider 'heterogeneity within national models' (Deeg and Jackson, 2007: 155). Widely used categories such as strong versus weak states (Dyson, 1983; Katzenstein, 1978b) are therefore not appropriate to capture the complexity of state-society relations in modern political economies across the board (Atkinson and Coleman, 1989: 47–8). The explanatory power of national typologies with their focus on commonalities at the macrolevel has been seriously challenged from that perspective. National economies, it is argued, do not function along the lines of stylised ideal types, but form 'complex amalgams' (Crouch, 2009: 90). For instance, spatial variation within a national economy can be considerable, as for instance the literature on local economies illustrates (Crouch et al., 2001, 2004).

Another source of heterogeneity is mesolevel variation within national capitalism across sectors (Atkinson and Coleman, 1989: 49; Freeman, 1986; Hollingsworth et al., 1994a: 8–9, 273–9; Levi-Faur, 2006a: 367–9).

Organisational structures, for instance, may vary significantly across countries, sectors and over time (see also Crouch, 1986; Streeck, 2006; Schmitter and Streeck, 1985). It is thus conceivable 'to focus on the sector as the key unit for comparative analysis' (Hollingsworth et al., 1994c: 8). Sector-specific studies such as Campbell's work on postal reform have thus come up with their own typological distinctions operating at the level of sectors. Campbell distinguishes between four types of postal reform following a 'mercantilist', a 'national', a 'market', and a 'hybrid model' (Campbell, 2002). Introducing new types at the level of sectors does, however, increase conceptual complexity, and neglects the question how sector-specific patterns relate to the wider socioeconomic context.

On the basis of in-depth comparative analysis of reforms in one sector, this book seeks to differentiate between sector-generic features that hold validity across countries (Vogel, 1996: 258), as opposed to nation-specific features of a sector (Levi-Faur, 2006a: 369). Whether such nation-specific features in one sector match with macrolevel assumptions about national typologies, is a key concern. The extent to which nation-specific features hold across sectors is not at the core of the analysis, but is addressed in Chapter 8 where postal reform is compared to reform in the telecoms and electricity sectors in the three countries studied. The empirical focus is on a sector that constitutes a hard case for change, and where country-specific features may survive longer than in other areas. Postal services are not exposed to technological dynamics and internationalisation to the same extent as telecommunications services, and the markets remain largely national. Postal reform therefore constitutes a crucial case since it is unlikely that we encounter fast and far-reaching change in this highly politicised and entrenched sector, which is why path dependence should be particularly relevant. Expectations derived from the capitalist typology in terms of the timing, dynamics and scope of change should thus apply. The country chapters examine in detail how the role of the state has changed as a consequence of privatisation, liberalisation and regulatory reform. The role of organised interests is also at the core of the analysis, with a special focus on industrial relations.

3

The social face of the regulatory state

The emergence of a 'regulatory state' (Majone, 1994, 1996a, 1997) has been identified as a major trend across varieties of capitalism, and academic research on the theme has flourished. Over the past few decades regulation has become a prominent theme among political scientists, to the extent that it has brought about the launch of new publication series, journals and study programmes (Lodge, 2008). Empirically, this research interest was caused by the 'deregulation revolution that wasn't' (Vogel, 1996). To capture the phenomenon of 'reregulation' (Héritier, 2001: 848; Levi-Faur, 2005), political scientists have coined various terms such as 'regulatory state' (Majone, 1994, 1996a, 1997), 'regulatory society' (Braithwaite, 2003) and 'regulatory capitalism' (Braithwaite, 2008b; Levi-Faur and Jordana, 2005). The emerging regulatory state has very much been associated with the creation of markets through regulation for competition. Yet unravelling the state as service provider and employer poses significant social policy challenges to the emerging regulatory state. Reregulation has thus to a large extent been about the realisation of social policy goals. The book puts this social face of the regulatory state front and centre, asking how the emerging regulatory state protects consumers and employees.

From the positive to the regulatory state

What Majone has described as the passage from the 'positive' to the 'regulatory' state can analytically be discerned into two dimensions as depicted in table 3.1. The first dimension is about the type of state, which opposes the positive to the regulatory state. The second dimension is about the role of the state, differentiating between direct intervention and delegated settings. Four distinct modes of policymaking result from a combination of these two dimensions: redistribution as the ideal type of policymaking in the interventionist, positive state; political regulation as the ideal type of policymaking in the interventionist, regulatory state;

Table 3.1: Policymaking in the positive and regulatory state

Role of the state Type of state	Intervening	Delegating
Positive	redistribution	corporatism
Regulatory	political regulation	independent regulation

corporatism as the ideal type of policymaking in the delegated, positive state; and independent regulation as the ideal type of policymaking in the delegated, regulatory state.

If we follow Majone's argumentation that what we have been observing in many policy areas, and in the network industries in particular, has been a transition from the 'positive' to the 'regulatory' state, this has important implications for the ways in which social policy objectives are going to be realised. The most fundamental claim made by Majone is the one about a shift in terms of the policy type involved: the positive state relies on redistribution, the regulatory state on regulation. Majone has situated this trend as a mechanism of 'strategic adaptation' in response to international competitive pressures, with the effect that 'rulemaking is replacing taxing and spending' (Majone, 1997: 139). This shift from redistribution to regulatory policies is at the core of the regulatory state hypothesis. Majone (1994, 1996a, 1997) has claimed that the state plays a fundamentally different role in the age of regulation as opposed to the role it played in the traditional welfare state: While the old, 'positive' state would have mainly relied on direct intervention and redistribution, the new, 'regulatory' state would mainly rely on arm's length policies and regulation (Majone, 1997: 149).

Thus the key distinction which underlies the dichotomy of the positive versus regulatory state is about the type of policy involved. The dichotomy therefore refers back to the typology established by Lowi (1964). His typological distinction between distributive, redistributive and regulative policies (less so the fourth type of constituent policy) remains an important point of scholarly reference. Regulatory policy is broadly defined as rulemaking which does not involve a (re)distribution of resources (Héritier, 1987: 39). For the sake of simplicity, I will draw the main line between regulatory policy on the one hand, and redistributive or distributive policies on the other hand. Empirically, the distinction between redistributive policies and distributive policies can be tedious, given that at least indirectly distributive policies also involve redistribution in view of limited financial resources. Majone has emphasised that the state plays a new role in the age of regulation. Rather than realising redistribution and macroeconomic stabilisation through taxing and spending, the state engages in rulemaking in order to correct market failures (Majone, 1997: 149). The regulatory state thus requires a certain degree of administrative capacity to formulate and impose rules, but since the costs of regulation are mostly borne by affected parties there is no need for an extensive budget as is the case in the positive state. Similarly, distinct functions can be attributed to the state each time. Since the regulatory state no longer relies on spending policies where implementation and potentially also administrative costs are borne by regulated business rather than by tax payers (Majone, 1994: 87; Ogus, 1994: 107), it is compatible with retrenchment and austerity policies. The transition from the positive to the regulatory state not only involves a retrenchment of the welfare state (Pierson, 1994), but has also targeted the public service sectors. In the positive state public ownership of service providers was an important form of state intervention (Majone, 1996b: 11–15). Service provision through public monopolies has been an instrument not only to realise state and national interests such as economic stabilisation (Starr, 1990: 35), but also to maximise public control through a politicised, discretion-based management (Burnham, 2001: 130). In reverse terms, privatisation is a means to reduce spending as well as the scale and scope of government, and to restructure the role of the state by shifting the balance between the public and private realm (Starr, 1990: 27–9, 30, 34–41). Privatisation decisions may also involve party politics to the extent that an incoming government seeks to break with the past by disentangling party politics which have become entrenched in ministerial and bureaucratic oversight of the national firm (ibid.: 39).

The need to realise social policy objectives does not disappear with the emergence of the regulatory state. The interdisciplinary literature on regulation has early on acknowledged that regulation goes beyond 'the traditional economic rationale' (Breyer, 1982: 16). Economic regulation aims at correcting market failure (Levi-Faur, 2011: 13; Prosser, 2006), which especially in newly created markets includes regulation for competition so as to limit the market power of incumbent operators (Majone, 1997: 143). Social regulation can be defined *ex negativo* to be 'that regulation which is not economic regulation' (Foster, 1992a: 291). More substantive definitions usually identify specific 'social' goals of regulation. These may include objectives such as income transfer and fairness (Breyer, 1982: 19, 20), or aggregate welfare and distributional justice (Ogus, 1994: 46–56, 2004: 35). Social regulation has a market correcting function as it 'aims to insert "social" elements into the market, by defining standards for coverage and benefit levels or by rectifying illegitimate inequalities' (Leisering, 2011b: 257–8). Prosser, in his legal analysis of public service law, which he defines as 'law designed to make basic public services available to all citizens without discrimination' (Prosser, 2000: 63–4), distinguishes between three ideal types of regulation depending on whether regulatory activity is based on economic principles, individual rights or social solidarity (Prosser, 2006: 365, 387; discussed by Baldwin et al., 2012: 22). In his understanding public services regulation constitutes a specific subcategory of social regulation (Prosser, 2006: 365) as it aims at social solidarity by granting universal entitlement to a certain level and quality of service provision. According to Majone the passage from the positive state to the regulatory state involves an altered institutional setting and alternative modes of policymaking. He has framed this change as a transition from 'social policy' to 'social regulation' (Majone, 1993). He distinguishes between the functions of distribution, which he attributes to the realm of social policy, and the function of allocation and stabilisation, which he attributes to the realm of social regulation (Majone, 1993: 157).

While the regulatory state hypothesis bears empirical validity and identifies an important trend in contemporary capitalism, the question is whether the new form of statism replaces the positive state, or whether it coexists with more traditional forms of statism which involve redistributive and distributive policies. Some authors have pledged for a polymorphic understanding of the two concepts, arguing that the distinction between the positive and the regulatory state is analytical rather than it bearing empirical validity (Levi-Faur, 2013). More recent studies have pointed to the emergence of regulatory welfare regimes in the public utilities on the one hand (Haber, 2010), and the emergence of regulatory elements of welfare state reform on the other hand (Leisering, 2011a; Mabbett, 2011). Paying closer attention to redistributive and distributive policies thus broadens the scope of research in regulation, which has focused widely on regulatory modes of policymaking. Liberalisation and privatisation reforms usually involve social costs that cannot easily be offset by regulation. Paradoxically, therefore, the transition towards the regulatory state may at the same time require the introduction of new redistributive policies. This resonates with Polanyi's argument about a double movement (Polanyi, 1957: 130), and the finding that structural reforms need to be accommodated by compensating reform losers for their losses (Mabbett and Schelkle, 2007). In response to the research question how the regulatory state protects consumers and employees, it is thus expected that redistributive and distributive policies will not disappear with the transition towards the regulatory state, but will complement and stabilise regulatory modes of governance.

Towards independent regulation

The second trend identified by Majone is about the predominant institutional settings in the regulatory state. According to Majone, the typical functions of the positive state require centralised structures such as 'a unified civil service, large nationalised enterprises and expansive welfare bureaucracies' (Majone, 1997: 152). By contrast, the regulatory state presupposes decentralised structures such as regulatory agencies operating 'at arm's length from central government' (Majone, 1997: 152), and rules may be set at the international or supranational level. The type of politics involved each time thus diverges, in the positive state it is 'majoritarian, party-political and national', in the regulatory state it is 'nonmajoritarian, technical and supranational' (Mabbett, 2011). The transition towards the regulatory state thus involves a process of depoliticisation, where policymaking competencies are shifted out of the majoritarian, political arena into a nonmajoritarian, bureaucratic arena. The transition towards the regulatory state therefore does not only involve a shift in policymaking from redistributive to regulatory policies, but also a shift from political to independent regulation. Here it is important to note that many scholars define 'regulation' in a way that excludes rule setting in the political arena. This holds for Selznick's classic definition of regulation as 'sustained and focused control exercised by a public agency over activities that are valued by the community' (Selznick, 1985: 363); or Levi-Faur's proposition to consider rules 'as regulation as long as they are not formulated directly by the legislature (primary law) or the courts (verdict, judgment, ruling and adjudication)' (Levi-Faur, 2011: 6). In this narrow sense regulation merely refers to the promulgation and execution of rules by administrations, bureaucracies and private actors, and excludes legislative or judicial rulemaking.

Independent regulation occurs where regulatory tasks have been delegated to so-called 'nonmajoritarian institutions' (Braun and Gilardi, 2006; Braun et al., 2002; Thatcher and Stone Sweet, 2002). Majone has described this mode of regulation as 'statutory regulation by independent agencies' (Majone, 1996b: 15–19). Thatcher and Stone Sweet (2002) have defined delegation as an authoritative decision that is formalised as a matter of public law, and where policymaking authority is being transferred away from representative organs towards nonmajoritarian institutions. The scope of political, majoritarian rule setting is thus expected to be limited in the regulatory state. This applies to legislation, which embodies the principles of representative democracy and ensures a direct link to the constituency through elected representatives. Legislation draws its legitimacy from majority rule (Offe, 1985b). In procedural terms it is the most politicised type of rulemaking (Flinders and Buller, 2006).

Since legislative decision making is a lengthy and costly process, governments may instead resort to decision making within the executive. Executive decisions can be located at different levels within governmental and ministerial bodies and thus involve varying degrees of politicisation. These have the advantage of being generally and directly applicable, while leaving more room for detail and facilitating reformulation. Executive decisions thus may involve gains in procedural efficacy in comparison to the lengthy process of parliamentarian policy formulation. Compared to independent regulation, the major setback of political regulation is its vulnerability to changing political majorities. Incoming governments and new parliamentary majorities can overturn prior policy choices. The delegation to unelected bodies constitutes a remedy to this time inconsistency problem as it allows to lock in a policy path over time, so that the choices of future governments will be constrained (Glazer, 1989; Vogel, 1996: 131). Delegation to independent regulators thus involves depoliticisation, understood as a 'process of placing at one remove the political character of decision making' (Burnham, 2001: 128). Such nonmajoritarian institutions have been granted specialised public authority that is distinct from that of other institutions, yet they are not representative organs as they are neither directly elected, nor directly managed by elected officials (Thatcher and Stone Sweet, 2002: 2–3).

There are a number of reasons for delegation, which have been discussed at length in the literature (e.g. Thatcher and Stone Sweet, 2002). Majone (2001) has suggested distinguishing between two separate logics of delegation, one where the major concern is about minimising agency loss by controlling the agent (agency model), and another one where the major concern is about maximising credible commitment through a trustee (fiduciary model). I have suggested elsewhere to conceptualise these dynamics as a continuum between commitment and control (Eckert, 2010), rather than as two distinct logics. The agency model functions along the lines of the principal agent logic (Aghion and Tirole, 1997; Moe, 1990). Governmental principals may be willing to delegate because they lack the required expertise or resources. They find another actor with those features and obtain the services of this agent in return for remuneration (Coleman, 1990: 146). Delegation is thus a means to reduce transaction costs and gain efficiency, yet it comes at the cost of losing out in controlling the outcomes. The principal agent framework assumes that the preferences of the principal do not coincide with those of the agent. This can lead to a situation where the agent does not enact the policies that the principal favours (Epstein and O'Halloran, 1999). The principal agency framework has conceptualised this discrepancy of preferences as agency loss (McCubbins et al., 1987; McCubbins and Schwartz, 1984). It is in the interest of the principal to minimise agency loss, while facing a trade-off to the extent that controlling the agent is costly.

Where the fiduciary logic applies, by contrast, political actors gain in policy credibility through delegation since decisions will no longer be subject to the volatile dynamics of the political arena (Bendor et al., 2001: 259–65; Bernhard et al., 2002: 693–5). The rationale is about 'tying one's hands' (Giavazzi and Pagano 1988, critically discussed by Schelkle, 2006) by giving up power to nonmajoritarian institutions. The latter are, depending on the degree of independence they are granted, not subject to political uncertainty (Moe, 1990, 1995; Horn, 1995: 16–19). In this scenario delegation is a means to assure commitment and to solve the time inconsistency problem through an agent who is not tempted by political opportunism (Dixit, 1996: 65). Under these assumptions it is beneficial for a political principal to choose an agent whose preferences differ systematically from her own (Majone, 2001: 104). By binding itself, a government may demonstrate vis-à-vis its constituents that it is truly committed to a certain policy path. Delegation thus guarantees the credibility and stability of policymaking where political principals face problems of credible commitment towards their constituents (Bendor et al., 2001: 260). When delegating, political actors may thus have fundamentally different motives depending on whether they predominantly seek to secure control or credible commitment.

When focusing more on the relationship of the political arena towards their constituents rather than towards their agents or trustees, a third scenario comes into play: political actors may want to shift the blame for unpopular policy outcomes rather than being held accountable because they maintain control over outcomes. Delegation may thus be driven by motives of blame avoidance instead of credible commitment. This 'blame game' (Hood, 2002) presupposes a certain degree of autonomy on the side of the agent or trustee, since the blame shiftee needs to take on the blame. Such a strategy may, however, result in a 'blame boomerang' (ibid.: 28) where the public holds the political arena accountable for undesired outcomes. From a political perspective, the principal agent framework is thus somewhat simplistic when conceptualising control mechanisms mainly as devices to avoid agency loss. From the perspective of input legitimacy, there will be a need to hold unelected bodies accountable for policy outcomes. There is, indeed, evidence that accountability mechanisms are frequently more developed in delegated settings in comparison to pre-existing political settings (Burnham, 2001: 129, 131, 149; Thatcher, 2002: 141–2).

How social goals are being realised by independent regulation is of key concern for this book. In the realm of economic regulation, the fiduciary logic is a more likely scenario. Particularly in former public monopolies, where the state traditionally pursued both operative and regulatory tasks, effective regulation for competition presupposes a certain degree of regulatory autonomy in order to secure credible commitment to liberalisation. Independent regulators are seen as the institutional guarantee for a policy output which provides for a level playing field and a favourable environment for investment. Regulation follows a long-term economic rationale, rather than short-term political considerations. By contrast, the agency logic is a more likely scenario where social policy goals are at stake. The literature on regulatory economics has pointed to accountability risks which follow from entrusting unelected bodies with such social tasks. Foster, for instance, warned that 'while doing so is practically inevitable, straying into social regulation should be kept to the minimum' (Foster, 1992a: 291). Compared to economic regulation, unelected bodies would thus be expected to operate within a policy area that has been clearly defined, and narrowly circumscribed by the political principal, so that regulatory action draws its legitimation as closely as possible from the political arena. The implementation of a universal service obligation, or uniform charges as examples of non-market pricing policies (Foster, 1992a), are social regulatory tasks which are frequently delegated to sector regulators. In the realm of social regulation, an accountability strategy of 'deference' is expected to be at work (Reiss Rubinstein, 2009), where the agency tends to decline responsibility for policy choices which have supposedly been taken elsewhere, and simply sees its role as an enforcement agency. In such situations the political arena can clearly not shift responsibility to the nonmajoritarian area, and deference by the latter would reinforce the blame boomerang (Hood, 2002: 28) mentioned above. Overall, therefore, it is expected that the transition towards independent regulation will be more pronounced in the realm of economic regulation, where regulators function as fiduciaries, as opposed to social regulation, where regulators function as agents.

Organised interests in the regulatory state

The delegation of regulatory powers to independent, nonmajoritarian actors will have repercussions on the ways in which organised interests exert influence on regulatory decision making. The division between capital and labour, which has traditionally translated into party politics and the left–right divide, is a constitutive part of the political arena. Corporatist arrangements in the delegated positive state have attributed public status to private interest groups (Offe, 1985a), mostly representing capital and labour. On top of the decline of organisational density leading to the segmentation of labour markets (discussed in Chapter 2), the depoliticisation involved in the delegation of regulatory tasks to nonmajoritarian institutions will additionally weaken these interests. High union density and an important role played by trade unions form part of a highly politicised arena (Burnham, 2001: 130). Unelected, supposedly apolitical bodies are thus not meant to directly respond to the interests voiced by trade unions and employer associations. If at all, their influence will be channelled via the political arena, and politicians may delegate a specified mandate of social regulation to nonmajoritarian institutions in this area. In contrast to their relations with regulated firms and consumer interests, independent regulators are not expected to cultivate particularly close links with employees in regulated sectors. Issues of health and safety in the workplace as a specific type of risk regulation mandated to regulatory agencies stand out from this general pattern (Hutter, 2001; Viscusi, 1983).

By contrast, business and user interests are at the core of regulated markets, and will form an integrative part of regulatory activity. Since regulated firms are directly affected by, and bear the cost of, regulation, they have an immediate incentive to seek to influence the regulator and will thus be key players in the regulatory game (Coen, 2005a and b; Martimort, 1999; Willman et al., 2003). The regulator–regulatee relationship has been analysed through the lens of the capture theory, which emphasises the role of private interests in the formation of public policy. In his seminal work on economic regulation, Stigler has conceptualised the predominance of private interest in regulation as an instance where 'regulation is acquired by the industry and is designed and operated primarily for its benefit' (Stigler, 1971: 3). Stigler, building on Olson's theory of collective action (1965), illustrated in his work that the regulatory process can be captured by relatively small business industries. Capture is, however, not a problem specific to independent regulation. Capture of regulators by regulated firms can be seen in analogy to capture of nationalised firms by politicians, bureaucrats and trade unions (Majone, 1996b: 18).

Besides the regulated firm, which has been studied intensively in the regulation literature, consumer interests have become better organised and more influential over time. According to Trumbull, 'consumer capitalism' is characterised by the predominance of consumer protection, which has developed as a 'new basic right of citizenship', and the 'emergence of consumers as a coherent interest group in society' (Trumbull, 2006: 9, 12). Such a consumer-oriented perspective would imply a relatively important role played by consumer interests in the regulatory game, an expectation which stands in contrast to the collective action logic according to which consumer interests are diffuse and weakly organised (Olson, 1965). It further links to approaches to risk regulation that have advocated greater protection for consumers rather than the industry, due to the latter's role as risk creator as well as resource and information asymmetries which go to the disadvantage of consumers (Beck, 1998; Schrader-Frechette, 1991). Alongside consumer risk, consumer information as well as price and quality will be key issues of consumer-oriented regulation (Trumbull, 2006: chapters 4, 5 and 7). In addition to ex ante regulation, courts will play a central role in enforcing consumer rights, which is why consumer capitalism connects to the rise of adversarial legalism (Kelemen, 2006: 119–21).

The role played by organised interests will thus vary significantly across actor categories. Old-style corporatist, highly politicised arrangements will become less relevant, while the regulated firms and consumers will be key stakeholders in the regulatory game. The upshot is to say that organised labour will become less relevant in the regulatory state, while business interests will prevail, and consumer interests will be on the rise.

A governance perspective on social regulation

The regulatory state hypothesis formulated in Majone's seminal work (1994; 1996a; 1997) has triggered an intense scholarly debate about the implications and scope of change involved in the passage from traditional forms of statehood to new forms of steering in the age of regulation. At the conceptual level, alternative terms have been suggested to move beyond Majone's state-centred perspective. Braithwaite proposed the term 'regulatory society' (Braithwaite, 2003) arguing that it better describes the involvement of a variety of societal actors. David Levi-Faur and co-authors coined the broader term of 'regulatory capitalism' to capture the growth of rulemaking within and beyond national borders, including business and societal actors, as well as international organisations (Levi-Faur, 2005: 20; Levi-Faur and Jordana, 2005). In this book I privilege the term 'regulatory governance' as the most comprehensive and neutral concept, compared to other alternatives. It is better suited than the term 'regulatory state' as it shifts the focus away from centralised rulemaking by state institutions towards private actors and international organisations. It is also more neutral than 'regulatory capitalism', as it does not go as far as to claim that pre-existing capitalist regimes will be transformed to the extent that they form a different type of regime. Instead, the governance perspective puts the accent on actors, structures and processes in regulatory policy-making. Governance is understood in broad terms to capture any instance of rulemaking that goes from hierarchical steering by state authorities to pure private self-regulation (Börzel, 2007: 61; Mayntz, 2005: 15). An alternative, narrow understanding of governance, in delineation to 'government', considers only instances of rulemaking that involve either non-hierarchical modes and/or private actors (Héritier, 2003; Héritier and Lehmkuhl, 2008). In the public utilities such a narrow understanding of governance would exclude much of the empirically relevant governance modes, given that the broader regulatory space continues to be shaped by public regulation, so that there is hardly any pure instance of self-regulation (Prosser, 2010: 5–6).

Social goals in public service regulation will relate to the availability, affordability and quality of services provided, as well as to working conditions, wage levels and job security. It is expected that the modes of regulation and policymaking will play a different role in these fields (see table 3.2). Redistributive policies will come into play where financial compensation for service provision is needed. Political regulation will relate to network features and service provision, imposing minimum requirements for network density or access to the network; introducing key principles in service provision such as a universal service obligation (USO), and identifying minimum standards relating to availability, quality and pricing of services. Implementing the regulatory framework is usually the task of sector regulators. Regulatory authorities may also be entrusted with setting rules within clearly defined areas such as price or access regulation. Employment related aspects are traditionally addressed by corporatist arrangements, but these will operate in a broad regulatory framework set by political regulation. Political regulation can also set minimum standards applicable to the whole economy or specific sectors, such as minimum wages. The political arena may also become active in wage bargaining processes. Here different degrees of intervention have been distinguished in the relevant literature (Hassel, 2006), ranging from centralised wage-setting practices by governments, tripartite agreements where the state is involved, to decentralised practices where the state steers at a distance. Independent regulation is not expected to play a major role when it comes to employment related issues.

Applied to the postal sector, the need for regulatory intervention appears paramount in both areas, service provision and employment. Regulatory provisions on service provision may formulate wider general interest goals, or impose highly specified conditions such as a USO. In the postal sector the USO refers to the provision of letter mail throughout a state's territory at a uniform rate, regardless of the length of the route of transport and remoteness of the recipient's location, (disregarding the actual costs incurred by delivery) (Ambrosini et al., 2006; Boldron et al., 2006). Thus the USO can be interpreted as a special case of redistributive pricing, achieving redistribution not through direct transfers, but through regulated prices (Cremer et al., 2008: 24–5). In a competitive environment the USO may aggravate what is called a graveyard spiral in the regulatory economics literature, a devastating financial spiral of increasing prices and continuing losses triggered by the entrants' capture of the most profitable business segments (Crew and Kleindorfer, 2005). In sparsely populated and remote areas entry costs are likely to be above revenues, so that only the universal service provider (USP) who is legally obliged to deliver services throughout the territory will be present in these unprofitable areas (Baldwin et al., 2012: 474). This raises the issue of financial compensation needed to cover the cost of the USO (Crew and Kleindorfer, 2008b). Besides the universal provision of mail delivery, the postal presence through its network of outlets has often assumed functions in terms of territorial and socioeconomic cohesion (Boldron et al., 2008; Cremer et al., 2008: 29), particularly in marginal rural areas (countryside villages) or newly urbanised areas that face social problems (Anderloni and Pilley, 2002: 15). In this context the services delivered by national post offices were often outside the core postal business, such as banking, or insurance services for the poor (Porges and Leong, 2006: 387). In order to safeguard the social benefits provided by the network of postal outlets, minimum requirements in terms of network density may constitute a part of the USO, or wider general interest goals may be formulated in the regulatory framework.

Employment related issues are also highly relevant in the labour intense postal sector. Historically, public operators have figured among the biggest employers in national economies, with postal employees often representing around 1 per cent of the active population (Cousquer, 1999: 222). For the last mile, that is mail delivery, wage costs constitute the major cost item, and there is no possibility to substitute the human workforce (Wachter et al., 2001). In order to secure viable working conditions and wage levels in a situation where new market entrants compete on cost, and where traditional patterns of corporatism may fail to cover the employees' social welfare, policy makers may opt for political intervention. Complementing postal corporatism, a sector-specific minimum wage or other minimum requirements related to working conditions and wage levels may be imposed on the operators by political regulation. How the four distinct modes of policymaking are expected to materialise in the postal sector, is depicted in table 3.2.

Table 3.2: Policymaking in the postal sector

Role of the state Type of state	Intervening	Delegating
Positive	**redistribution** financial compensation service provision	**corporatism** employment conditions wage levels
Regulatory	**political regulation** general interest goals, USO, price levels, network density, minimum wage	**independent regulation** implementing USO, tariff regulation

Applying the conceptual framework not to the social goals pursued in a specific sector, but in order to capture expected variation across countries, policymaking can be expected to vary as summarised in table 3.3. In line with the expected interaction between redistributive and regulatory policy modes, redistribution should constitute a fall-back option in all three types of capitalism. Corporatism obviously constitutes the best match with the CME model, which relies on a strong organisational basis of stakeholders. Political regulation is expected to be the predominant mode in the SME, in the absence of strongly organised interests, and a tradition of direct state intervention. Finally, independent regulation constitutes the best match with LMEs with its 'arm's length state-economy relations' (Hancké et al., 2009: 291), and a weak degree of interest organisation. The ideal-typical regulatory state discussed by Majone thus constitutes the best fit with the LME-type of capitalism, while it requires more adaptation in CMEs and SMEs. Independent regulation matches the 'restricted state', (Crouch, 1986: 186) cultivating clear state–society boundaries as a distinctive feature of liberal political economies (ibid.: 180). Empirically, liberal market economies have indeed been the pioneering countries in regulatory reform, which also explains that theories of delegation are of American origin (as discussed by Pollack, 2002). From a governance perspective the question is how the coordinated and state-led variant are accommodating independent regulation as a new tool of governance, and how this impacts on established governance tools such as corporatism and political regulation.

Revisiting the interdisciplinary literature on regulation, this chapter has shown that the role of the state and organised interests has changed with the rise of regulation. There has been an important shift from distribution and redistribution to regulation, but redistributive policies are not expected to disappear. The argument that the regulatory state relies on a redistributive and distributive underpinning bears crucial policy

Table 3.3: Policymaking across types of capitalism

Role of the state Type of state	Intervening	Delegating
Positive	**redistribution** fall-back option all types	**corporatism** predominant in CMEs
Regulatory	**political regulation** predominant in SMEs	**independent regulation** predominant in LMEs

implications in a time of austerity, when it will not be easy to compensate the losers of change. Independent regulatory authorities are expected to be key players in economic regulation, but less so in social regulation, where the political arena is more likely to intervene. Organised interests are affected by the transition towards the regulatory state. Business interests play a key role in the regulatory game, and consumer interests are on the rise. By contrast, more traditional patterns of interest organisation are at the periphery of the regulatory state, and are likely to be weakened.

4

A European model of public service regulation?

Public service reforms and regulation in the member states of the EU have been driven and shaped by supranational law. An emerging European framework has imposed stepwise liberalisation and regulatory reform on the member states. From a comparative capitalist perspective this raises the question of whether the public service sectors in the EU converge on a single model of reform and regulation, or whether diversity continues to persist. In order to delineate the European impact on domestic change this chapter deals with the European approach to reform and regulation in three key utilities, namely telecoms, postal and electricity. The discussion of the *acquis* which has emerged from the 1980s onwards in these sectors specifically focuses on reregulatory measures seeking to realise social goals.

Given that on the telecoms and electricity sectors I can draw on a comprehensive body of secondary literature (e.g. Bartle, 2002, 2005; Black, 1977; Buchan, 2010; Eberlein, 2008, 2012; Eising, 2002; Eising and Jabko, 2001; Humphreys and Padgett, 2006; Jabko, 2006; Matláry, 1997; Prosser, 2005; Sandholtz, 1992, 1998; Sandholtz and Zysmans, 1989; Thatcher, 1999, 2001, 2004a, 2004b, 2007a), the original contribution of the chapter is the discussion of postal services. Where EU-driven postal reform has been discussed in the political science literature, this has taken the form of smaller book chapters (Schmidt, 1998: 274–86; Smith 2005a; Thatcher, 2007b) or sections in journal articles (S.K. Schmidt, 2005; Smith, 2001). The following sections draw on primary documents, legislative acts, studies and press coverage (especially through *Agence Europe*, quoted as 'AE' with publication date throughout the text), and secondary literature where relevant. The first three sections revisit the emergence and evolution of a European regulatory framework over time, differentiating between three distinct phases as pictured in table 4.1. During an initial phase between 1988 and 1998 market opening was launched in all three sectors, followed by a phase of economic and social reregulation from 1999 to 2003. Since then a third round of supranational

Table 4.1: Timeline of European legislation on telecoms, electricity and postal services

	First phase											Second phase					Third phase					
	88	89	90	91	92	93	94	95	96	97	98	99	00	01	02	03	04	05	06	07	08	09
T	■		■		■			■	■	■	■		■		■							■
E			■						■							■						■
P											■				■						■	

Information compiled by author

rule setting between 2004 and 2009 aimed at consolidating the regulatory framework. A last section elaborates on the extent to which we can speak of a European dimension of social regulation in these sectors.

Launching market opening in the public utilities (1988–98)

The Single European Market (SEM) is one of the cornerstones of European integration (Egan, 2010; Leuffen et al., 2013; Young, 2010), yet market integration only started to become a political reality from the mid-1980s onwards. In 1985 Commission President Jacques Delors and the British Commissioner Lord Cockfield presented the White Paper on 'Completing the Internal Market' (COM 85/310) and in the same year an Intergovernmental Conference endorsed a programme to complete the SEM by 1992 within the framework of the Single European Act. The spill-over from the free movement of goods to market integration of services took some time. The liberalisation of utilities started to take off by the end of the 1980s, fuelled by the Commission's competencies under competition law and a dedicated sectoral approach to market opening. Under article 90.3 of the Treaty establishing the European Community (TEC; now article 106 TFEU, Treaty on the functioning of the European Union), the Commission has the possibility to directly impose a Commission directive on the member states that would require them to liberalise public utilities, as long as the application of these provisions does not impede on the provision of 'services of general economic interest' (SGEIs) stipulated in article 90.2 TEC (for a detailed discussion see Bekkedal, 2011). Such limitations on the application of competition rules on SGEIs have been upheld by several court decisions, such as the Corbeau ruling in 1993 or the Almelo ruling in 1994 (Soriano, 2005).

Once liberalisation had spread to the public utilities by the mid-1990s, issues relating to public service provision in these sectors have attracted the attention of European policy makers (Héritier, 2001: 828–9). In 1996 the Commission services published a first communication on 'services of general interest' (SGIs, European Commission, 1996), and in 1997 the treaty was amended by an article on SGEIs as a fundamental principle of the Community (article 16 TEC, article 14 TFEU). Since then, various proposals have been issued on SGIs (European Commission, 2003, 2004, 2000, 2011a), involving vivid policy debates (for a detailed discussion see Héritier, 2001: 828–9; Prosser, 2005, chapter 7), which so far have not resulted in a common legislative framework. By contrast, the Commission has developed a rather detailed approach to SGEIs under its competition law prerogatives, publishing a reviewed legislative package on the application of state aid rules in 2012 (European Commission, 2012a), including specified provisions applying to compensation for public service provision (Commission decision 2012/21/EU, European Commission, 2012b).

Initially, postal and telecommunications services were not on the European agenda, and integration in these sectors was not laid down in the treaties. National governments did also not envisage to cooperate on related issues, illustrated by the fact that the postal ministers met only twice between 1959 and 1977 (Schneider and Werle, 1990: 87). This absence of a European policy on related issues cannot, however, be attributed to a lack of political salience of this area (Laborie, 2006). In the run up to the Treaties of Rome, the Spaak report had, indeed, urged the founding members to become active in the area of the public utilities (The Intergovernmental Committee established by the Messina Conference, 1956). In the area of postal policy, the report recommended the creation of a postal union, arguing that the postal traffic between member states was particularly important. Within this union, a special tariff should be introduced for cross-border letters, transit fees should be abolished, and air transport should be ensured without imposing a special tax. Common efforts to improve the cross-border infrastructure for telecommunications as well as joint research activities would also fall under the activities within the postal union proposed by the report. With regard to energy, the Spaak report did not envisage the extension of market integration to this sector due to its specific features, but recommended cooperation to safeguard a sufficient level of investment and security of supply.

None of these suggestions were immediately taken up by the member states of the European Communities (EC). Instead, other international organisations took over the task of coordinating national policies in these areas (Patel, 2013: 649–50). A European Conference of Postal and Telecommunications Administrations (CEPT) was established in 1959 by nineteen European countries and over time expanded to become an intergovernmental organisation of forty-eight members. The Communities have, for a considerable period of time, therefore not been the focal point for cooperation in the area of telecoms and postal policy.

This changed dramatically once the scope of the single market agenda was broadened to include the public utilities. The telecoms sector has been the frontrunner in the liberalisation of European utilities and has been intensively researched by political scientists (e.g. Bartle, 2005; Jordana, 2002; Sandholtz, 1998, 1992; Sandholtz and Zysmans, 1989; Thatcher, 1999, 2001, 2004b). First steps were taken between 1979 and 1987, resulting from cooperation between national policy makers and the European Commission (Thatcher, 2001: 562), and by the end of the 1990s a regulatory framework had emerged (Bartle, 2005: 68–71). A key date was January 1998, when exclusive rights for voice telephony were abolished in most member states. Already in 1979, the so-called Davignon report proposed the creation of a single market for telecommunication services. In 1983, the Commission published a communication, followed by the 1987 Green Paper (COM (87) 290), envisaging partial liberalisation. In 1988 and in 1990, two Commission directives were adopted, liberalising terminal equipment (88/301/EEC) and telecommunication services (90/388), respectively. The right of the Commission to issue such directives based on article 90.3 TEC (now article 106.3 TFEU), upheld by judgements from the European Court of Justice (ECJ) in 1991 and 1992, proved controversial, given that neither member states governments represented in the Council, nor the European Parliament had a say in the decision making process (Schmidt, 1998, chapter 4). This conflict was about the allocation of competencies rather than policy substance, given that the very principle of expanding European regulation on telecoms was uncontroversial (Thatcher, 2001: 546). Another Commission directive (96/19/EC) was passed in 1996, stipulating full liberalisation to be achieved by 1998.

From 1997 onwards, the Council and the European Parliament were involved in the decision making process. It is thus fair to argue that the European telecoms policy has been developed by the European Commission and national governments as partners, based on compromise in the details and an overall agreement on the expansion of EU-level regulation in the sector (Thatcher, 2001). But from now on there was also a need to secure the support of the European Parliament, which effectively pressed for a stronger commitment to general interest goals (Héritier, 2001: 839–40). When negotiating this first round of legislation, prior reforms in some member states such as Finland, Sweden and Britain played a key role in shaping the debate. A case was made for liberalisation based on such reform experience, helping to overcome political resistance. Within the Council member states were split into a camp of liberalisation frontrunners, led by Britain, and followed by the northern countries; another group of member states composed mainly of France, the Benelux and southern European countries (AE 27 November 1995) opposed reform, alongside the political left and trade unions in many other member states (Thatcher, 2004b: 296). Reform opponents were voicing concerns regarding the effects of competition on service provision and employment.

Debates surrounding these issues became particularly salient once full liberalisation was envisaged by the European Commission. Commissioner Bangemann, who sought to secure support for his reform agenda, in 1995 argued that while reform would lead to job losses in traditional segments of the business, these losses would be offset by the creation of new jobs in other segments (European Commission, 1995: 3). By 1997 the European Commission underpinned such assessment with additional evidence, publishing the results of a study on employment in the European telecoms sector (European Commission, 1997). Regarding service provision member states took very different positions, with those like France and Belgium demanding a wider concept of the universal service, and those like Britain wanting to restrict universal service obligations to voice telephony (AE 26 June 1996). To secure the support of the more reluctant member states, liberalisation measures were balanced by regulatory safeguards to secure public service provision (also discussed by Thatcher, 2001: 565).

In this first phase of reregulation European policy makers thus pioneered both liberalisation and the definition of an EU-wide universal service obligation (for a legal analysis see Prosser, 2005: 177–81; Sauter, 1998: 130–40). In its initial conception the notion referred to universal access, meaning that every person, regardless of her geographical location should be connected to the telephone system (Prosser, 2005: 177). Given that universal access was not granted across the member states where consumers often had to wait for considerable periods until they were connected (Sauter, 1998: 123), imposing such a requirement helped to rally support for liberalisation. The term 'universal service' first appeared in the 1987 Green Paper, and figured as a key objective in a 1993 Council resolution (93/C213/01), while the first voice telephony directive (directive 95/62) as well as the 1996 Commission directive on full liberalisation (96/19/EC) defined the scope of such an obligation. The directive on open network provisions (97/33/EC) defined the universal service in its article 2 (reiterated in article 2 of the voice telephony directive 98/10/EC), and furthermore obliged member states to establish a funding mechanism for sharing the cost of the USO. The balance to be struck between liberalisation and service provision is most clearly set out in the 1998 directive (98/10/EC) establishing the universal service as a European goal that cannot be realised at national level, and putting territorial coverage front and centre (article 3).

Member states were also split during the negotiation of postal reform, but the level of domestic opposition, as well as the level of disagreement about the general direction to take, was far more pronounced than on telecoms reform. The political conflict over the legal basis and procedures to use, which had characterised the early stage of telecoms liberalisation, re-emerged in the postal sector, and this time translated into an intra-institutional conflict. Building on the experience in the neighbouring telecoms sector, the European Commission put forward first policy proposals in the mid-1990s. While the Commissioners at the Directorates General (DG) for Competition and the Internal Market, Karel Van Miert and Martin Bangemann, in policy substance, agreed on postal liberalisation, they disagreed on procedural grounds. Miert had envisaged making use of the Commission's prerogatives under competition law (AE 25 July 1995), and his DG had started to prepare a notice on the application of competition law in the postal sector (SEC/1995/830 final). Such steps were taken before a draft directive had been proposed by the Internal Market DG in December 1995 (COM (95) 227). National governments had reason to fear that the European Commission would proceed as in the telecoms sector (Schmidt, 1998: 278–80) and introduce liberalisation through a Commission directive based on its competition law prerogatives. They therefore exerted pressure on the Commission to refrain from publishing the notice unless political agreement had been found on the draft directive (AE 26 October, 27, 28 November 1995 and 29 January 1996).

In its draft directive the Commission highlighted unsatisfactory performance levels and discrepancies in the quality of mail services across Europe. Aware of the political sensitivity surrounding the postal universal service, the proposal allowed for generous price and weight limits to determine the reserved area (less than five times the basic tariff and below 350 grams). The Commission was however determined to open up direct mail and incoming cross-border mail, proposing that these markets should not be sheltered from competition beyond 2000 (article 8.2 COM 1995/227 final). Political controversy thus unfolded on the liberalisation of these profitable market segments. In response to concerns raised over service provision and employment in the sector, the European Parliament overall sought to slow down and limit liberalisation (AE 9 May 1996), and the Council agreed to include direct mail and incoming cross-border mail into the reserved area without setting a time line (article 7.2 of directive 97/67 EC). The first postal directive, furthermore, put the universal service front and centre, defining minimum levels for its scope and quality. The directive required the legislator to decide no later than 1 January 2000 on further steps in the light of economic, social and technological developments, and introduced a sunset clause stating the validity of the directive until the end of 2004 (articles 7.3 and 27 of directive 97/67 EC).

The policy output of the first round of European postal legislation thus came about, to the disappointment of the liberalisation frontrunners Finland, The Netherlands and Sweden. These countries vetoed the directive in the Council (AE 2 December 1997). Germany and the Netherlands did also form part of the supporters' camp, along with private operators and user groups (AE 29 April, 26 June, 20 December 1996 and 5 May 1997). A coalition led by the French gathering Belgium, Ireland, Spain, Portugal, Italy, Greece and Luxembourg opposed liberalisation alongside sector trade unions (AE 11 May 1995, 23 February 1996). In view of the diverging preferences of national governments, which basically reflected the positions of national post offices, the association of the incumbent operators, PostEurop, could not come up with a uniform position representing its members (Interview, PostEurop 1). National positioning was also the main cleavage among members of the European Parliament (MEPs), while party affiliation played a secondary role (Interview, EP). The dividing line between liberalisation supporters and opponents was more pronounced than in the telecoms sector, and during this first round of negotiation Britain took an ambivalent position and did not form part of the liberal camp. In most member states vested interests and domestic opposition made change difficult, with powerful trade unions and a lack of public support (discussed in detail in Chapters 5, 6 and 7 for France, Germany and Britain). As a result, first steps taken to open up national postal markets were extremely cautious, engaging in an incremental and lengthy process towards full liberalisation (as discussed by Smith, 2005a: 127–8; Thatcher, 2007b: 238). And the level of social reregulation was considerable, positioning the safeguard of a universal postal service at the core of the emerging regulatory framework.

Tackling the liberalisation of electricity markets proved to be another challenging task for European policy makers where, unlike the telecoms sector, powerful incumbents worried that they would lose their dominant market position and thus lobbied their national governments to oppose change. Establishing 'the market as a norm' required a cautious approach in view of the politics involved, resulting in an incremental and controlled process of liberalisation (Jabko, 2006, chapter 6). The extent to which member states have shaped policy outcomes as compared to the influence exerted by other players such as the Commission, the European Parliament and the ECJ, has attracted considerable attention in the political science literature (e.g. Bartle, 2005: 73–9; Eberlein, 2008: 75–6; Eising, 2002;

Eising and Jabko, 2001; Héritier, 2001: 840–4; Héritier and Soriano, 2002). The way towards market opening proved lengthy and difficult, in particular owing to fervent French opposition to give up on its public monopoly.

Already in the late 1980s, the European Commission launched the idea of an internal energy market, publishing a communication on energy policy in 1988 (COM (88) 238 final), followed by a Green Paper *For a European Union Energy Policy* in 1995 (COM (94) 659 final). The Commission sought to shape the debate positively, highlighting potential economic gains from market integration in the form of job creation and lower prices (declaration by the Commissioner designate Christos Papoutsis, AE, 10 January 1995). The Commission already sought to establish a legal basis by including energy policy into the treaty at this stage, but this would only happen more than two decades later. In the negotiations following the Commission proposal, the major controversy unfolded over the issue of third-party access. France was strongly in favour of allowing for a single buyer model alongside negotiated access, which from a French perspective would be necessary to ensure a sufficient level of long-term investment in infrastructure. Britain, rallying support from other liberalisation leaders, opposed the French proposal, while a third group of member states took a middle position (AE, 3 March 1995).

On the side of organised interests trade unions, organised within the European Public Services Committee, the European Federation of Chemical and General Workers' Union and the Miners' European Federation, strongly opposed liberalisation as a threat to security of supply and jobs in the sector (AE 2 June 1995, 28 November 1995, 13 December 1995). Business interests were split: the Confederation of British Industry acted as a vocal supporter of liberalisation; the association of the European Electricity Companies, Eurelectric, took a middle position representing the very different interests of its members, and thus advocated the coexistence of different access models; European industry associations representing energy-intense sectors and the International Federation of Industrial Energy Users lobbied for market opening, hoping for lower prices that would boost their competitiveness (AE 2 May 1995, 13 December 1995). The division between liberalisation supporters and opponents also translated into very different positions on public service regulation. A coalition composed of France, Belgium, Italy, Spain and some other member states insisted that a central role would be attributed to public service provision, allowing member states to impose public service obligations on its national operators, in the realm of safety, environmental protection, availability of supplies, quality and price. Germany, backed by Austria and Britain, was opposed to such provisions which would give member states too much leeway in implementing market opening (AE 3

May 1996). The European Parliament overall was in favour of a strong emphasis on public service obligations in the sector (Cameron, 2002: 144). A political agreement, putting an end to tedious negotiations that on several occasions were deadlocked, was eventually reached in June 1996 thanks to a compromise struck mainly between Germany and France under the Italian presidency (AE, 14 and 21 June 1996, also discussed by Eising and Jabko, 2001). In substance, the outcome helped to gain support from all parties, allowing for both negotiated third-party access and the single buyer model, envisaging incremental market opening and adding strong emphasis on public service aspects (also discussed by Bartle, 2005: 76–7; Héritier, 2001: 842–3). Following successful negotiations among member states, the European Parliament had given up on its amendments and accepted the Council's common position without any changes (AE 11 December 1996). As these amendments would have addressed harmonisation of social protection standards for the sector's workers and job security, this decision was a disappointment to the trade unions (AE 20 December 1996). The directive on the internal electricity market (1996/92/EC) came into effect on 30 January 1997.

In order to secure sufficient political support for the liberalisation agenda, market opening was accompanied by a significant level of reregulation. In particular, France and a group of southern member states were insisting on introducing an EU-wide regulatory framework which would guarantee minimum standards for service provision across all member states. As a result, EU-driven reform in the public utilities combined market opening with social cohesion to align member states and the European Parliament (Héritier, 2001). This was the case in the high-tech telecoms sector, where change was driven by important economic and technological factors, and even more so in the politically entrenched postal and electricity sectors.

Reregulating for competition and in the public interest (1999–2003)

Once the principle of market opening had been established for the public utilities, further measures were passed in order to make competition a policy reality, while at the same time controlling for public interest goals. All three sectors went through another round of legislation between 1999 and 2003, resulting in a second legislative package on telecoms (2002), postal services (2002) and electricity (2003). The following sections discuss how European policy makers responded to the economic and social challenges of continued reregulation.

Following the incremental and stepwise evolution of the *acquis* in the telecoms sector during the 1980s and 1990s, this second phase of regulation aimed at simplifying and streamlining existing rules, securing compliance at the domestic level, and adapting the framework to new technological developments (also discussed by Bartle, 2005: 71–3; Prosser, 2005: 181–2). By 1999 the Commission had carried out a review (European Commission, 1999) which urged the need to broaden the scope of the regulatory framework to the wider area of electronic communications, as these were rapidly evolving with new developments such as the Internet or cable TV. The Commission suggested passing a comprehensive legislative package composed of a framework directive to be complemented by directives on authorisation, access and interconnection, universal service, and privacy and data connection. Major political controversies during the formulation of the second legislative package concerned the role of national regulatory authorities in the multi-level governance architecture, as well as their prerogatives with respect to public service goals. Member states effectively blocked attempts to centralise regulatory powers. Instead, cooperation among national authorities was strengthened within a European regulators group (ERG) which was set up in 2002 (for a detailed discussion see Thatcher and Coen, 2008: 823–4).

Member states were split on the issue of whether national regulators should implement wider social objectives. A group of southern countries, led by France, favoured an extensive definition of the universal service which would give the regulators some discretion on social issues. By contrast, a group of liberalisation supporters, led by Britain and Germany, feared that such provisions could be used to restrict competition (Thatcher, 2001: 570). The second telecoms package, passed in 2002, constituted a compromise between these diverging preferences. It was composed of measures on the competition in the telecoms markets (Commission directive 2002/77/EC), on access to, and the interconnection of, networks (directive 2002/19/EC), on authorisation (directive 2002/20/EC), on regulatory harmonisation and the creation of a regulatory body (directive 2002/21/EC and Commission decision 2002/627/EC), the universal service and users' rights (directive 2002/22/EC), and data protection (directive 2002/58/EC). In the realm of social regulation, the second package emphasised the role of national regulators in contributing to the fulfilment of broader policies in the area of employment and in ensuring citizens' access to a universal service (directive 2002/21/EC). The directive on universal service and users' rights emphasised that 'liberalisation of the telecommunications sector and increasing competition and choice for communications services go hand in hand with parallel action to create a harmonised regulatory framework which secures the delivery of universal service' (directive 2002/22/EC (1)) and laid down detailed requirements in this regard. In particular, the directive required that consumers be connected to a public telephone network which allows for functional access to the Internet (article 4.2).

In the postal sector the Commission was more ambitious in achieving progress on market opening than in the previous phase, given that in the late 1990s a number of competition cases had fuelled a renewed debate (Smith, 2005a: 111). At this stage the political battle throughout policy formulation was about the pace and scope of future market opening steps. Commissioner Bolkestein had originally envisaged increasing the competitive share of the market up to 30 per cent of total volume (AE 11 May 2000), but the Commission proposal published in May 2000 (COM (2000) 319 final) eventually stipulated a reduction in the weight and price limits of reserved services from 2003 onwards, to 50 grams and two and a half times the basic standard tariff, which amounted to roughly 20 per cent of total mail volume (AE 30 May 2000). The Commission also allowed for direct mail as well as incoming cross-border mail to be included within the reserved sector, but suggested to exclude outward cross-border items (at the time approximately 3 per cent of total postal revenues). Further liberalisation steps were envisaged to be taken by January 2007, following a Commission proposal by December 2004 and an agreement under co-decision to be achieved by December 2005. An extension of the universal service was not foreseen, but rather procedures for reviewing its adequacy and scope.

As was the case during the negotiations of the first directive, member states were again split into two camps, a pro- and an anti-liberalisation camp. On the side of stakeholders, the newly created 'Free and Fair Post Initiative' (Interview, FFPI) representing private operators and big costumers sought to counterbalance the trade unions' and incumbents' lobbying against liberalisation of the letter market (AE 13 February 2002). FFPI allied with the well-established associations representing the liberalised segments of the market such as express mail (European Express Association, EEA) or direct mailing (Federation of European Direct and Interactive Marketing). Among the incumbents, the British Post Office strongly lobbied with MEPs to counter the Commission proposal, backed by its French and Italian counterparts (AE 13 December 2000). The main arguments of opponents related to concerns about employment in the sector, and service provision. In the ensuing political discussions, neither the suggested scope of the next liberalisation step, nor the timeline met with support from the member states.

During the policy formulation process, France as the leader of the reform opponent's camp was in a privileged position to set the agenda when it was holding the Council presidency in the second half of 2000. The French voiced their concerns to see universal service provision being watered down by liberalisation. In September 2000, French MEPs and MPs addressed an appeal to the European Commission asking it to review its draft directive in this respect (AE 21 September 2000). Within the EP, German *rapporteur* Markus Ferber, CSU, established the grounds for compromise between the Commission's proposal on the one hand, and the opponents' position on the other hand by putting stronger emphasis on universal service provision as well as social and territorial cohesion (Interview, EP). Adopting their report by mid-December 2000, the parliamentarians expressed their preference for slowing down liberalisation in order to safeguard universal service provision (AE 28 November and 14 December 2000). Such efforts within the European Parliament (EP) resonated with the position of the French Council presidency. The French put forward a compromise proposal in December 2000 gaining support from Greece, Ireland, Italy, Spain, Portugal and Greece, while Austria, Denmark, Finland, Germany, The Netherlands and Sweden were opposed. Britain took a middle position, not expressing support for either of the two camps. With these two groups remaining antagonistic, and the French being inflexible on their position in view of cantonal and local elections upcoming by mid-March 2001, no agreement was achieved under the French presidency (AE 22 and 28 December 2000).

A first step was taken at the Stockholm summit held on 23 and 24 March 2001 under the Swedish presidency, where heads of government urged the Council to move forward (AE 25 March 2001). Eventually, negotiations were relaunched in October 2001 under the Belgian presidency, based on a compromise paper that was suggested jointly by the presidency and the Commission. This compromise envisaged a phased approach to liberalisation, reducing the upper threshold for reserved services to 100 grams from 1 January 2003, and 50 grams from 1 January 2006 onwards. By 2006, the Commission was required to present a prospective study on the impact that complete liberalisation, if implemented until 2009, would have on universal service provision in the member states. The compromise further allowed for outgoing cross-border mail being reserved under certain conditions. The Telecoms Council endorsed this text in October 2001 (AE 15 October 2001). Thus, the camp favouring a rapid liberalisation together with a fixed date for full opening did not manage to sway those in favour of a gradual liberalisation. As a result, the decisive stage would be subject to another round of negotiations. Among the pacesetters, The Netherlands voted against the agreement and Finland abstained, while Germany rallied around the majority (AE 16 October 2001).

The resulting second directive (2002/39/EC) constituted not more than a transitory step, yet confirmed the ultimate objective of the process: the next liberalisation steps would have to be taken in 2003 (above 100 grams, tariff three times higher than the standard letter), and in 2006 (above 50 grams, tariff two and a half times higher than the standard letter). If necessary for the provision of universal service, member states could continue to reserve direct mail as well as outgoing cross-border mail within the same weight and price limits. A sunset clause (article 7.3) stipulated that the Commission, on the basis of a prospective study, was to assess the impact of full liberalisation for each member state and submit a proposal by the end of 2006. This proposal could confirm, if appropriate, 2009 as the final date. The directive did not introduce major changes regarding the USO. It also committed the Commission to submit a study covering economic, social, employment and technological aspects, and the effects on quality of service by the end of 2004 (article 23). The Commission had provided data on service provision throughout policy formulation, pointing to the positive effects that the first directive had generated on universal service provision (European Commission, 2002). The assessment on employment effects was mixed, but the Commission sought to emphasise that job losses were counterbalanced by employment growth within the competing private operators (European Commission, 2002: 6, 36–8). This assessment is reproduced in the text of the directive (consideration 13). The directive adds a consideration on employment related aspects, stating that 'a high level of employment and social protection' as well as 'maintaining cohesion in social and employment terms' (considerations 5 and 6) as objectives of European policy should be pursued in the sector. Overall, the second directive constituted a significant step towards a more competitive outlook of the postal sector, although it ran short of introducing full market opening.

In contrast to the postal sector, agreement was reached on full liberalisation in the electricity sector during this second round of policy formulation. This new round of negotiations coincided with the Commission taking infringement action against France, Belgium and Luxembourg for non-transposition of the 1996 directive (AE 24 November and 22 December 1999, 15 February and 13 June 2000, 26 September 2001). In May 2000, the Commission, led by energy commissioner Loyola de Palacio, made proposals to accelerate the liberalisation of Europe's electricity markets (AE 15 and 16 May 2000), and proposed legislation in spring 2001 (COM (2001) 125). Such efforts were backed by some member state governments, particularly the British and Spanish prime ministers Tony Blair and José Maria Aznar (AE 31 October and 3 November 2000), and industry interests such as those represented within the Union of Industrial and Employers' Confederation of Europe (UNICE, AE 18 May 2001). Liberalisation opponent France could rally support from Germany as the Commission's regulatory reform proposals went against the German interest to maintain its decentralised regulatory regime (AE 14 May 2001). In the course of policy formulation, trade unions also raised their concerns regarding job losses. According to a study prepared by the European Federation of Public Service Unions and the Public Services International Research Unit, job losses had occurred everywhere in the EU except France, with the biggest decline in Britain of minus 40–50 per cent between 1990 and 1998 (AE 22 February 1999). In view of such debates the Commission generated input in the form of a positive assessment of past achievements, for instance by providing data on price reductions for both industry and households in its 1999 report on the implementation of the first directive (AE 7 May 1999). When French opposition prevailed, the Commission threatened to move ahead with liberalisation, using its competition law prerogatives by issuing a Commission directive (AE 17 January 2002). In order to rally support, the Commission furthermore proposed changes to its draft directive which strengthened the public service notion, regulatory independence, requirements regarding consumer information and the protection of vulnerable consumers (AE 12 June 2002). A political agreement among the member states was reached in November 2002, envisaging a phased approach to liberalisation and public service guarantees (AE 21 November 2002).

Following successfully concluded negotiations, the second legislative package was published in July 2003. In view of member state opposition the electricity directive (2003/54/EC) allowed for a longer transition towards full competition than originally envisaged by the Commission (discussed by Bartle, 2005: 77), opening the markets for all non-household customers by July 2004, and for all other customers by July 2007 (article 21). In institutional terms the introduction of independent regulators at this stage became a mandatory requirement, and their cooperation was formalised within a European Regulators Group for Electricity and Gas (ERGEG, created by Commission decision 2003/796 EC; for a detailed discussion see Eberlein, 2008: 82, 86–8; Thatcher and Coen, 2008: 824–5). The scope of the public service obligations in the sector was broadened, formulating a universal service obligation and the duty for member states to introduce adequate safeguards to protect vulnerable customers (article 3).

During this second phase of reregulation, striking a balance between economic and social goals formed the core of the policy debates in all three sectors. In telecoms, given that full liberalisation had already been agreed, key issues revolved around the allocation of regulatory powers and the question to what extent sector regulators should be allowed to implement broader social goals. In the postal sector support from reform opponents for further steps towards full liberalisation could only be gained in return for a stronger emphasis on social aspects in the regulatory framework. And, finally, a political deal on full market opening of electricity markets was struck on the basis of a phased abolition of monopolies and regulatory discretion being left to the member states in the realm of public service goals and the protection of vulnerable customers.

Consolidating regulatory regimes (2004–9)

While a third round of legislation was needed in the postal sector to secure political agreement for full market opening, the EU in 2008 and 2009 engaged in another round of legislation on telecoms and electricity, in order to improve the compliance record, and to consolidate the sector-specific regulatory regimes. At this stage, policy formulation took place in the wider context of the economic and sovereign debt crisis which struck the EU from 2007 onwards.

In the telecoms sector the third legislative package was published in December 2009, and the rules included in the package were to be transposed into national law by May 2011. As in the past, controversies in the policy formulation process evolved around the allocation of regulatory powers, but also around new issues such as restricted access to electronic communications networks and network neutrality. Attempts by the Commission to centralise regulatory powers at the European level within a 'European Telecom Market Authority' (Commission press release no. IP/07/1677) were rejected by both the Parliament and the Council (AE 24 September 2008). Creating such a supranational regulator would indeed have been a radical departure from the intergovernmental outlook of the institutional framework which had emerged over the past two decades (Simpson, 2009). Instead, legislators opted for a decentralised arrangement, creating a Body of European Regulators of Electronic Communications (regulation (EC) no. 1211/2009) with very limited formal powers. The outcome has been explained by the effective resistance of lower-level bodies, as these were keen to safeguard the regulatory powers they had received in previous rounds of delegation (Thatcher, 2011). Service provision aspects were considered in detail, yet the scope of the USO defined in the directive (articles 3 and 4 of the directive 2009/136/EC) did not change in comparison to the 2002 directive. The package strengthened consumer rights in several areas such as switching operators, more transparent contract information, and standards concerning online privacy and safety for the consumers

(European Commission MEMO/09/491). Political deadlock was caused by a controversy between the European Parliament and the Council over the possibility for member states to restrict end users' access to the network, which by November 2009 was resolved (EurActiv, 2009) by introducing a so-called 'internet freedom provision' into the final text (article 1.3a of the directive 2009/136/EC).

The third round of legislation in the European postal sector did also not depart from previous patterns. In October 2006 the European Commission issued a draft directive (COM (2006) 594 final) together with a prospective study (COM (2006) 596), a detailed implementation report (COM (2006) 595 final) and an impact assessment (SEC (2006) 1292). The Commission proposal envisaged the introduction of full market opening across the EU by 2009. Member states and national incumbents again were split into two opposed camps (AE, 11 December 2006). On the side of opponents, national post operators in Belgium, Cyprus, Spain, France, Greece, Italy, Hungary, Luxembourg and Poland lobbied against full liberalisation. They commissioned a study which argued that safeguards were needed to secure the financing of the universal service and that a reserved sector was an effective means to that end (Oxera, 2007). Trade unions mobilised strongly and postal workers from all over the EU went jointly on strike in June 2007 (*Financial Times*, 2007; *Le Monde*, 2007). On the side of supporters, the historic operators from Germany, Finland, The Netherlands and Sweden supported the Commission proposal (TNT, 2006), as did associations representing private operators (EEA, FFPI). Member state positions broadly coincided with the stance of their public operator: Belgium, Cyprus, France, Greece, Italy, Hungary, Luxembourg, Poland and Spain expressed their reservations about the initiative, raising concerns about the funding of universal service provision in a liberalised environment; on the other side, Germany, The Netherlands, Finland, Sweden and this time also Britain supported swift market opening. For the first time, Britain formed part of the supporters' camp in the European postal reform debate, given that in the meantime the British had caught up on domestic reform, being the second member state after Sweden to fully liberalise the letter mail (discussed in detail in Chapter 7).

The division among member states was again broadly reflected among MEPs, where overall there appeared to be a consensus in favour of slowing down the liberalisation process. French and Belgian MEPs wanted to postpone the timetable arguing that sufficient financing mechanisms for the USO had not been secured. In order to reach agreement, a compromise proposal was put on the table along the following lines (A6–0246/2007): delaying full liberalisation until 2011, allowing derogations to member states facing particularly difficult preconditions, and introducing a 'reciprocity clause' which should protect liberalised markets from entry of foreign operators which were still protected by monopoly at home. These suggestions were backed by the transport committee on 18 June 2007, and the EP concluded its first reading on 11 July 2007 (EP, 2007). The first preparatory discussions at the Council took place under the Finnish presidency in December 2006, and in January 2007 the Germans took over the presidency with the ambition to secure support for full liberalisation in 2009 (AE 3 January 2007). Again, a nexus was established by German politicians between full liberalisation at home, foreseen by January 2008, and the pace of EU induced reform. The German chancellor sent a strong signal that Germany would go ahead with liberalising its market, no matter what the outcome would be at the European level. Angela Merkel did, however, warn that further delay of EU-wide opening would lead to an unacceptable distortion of competition on the German market, and thus favoured the Commission's timeline (Mai, 2007). In this endeavour Germany faced substantial opposition from France, where internal market issues were highly sensitive post-referendum and in the run-up to presidential elections in June 2007, but also from other member states such as Belgium, Italy and Luxembourg (AE 15 May 2007). It therefore did not seem opportune to engage in public deliberation at this stage, which is why the German presidency addressed the highly sensitive issues during an informal lunch and bilateral meetings in early June. More technical aspects were discussed and prepared at working group level (Interview, Council). The French presidential elections effectively caused a complete deadlock in the negotiation process and thus prevented the German presidency from achieving any tangible results (Ricard, 2007b).

Things only began to move forward under the Portuguese presidency in the second half of 2007. Based on the European Parliament's first reading, grounds for compromise could be gained during subsequent negotiations in the Council. In order to reassure those member states, and particularly so France, being concerned about the financing of the universal service in a liberalised regime, the Portuguese suggested adding an annex to the directive laying out the calculation of the net costs of universal service. A large majority of delegations favoured the postponement of the final date for full liberalisation, and several member states asked to be granted a derogation from the EU-wide date. Political agreement was found at the Council meeting on 1 October 2007. The EP committee backed the Council's common position in December without amendment, endorsed by the plenary vote on 31 January 2008 (EP, 2008). Both the example set by full liberalisation in Britain and the German determination to open the domestic letter mail market by January 2008 had a decisive impact on the debate (Interview, EP). The British case had illustrated that it was possible to open the market in a big, geographically disparate country with a long postal tradition and an important trade union. The liberalisation of the German letter market also had an important signalling effect, given it is the biggest in Europe and centrally located.

Updated European legislation (articles 2 and 3 of the directive 2008/6/EC) stipulated full liberalisation by January 2011 and granted a two-year transition phase to eleven member states (the Czech Republic, Greece, Cyprus, Latvia, Lithuania, Luxembourg, Hungary, Malta, Poland, Romania and Slovakia). In order to prevent unfair competition, a reciprocity clause (article 3.3) stated that between 2011 and 2012 member states that had fully liberalised could refuse entry to monopoly operators. The directive set requirements with regard to transparent and separate accounting to prevent cross-subsidies between services subject to a universal service obligation and other parts of the business (article 14). On independent regulation, the directive emphasised the need for effective structural separation between operational and regulatory tasks where member states 'retain ownership or control of postal service providers' (article 22), and strengthened the competencies of national regulators in gathering information from the operators (article 22a). For the first time, European law referred to cooperation mechanisms between national regulators (article 22.2). In 2010 the Commission, backed by supporting evidence provided by a study on postal regulation (WIK-Consult, 2009b), created a European Regulators Group for Postal Services (Commission decision 2010/C 217/07).

Another round of negotiations on energy policy was launched in September 2007 with the publication of the Commission's proposal for a third energy package. This policy initiative came at a time when most member states still did not comply with existing legislation: in April 2006 the Commission had sent letters of formal notice to seventeen member states (IP/06/430), and in 2008 brought three member states before the Court of Justice for failure to transpose the energy directives (IP/08/85). When the negotiations were concluded in summer 2009, the Commission launched infringement proceedings against twenty-five member states for not complying with applicable existing law (IP/09/1035). The major controversy during negotiations on electricity regulation was about ownership unbundling. France and Germany, rallying support from the Benelux countries, teamed up as the main opponents to unbundling. These countries sought to defend their national models of vertically integrated operators (AE 7 March 2007). The European Trade Union Confederation as well as the European Federation of Public Service Unions shared such reservations against ownership unbundling, arguing that Britain sought to export its deficient liberal model to the continent (AE 12 January 2007).

On the other hand, a group of eight member states led by Denmark as well as the European Parliament lent support to ownership unbundling (AE 25 June and 10 July 2007). Although the Commission could not push through its preferred option of breaking up such vertical integration, it exerted an important role in the process, notably through its competition law prerogatives (Eikeland, 2011). The third electricity directive (2009/72/EC) introduced various unbundling options which ran short of full ownership unbundling, and introduced several institutional innovations. In particular, it created a new Agency for the Cooperation of Energy Regulators (created by regulation EC no. 713/2009) which replaced the pre-existing regulators' group ERGEG. Moreover, new legislation attributed a formal mandate to cooperation between transmission system operators (TSOs) within the newly created European Network of TSOs (ENTSO). The directive also addressed the increasingly salient issue of rising energy prices, and for the first time explicitly referred to the risk of energy poverty.

In this last phase of European legislation, full market opening was finally embraced in the postal sector. But even in the rapidly evolving telecoms sector institutional rigidity was quite pronounced, where member states effectively blocked a significant shift of regulatory powers towards the European level. The debate on electricity reform was dominated by two issues related to effective competition (unbundling) and affordability of services (energy prices). In all three sectors the double economic and social dimension of public services has continued to be of key concern to policy makers in the context of the economic and sovereign debt crisis: on the one hand, liberal-minded ideas favouring competitive markets and privatisation have gained new currency for those arguing in favour of economic growth while at the same time rolling back the state; on the other hand, job creation and affordability of services have become politically ever more salient in a context of increasing unemployment and social inequality.

The European dimension of social regulation

The previous sections have illustrated how European policy makers have sought to pay tribute to very different state traditions and socioeconomic preconditions when liberalising and reregulating the public service sectors. In all three sectors social concerns raised with respect to service provision and employment have played a central role in the course of political debates, yet the emerging regulatory regimes have not integrated related aspects to the same extent. Imposing sector-specific USOs across the EU has been the most substantial form of social regulation, whereas

Table 4.2: Sector varieties of European social regulation

	USO	General interest	Employment
Telecommunications	Universal access fixed network including Internet, non-discriminatory tariffs in disregard of location	Protecting vulnerable customers, data protection, net neutrality, freedom of access to electronic communications, transparent consumer information	Activity of national regulatory authority contributes to broader policies in the area of employment
Postal	Universal delivery and collection, uniform tariff in disregard of location	Access to essential local services and electronic communications, consumer protection	Regulation of employment conditions a national prerogative, authorisation may be subject to the respect of working conditions
Electricity	Universal access, reliability of supply	Environmental protection, security of supply, consumer protection, protect vulnerable customers, combat energy poverty	–

broader requirements concerning the provision, quality and affordability of public services are less pronounced, and reregulation on employment related aspects hardly exists. It is thus worthwhile to contrast service- and employment related aspects of social regulation across sectors (see table 4.2) and to situate them in the wider context of European debates on SGIs on the one hand, and social policies on the other hand.

Regulatory harmonisation of service provision aspects is most advanced where an EU-wide USO has been defined. This applies to all three sectors, although the precision of relevant provisions diverges. An EU-wide USO was first defined in the telecoms sector, initially focusing on universal geographical access, and subsequently moving towards wider social and redistributive goals (Prosser, 2005: 177). The directives on open network provisions (article 2 of directive 97/33/EC) and voice telephony (article 2 of directive 98/10/EC) defined the universal service as 'a defined minimum set of services of specified quality which is available to all users independent of their geographical location and, in the light of specific national conditions, at an affordable price'. Such guarantees were reiterated in subsequent legislation, with a rather comprehensive definition of the universal service in the 2002 directive on universal service and user rights (article 3 of the directive 2002/22/EC). The directive broadened the scope of the USO to other electronic communications, stipulating in particular that fixed access should be 'sufficient to permit functional Internet access' (article 4.2). The 2009 directive, in addition, referred to the need to improve access to high-speed broadband services (considerations 9, 60 of directive 2009/136/EC), but did not, at this stage, integrate such a requirement into the definition of the USO. In its preparatory work for a potential fourth legislative package on electronic communications the Commission identified universal provision of broadband services as a major challenge for investment and funding in a Union with very different levels of broadband coverage and income levels (European Commission, 2011b). Given such divergence, the inclusion of broadband services within the scope of the USO in the next round of reregulation is a rather unlikely scenario. The financing of the USO in telecoms can be secured by two options, providing compensation by public funds or by introducing cost-sharing mechanisms between operators (article 13 of directive 2002/22/EC).

The minimum standards laid down by the USO in the postal sector are comprehensive and comparatively stable, as they have been maintained throughout the three rounds of policy formulation. In view of the very different geographical preconditions across Europe the postal directive does not impose any minimum standards in terms of the number and density of the network on the member states. Here European legislation simply stipulates that member states 'shall take steps to ensure that the density of the points of contact and of the access points take account of the needs of consumers' (article 3.2 directive 1997/67/EC). The provisions on postal services are more detailed where 'member states shall ensure that users enjoy the right to a universal service involving the permanent provision of a postal service of specified quality at all points in their territory at affordable prices for all users' (article 3.1 of the directive 2008/6/EC). The minimum requirement is that member states ensure the processing and delivery of postal items weighing up to 2 kg and postal packages up to 10 kg, to be guaranteed at least on five working days a week, with one clearance and one delivery per day (article 3.3 of directive 2008/6/EC). The member states furthermore have to notify the Commission of the identity of the USP (article 4), they shall ensure the financing of the universal service (articles 1, 7), and prices shall be affordable to all users independent of their geographical location (article 12). The current framework allows for funding through three options, namely through a compensation fund, cost-sharing or public procurement (for a detailed discussion Eccles, 2011). In addition, the annex to the 2009 directive provided for 'guidance on calculating the net cost, if any, of universal service'.

As in the telecoms sector, the adequacy of the postal universal service is under scrutiny. A detailed study on the evolution of postal markets and service provision suggested a more flexible approach to the universal service (WIK-Consult, 2013b: 299–307). Providing public funds for a communication technology in decline, the study argued, would involve opportunity costs, since funding provided should better be spent on newer technologies. The study also pointed to very different situations in the member states, where aggregate mail volumes in the newer member states were found to be at substantially lower levels than in the older member states. These member states would thus waste resources in funding a universal service transgressing the future needs of the society. Overall, the study made a case in favour of a revised and leaner USO. Here it referred to data gathered by the British regulator Ofcom on consumer needs (WIK-Consult, 2013b: 216–17). Given that in European postal reform the universal service concept was of far greater importance than in other public utilities (Prosser, 2005: 202), rallying support from the European Parliament and the member states for deregulation on the issue will be a politically challenging endeavour.

In the electricity sector the USO is not as prominent as in the other two sectors. The first directive used the notion of a 'public' (article 2.2 of the directive 96/92/EC) rather than a 'universal' service. This changed with the second package, when the 2003 electricity directive (article 3.3 of the directive 2003/54/EC) defined the universal service as 'the right to be supplied with electricity of a specified quality within their territory at reasonable, easily and clearly comparable and transparent prices' to be granted to all household customers and potentially also to small enterprises. To secure universal service 'member states may appoint a supplier of last resort' and 'shall impose on distribution companies an obligation to connect customers to their grid' (article 3.3).

Wider general interest goals, which relate to social solidarity goals such as the protection of vulnerable customers or environmental goals such as clean energy, have been formulated in all three sectors. In the telecoms sector the protection of vulnerable customers was already addressed in the 1998 voice telephony directive (article 3.1 of directive 98/10/EC), stipulating that services should be affordable to 'vulnerable groups of users such as the elderly, those with disabilities, or those with special social needs'. The 2002 framework directive emphasised that 'users, including disabled users, derive maximum benefits in terms of choice, price and quality' (article 8 of directive 2002/21/EC). The revised 2002 universal service directive introduced new provisions concerning affordability, requiring that member states offer 'tariff options or packages to consumers which depart from those provided under normal commercial conditions, in particular to ensure that those on low incomes or with special social needs are not prevented from accessing or using the publicly available telephone service' (article 9 of directive 2002/22/EC).

New issues concerning fundamental rights and consumer protection emerged with the rapid evolution of electronic communications. As part of the second package the directive on the processing of personal data and the protection of privacy (directive 2002/58/EC) has addressed related issues, and the 2009 package introduced several changes which were taken a step further with the 'connected continent legislative package' proposed in 2013 (European Commission, 2013, Commission press release no. IP/13/828). Concerning potential restrictions to the freedom of access of users to electronic communications, the universal service directive stipulated that member states have to 'respect the fundamental rights and freedoms of natural persons' (article 1.3 of directive 2009/136/EC). The debate on net neutrality is ongoing and has led to major political conflict. The 2009 package contained a declaration by the Commission on net neutrality, which announced monitoring activities and envisaged further policy measures. In its 2013 proposals the Commission envisaged measures which were deemed to end discrimination of Internet users and strengthen consumer rights with stricter rules on contract information concerning the quality and speed of services provided. Critics have, however, argued that net neutrality was put at risk where the proposals would allow for differentiated offers in terms of speed and quality. The debate proved particularly controversial in the European Parliament where MEPs were split over the issue along political lines, with a coalition of liberal, Green and centre-left parliamentarians rejecting any discrimination over Internet traffic (Hirst, 2014). Another element of the proposals is to end roaming charges for incoming calls and to phase out roaming charges altogether (European Commission, 2013: 6). The European Parliament supported a complete ban of roaming charges by the end of 2015 during its first reading of the telecoms package completed in April 2014 (EP, 2014).

Given that the minimum requirements for an EU-wide USO of mail and parcels provide for quite some detail, there is less room for wider general interest goals in the postal sector. The postal directive emphasises that 'postal services fulfil a vital role which contributes to the objectives of social, economic and territorial cohesion' and that 'postal networks have important territorial and social dimensions which make universal access to essential local services possible' (consideration 5 of directive 2008/6/EC). The text also refers to the role of rural postal networks for local businesses, employment and access to new electronic communication services (consideration 19). Consumer protection has also been a key issue in European postal regulation, referring to relevant institutional structures (e.g. independent regulatory authorities, consumer bodies) and procedures (e.g. complaint procedures).

Wider general interest goals in the electricity sector have been introduced into the legal framework referring to the notion of a public service. The 1996 directive stipulated that member states 'may impose on undertakings operating in the electricity sector, in the general economic interest, public service obligations which may relate to security, including security of supply, regularity, quality and price of supplies and to environmental protection' (article 2.2 of the directive 96/92/EC). At this stage of policy formulation environmental aspects figured more prominently in supranational law than social cohesion aspects, with provisions referring to environmental protection, land use, energy efficiency (e.g. in article 5). This changed with the 2003 directive, which for the first time referred to universal service as discussed above. The directive furthermore emphasised the need 'to protect vulnerable customers, including measures to help them avoid disconnection' (article 3.5 of directive 2003/54/EC). How such protection is going to be achieved is left to the member states, and 'may include specific measures relating to the payment of electricity bills, or more general measures taken in the social security system' (consideration 24). The redistributive aspect of electricity supply has become ever more salient with rising energy prices and the detrimental effects of the economic crisis on the financial sustainability of lower income households. The third directive for the first time refers to the problem of 'energy poverty' and urges the member states to adopt national action plans in this respect (consideration 53, article 3.8), and to adopt measures aimed at protecting vulnerable customers (article 3.7). The directive, furthermore, strengthens the protection and rights of consumers, referring to issues such as information on energy consumption and switching of suppliers. Energy prices were dealt with prominently when the Commission presented its energy and climate goals for 2030 (European Commission, 2014a), dedicating a communication and study to the issue of energy prices and costs in Europe (European Commission, 2014b). The study found that overall electricity retail prices had increased significantly, partly due to higher network tariffs and energy taxes as well as renewable subsidies, while price levels differed largely between member states.

Employment related issues have time and again figured prominently in the debate and have mobilised resistance against change. Yet the European level did not become active in this field, given that social and employment policies largely remain in the national remit. There was, however, an effort to generate comparative data and to assess the potential effect of liberalisation on employment patterns and conditions. In the telecommunications sector, the Commission, from the outset, sought to frame employment aspects of liberalisation positively, pointing to potential job growth created by new operators, which would offset losses in traditional segments (European Commission, 1997). In the context of the economic and financial crisis which led to rising levels of unemployment, the topic has gained new political salience. In its connected continent package proposed in 2013 the Commission therefore strongly emphasised that the revised legislative framework would help to create jobs in the electronic communications sector (European Commission, 2013). Social regulation on employment related goals does not form part of the sector-specific regulatory framework in telecoms. The only reference is in the framework directive which states that the activities of national regulatory authorities may relate to broader policies such as those on employment or social cohesion (consideration 7, article 2002/21/EC).

The employment issue figured more prominently in the labour intense postal sector. All postal directives imposed a reporting duty on the Commission to assess the effects of liberalisation on employment. The Commission regularly contracted studies to this end (PricewaterhouseCoopers, 1997; Ramboll, 2002; WIK-Consult, 2013b: 255–87). Overall, these studies emphasised job creation within the new operators, and attributed job losses to factors other than liberalisation. A downwards trend of wages paid in the sector was mainly explained by pre-existing wage premiums and a decreasing profitability of the sector due to electronic substitution (WIK-Consult, 2013b: 268–9). This line of argument also re-emerged in European secondary law, where the second directive made a case that job losses within the USPs would be offset by the job creation among private operators (consideration 13 of the directive 2002/39/EC). The third directive, in addition, highlighted that European law would not touch upon member state prerogatives to regulate employment conditions in the sector (consideration 16 of the directive 2008/6/EC). The directive explicitly referred to the possibility that authorisation may 'be made subject to or impose an obligation to respect working conditions laid down by national legislation' (article 9). Employment related aspects of electricity liberalisation are not addressed in supranational law. Trade unions did, time and again, raise their concerns, but policy makers did not prove responsive to requests to insert social standards into the emerging sector-specific framework. In the first round, the European Parliament, as discussed previously, had given up on amendments aiming at social protection standards for the sector's workers and job security, for the sake of political compromise. And during the second round of policy formulation a study prepared by trade unions on job losses in the sector did not result in targeted policy measures. The only reference on employment to be found in the European electricity directives is that public service guarantees granted to small enterprises may indirectly help to create employment (consideration 19 of directive 2003/54/EC).

The European dimension of social regulation is most developed in connection with service provision and consumer protection, and is weakly developed with regard to employment. Even where supranational law does impose an USO in the sectors, ample discretion is left to the member states. This also holds for wider general interest goals pursued in the directives, where it is up to the member states to put general principles into policy practice. Despite the common trend towards liberalisation and regulatory reform the European framework allows for policy choices which can best be characterised as 'convergence within national diversity' (Lütz, 2004). The extent to which regulatory approaches continue to vary across sectors and policy areas does not point to increasingly convergent paths in a longer perspective. The fact that European policy makers have not made any progress in agreeing on a horizontal, cross-sector framework for SGIs is just another indicator for persisting divergence. The upshot is to say that where a single European model of public service regulation does not exist, national traditions of public service reform and regulation will prevail.

5

Delaying delivery: postal reform in France

In the state-led variant of capitalism government sought to steer reform centrally, while fragmented patterns of interest organisation hampered societal input. Legitimating state-led reforms has however proven particularly difficult in this sector, and governments could not simply impose reform, even less so since trade union mobilisation resonated with public unease about change (Schmidt, 2002: 64–5, 83–4; Thatcher, 2007a: 143). Postal policy in France, attributed to the 'national' or 'public model' in the literature (Campbell, 2002, chapter 7), was dominated by social and political concerns for a considerable time, and the introduction of independent regulation is a recent development. As discussed in Chapter 4, the French fervently resisted reform in EU-level negotiations, leading the reform opponents' camp in subsequent rounds of policy formulation. At the domestic level, the transposition of European directives came with significant delay. The French political elite in a first phase resisted EU-induced change, and in a second phase used external pressure as an empowerment for imposing liberalisation and regulatory reforms. Privatisation has been embraced much later than in other sectors in 2010, mainly as a reaction to lobbying efforts of the USP. Throughout the process national governments intervened directly to compensate for the social costs of reform. The following sections briefly review the history of French postal reform, analyse the transition towards independent regulation, elaborate on the role of organised labour in the postal sector, and present findings related to the development of the postal network and mail delivery.

Don't touch the *service public*! Liberalisation and privatisation *à la française*

> Il faut bien souvent que Bruxelles exerce de la pression sur nous pour qu'on se mette en conformité avec les directives européennes...On attend le dernier moment, on recule, et quand on ne peut plus faire, on le fait.

> Souvent on prend du retard et après il faut aller au pas de charge pour le rattraper. Même si on le rattrape, après il faut aller avec des mesures fortes. (Interview, CFDT)
>
> ('It is quite often necessary that Brussels pushes us to comply with European directives... We are waiting until the very last moment, we are postponing, and only if we cannot manage otherwise, we'll do it. Frequently we are belated, and then we have to move at double speed to catch up. Even if we manage to catch up, we are forced to introduce drastic measures', translated by author)

Postal services are deeply engrained in the social fabric of the French as the emblematic incarnation of the *service public* (Vezinat, 2008: 2). The postal operator has played a traditional role in enhancing socioeconomic cohesion throughout the French territory. French postal history (de Rothschild, 1984) dates back to the reign of Louis XI, who established the equestrian mail, and the legal monopoly created by a decree of Colbert in 1681. Inter-city services for letter distribution (*Petite Poste*) joined the Royal Post Office (*Grande Poste*) – that is, the state-approved service for collection and delivery, in 1780. Banking services for the broader population have been provided since 1818 with the creation of the so-called *Livret A*, a basic and affordable banking account provided by the post office. Not only has this type of account helped to increase access to banking services within socially disadvantaged groups, the funds of these accounts have also played an important role in financing social housing (Camdessus et al., 2007: 12). The principle of a unified postal tariff throughout the territory became reality with the introduction of the stamp in 1848, and a postal ministry was created in 1879. In 1925 the post, telegraph and telephone (PTT) administration was formally established by law, disposing of special financial resources separated from the state budget, and in 1946 postal employees were granted civil-service status. Overall, the post office in France has been an important administrative instrument to foster centralisation, while at the same time safeguarding social cohesion throughout the territory.

First discussions on postal reform emerged in the 1960s, with subsequent governments reflecting on options to separate the telecoms and postal branches. The governments of Raymond Barre and Giscard d'Estaing were particularly articulate on sector reform (Campbell, 2002: 246). Throughout the 1980s, different attempts to introduce change in the telecoms and postal sectors failed. Time and again French governments shied away from reforming the public utilities, whereas other parts of the national economy underwent transformative change (Schmidt, 2002: 81). In 1984 a special report on the future of the French post office (Chevallier,

1984) suggested separating postal and telecommunications operators, but no action was taken. In 1987 the PTT minister Gérard Longuet put forward a consultative document in preparation for a legislative proposal which included plans to alter the organisational structure of the French incumbent (*projet Longuet*). Such plans were, however, withdrawn as a response to massive strike actions in the postal and other highly unionised parts of the public sector, such as rail and metro, between 1986 and 1987 (Howell, 1992: 219).

Paradoxically, postal reform gained momentum with the renewed Socialist victory in 1988. In 1989 Prime Minister Michel Rocard launched his modernisation programme, publishing a circular on the renewal of public services (Ministère de la Fonction Publique et des Réformes Administratives, 1990). According to Guyomarch, the Rocard reforms should be seen in the tradition of the Deferre decentralisation measures adopted in the 1980s, when the Socialists had shifted away from an interventionist and centralised approach. The Socialists furthermore acknowledged the need for greater responsiveness to business needs as well as increased responsibility for civil servants, while they did not as such put into question the role of the state in the public service sector (Guyomarch, 1999: 173–9). Thus, while initially the incoming PTT minister Paul Quillès had announced that he would maintain the status quo, a comprehensive reform package was proposed by the Rocard government (Rocard, 1988).

Strike action by some 1,000 lorry drivers in 1988, which effectively paralysed mail sorting centres, helped to change the political rationale (Darrigrand, 2002: 138). The ministry used this episode to legitimise change, portraying reforms as a means to overcome social tensions and militancy within La Poste. The transposition of the first European directives in the telecoms sector furthermore required change within the French PTT administration, and management within France Télécom urged for modernisation in order to prepare international competition. The incumbent succeeded in gaining governmental support, partially in view of the additional revenue for the treasury to be generated through privatisation (Thatcher, 2007a: 177–82). A commission was set up under the chairmanship of the former trade unionist Hubert Prévot in order to facilitate the negotiation process, delivering its report in 1989 (Prévot, 1989; for a detailed discussion rf. Darrigrand, 2002: 139–41). The positions adopted by the numerous trade unions present in the sector diverged significantly. The left-wing General Confederation of Labour (CGT) rejected the very idea of changing the PTT statute, fearing that such reorganisation would mainly be at the expense of the employees, and would jeopardise their civil servant status (Interview, CGT-PTT). The more centrist and moderate trade unions French Democratic Confederation of

Labour (CFDT) and French Confederation of Christian Workers (CFTC) were willing to compromise (Interview, CFTC; Interview, CFDT). The deal struck was to go ahead with structural separation, while at the same time maintaining the civil servant status of employees at France Télécom and La Poste. The Act (90–568), complemented by a decree (90–1214), amended the Post and Telecommunications Code. Two public entities for postal services and telecommunications were established, which functioned separately as of January 1991. Legislation, furthermore, defined public service obligations and introduced some institutional innovation. A long period of the PTT state administration, which had been created back in 1925, came to an end. The new entities were established as industrial and commercial public corporations (Chevallier, 2003: 106). The reform was, however, far from leading to the state's retreat. Instead, the political arena and, in particular, the PTT ministry continued to have important powers on postal policy through a dense network of institutional arrangements (for a detailed discussion see Campbell, 2002: 252–8). The law in procedural terms secured political influence with the introduction of a schedule of conditions and the contractual plan, alongside organisational structures such as the National Council for Postal Services and Telecommunications, the Higher Committee for Public Services provided in the Postal and Telecommunications Sector and La Poste's Administrative Council.

No major reform was introduced until European law required further domestic change towards the end of the 1990s. When Chirac became president in 1995, the Juppé government issued a circular on state and public service reforms which notably aimed at improving accessibility and quality of services (discussed in detail by Guyomarch, 1999: 175). A general strike declared by civil service unions in 1995 caused reform blockage and the project was called off (Bezes, 2001: 114). When the first European postal directive was introduced in 1997, France for a second time was governed by a *cohabitation* (i.e. the coexistence of a directly elected president and a prime minister who belonged to two opposing political parties). Chirac had dissolved the parliament in spring 1997 to anticipate the vote scheduled a year later, yet a majority of the French electorate turned to left-wing parties, so that the president had to appoint a Socialist politician as his prime minister. Lionel Jospin entered the scene promising to give economic and social policy a leftist touch (Levy, 2002: 337). In the telecoms sector he sought to maintain a strong public role and guarantee employee protection (Thatcher, 1999: 156), and in the labour-intense postal sector he proceeded with caution. On postal issues there was no majority supporting reform in the upper chamber, dominated by the right. Senators across the political spectrum attributed prior concern to aspects of territorial cohesion and were keen to realise social goals through reregulation (Delfau, 1999; Larcher, 1999, 2003). A committee advising the government on postal and telecommunications services (CSSPpt) voiced its preference for a comprehensive reform of existing legislation (Campbell, 2002: 255–6), but instead the government transposed the European directive in a piece of legislation on spatial planning and sustainable development (Act 99–533). It defined the reserved area by using the highest weight and price limits proposed by the European directive, and abstained from changing the institutional set-up in the sector so that regulation remained in the hand of the lead ministry. Thus, structural separation had not been realised at this stage, so that the regulator continued to be 'inside the operator' (Rodrigues, 2002: 251). In a competition case on mail preparation services the Commission decided that the French did not, therefore, respect the required separation between operational and regulatory tasks (decision 2002/344/EC). To respond to these objections, the French government in 2001 adopted two decrees (2001–122 and 2001–1335) which specified the USO, introduced stricter accounting rules and established a mediator to deal with user complaints. Not satisfied with institutional change introduced by France, the Commission published a reasoned opinion in June 2002 where it asked 'France to reinforce the independence of its national regulatory authority for the postal sector' (press release IP/02/932 of 30 June 2001). In July 2003 the Commission issued another reasoned opinion for the French failure to implement the second postal directive by 31 December 2002 (press release IP/03/1005 of 14 July 2003), and in December 2003 referred these matters to the European Court of Justice (press release IP/03/1754).

It was clear by then that minimum reform efforts were not sufficient to secure compliance with EU legislation. This time policy formulation coincided with a phase during which the public mood on European issues was particularly gloomy. Both the so-called Bolkestein directive and the draft constitutional treaty proved highly unpopular in France. The new postal law (no. 2005–516) was in fact adopted only a few days before the French cast their 'Non' against the draft treaty in May 2005. Local politicians and trade union activists alike sought to slow down change and fought for social safeguards. With upcoming regional elections in September 2004, Senators vividly voiced their concerns about the negative impact the reform could have for territorial cohesion (report no. 162, recommendation no. 171 [2003–2004]). The text, adopted in first reading by the Senate in January 2004, attributed a more comprehensive public service mission to La Poste than the proposal initially did in order to address social concerns (text no. 46 [2003–2004]). Discussions also proved difficult in the lower chamber where parliamentarians were preoccupied with the safeguard of universal service provision, the working conditions in the sector and the future of the postal bank (report no. 1988, 21 December 2004).

After difficult negotiations involving the joint committee procedure, both chambers adopted the final text on 12 May 2005. The Act secures compliance with the first two postal directives in the area of liberalisation and regulatory reform, but also adds social guarantees concerning territorial cohesion, universal service provision and industrial relations. Furthermore, the reform was used to expand the range of financial services offered by La Poste, already envisaged in the 1990 Act, by creating a separate banking branch (article 16 of the Act). The biggest French banks lobbied heavily against the project, and lodged an appeal with the European competition authority (Arnold, 2005). In November 2005 the government's decision to create a postal bank was, however, confirmed, announcing its operation for January 2006 (Michel, 2005). The European Commission in 2007 imposed that the duopoly held by the postal bank and the public bank Caisse des Dépôts to distribute the so-called *Livret A*, a cost-free banking account providing basic services, should be abolished in order to allow all banks to offer this type of account (Ricard, 2007a). This decision had been suspended in response to a high-level request: President Chirac in early 2007 asked the president of the European Commission Barroso, to wait with the decision until after French elections in June 2007. Later on the French government, lobbied by the postal bank (La Banque Postale, 2006), continued to contest the validity of the decision on the grounds that the generalisation of the *Livret A* would destabilise a working scheme used to finance social housing and fight exclusion from banking services (Ricard and Michel, 2007). Such resistance, however, proved ineffective, and France had to comply. Since 2009 all banks are therefore allowed to offer this type of financial service to their customers.

Postal policy again became a topical issue in autumn 2006 once the Commission had proposed a third postal directive. The prospect of full market opening caused massive protest in France against the Commission's perceived neoliberal agenda and united the trade unions in outright rejection of the liberalisation proposal (*Les Echos*, 2006). In view of presidential elections upcoming in September 2007, the right-wing Villepin government proved responsive to such concerns, expressing French reservations against the proposal in a letter addressed to Internal Market Commissioner McCreevy (AE 21 November 2006). The French also adopted an official position favouring the safeguard of the reserved sector in the absence of viable financing mechanisms for the USO (Comité interministériel sur l'Europe, 2006). As discussed in Chapter 4 negotiations at the European level were deadlocked until Sarkozy took over as the new French president.

Sarkozy, who had called for rather radical socioeconomic reforms during his campaign (*Le Monde*, 2005), was a deal maker in the previously stalled negotiations at the European level (Interview, EP; Interview, Council).

Domestically, EU-induced full liberalisation by the end of 2010 fuelled an unseen debate on privatisation, driven by the incumbent's lobbying efforts to gain more commercial freedom and access to private capital (*Le Monde*, 2008f, 2009a). The government eventually decided to expand its privatisation agenda to the postal sector, an endeavour which in the past was doomed to fail: in 2000 a governmental proposal had been overthrown by French banking associations and trade unions (Vezinat, 2008: 5); and in 2005, when the Villepin government engaged in an ambitious privatisation programme, the postal sector was not even part of the agenda (Villepin, 2005). It can be argued that the situation was fundamentally different in 2007 when the president, unlike his predecessors, had been elected with an explicit mandate to engage in far-reaching reforms (Levy, 2008: 431). Plans discussed within La Poste and governmental circles became public in July 2008 (Michel, 2008a), resulting in an uproar among sector unions (CGT-FAPT, 2009; *Le Monde*, 2008c). The government set up an expert body in September 2008 with the task to come up with policy proposals concerning the incumbent's future development in a liberalised market. The so-called Ailleret commission, named after its president, presented its report in December the same year (Commission sur le développement de La Poste, 2008). The report concluded that the status quo was not sustainable, pointing to the operator's debt of around €6 billion, mail volumes declining at a speed which transgressed the assumptions of the strategic plan for the period covering 2008–12, and an overall turnover far below competitors such as Deutsche Post. The report therefore suggested an increase in equity through public capital and proposed to transform La Poste into a limited company, yet at the same time ruled out private investment in a climate of economic uncertainty (Commission sur le développement de La Poste, 2008: 31–4). The camp of opponents, rallying trade unions and the political left, mobilised strongly against these proposals through campaigning and industrial action (*Le Monde*, 2008c and g, 2009c; Michel, 2009). They argued that the change of statute would be a first step towards privatisation, with the latter ultimately causing job losses, post office closures and increasing postal rates. Trade unions supported by local politicians launched a petition against privatisation and called for a national referendum on the future of La Poste (*Le Monde*, 2008a and d). Right-wing parties were torn between the rationale put forward by La Poste and the danger that the left would capitalise on the issue in the upcoming June 2009 EP elections (*Le Monde*, 2008b and h).

The reform, which should have been concluded before the summer break 2009, was however put on hold at the height of the economic and financial crisis (*Le Monde*, 2009b). Political agreement was eventually secured in early 2010. The new law (no. 2010–123) as of 1 March 2010 transformed La Poste into a public limited company and transposed the third postal directive into national law. Increases in capital became effective in 2012 and 2013 when the public banking group Caisse des Dépôts invested some €2.7 billion in La Poste (Caisse des Dépôts, 2013: 100). During the 2012 elections Sarkozy was defeated by the Socialist candidate Hollande. During his campaign, Hollande had announced that greater emphasis would be put on industrial and social policy objectives. He explicitly addressed postal reform, promising to provide policy responses in order to address the concerns raised by citizens and employees (Parti Socialiste, 2012). Facing a surmounting public deficit, it is, however, not unlikely that an IPO of La Poste may at some point in the near future form part of the government's austerity programme.

Statism reloaded: the transition towards the regulatory state

> France has opted for a public authority by appointing the Minister for Economic Affairs, Finance and Industry as the national regulatory authority for the postal sector. However, the Minister is also responsible for certain tasks in connection with State property in La Poste as well as for its economic and financial performance. France has therefore still not fully complied with this essential component of EU law on postal services over four years after the deadline for implementation. (European Commission, press release dated 17 December 2003, IP/03/1754)

> The fact that regulators are initiating and introducing economic analysis mechanisms will improve the quality of the political debate (Joëlle Toledano, former board member of the French Authority for the Regulation of Electronic Communications and Postal Services (ARCEP) and former chair of the European Regulators Group for postal services (ERGP))

Although the French postal landscape has changed over time, the role played by the state is amazingly stable. While the postal service provider ceased to be part of the ministerial administration with the transformation into a public corporation in 1990, it remained in the realm of ministerial oversight, the so-called *tutelle* (article 1 of the Act 90–568). It did, however, enjoy greater commercial freedom (articles 14–16) notably in the area of negotiating tariff agreements, raising external funding and holding corporate property such as buildings. Under the 1990 Act a ministry with special responsibility for postal services within its Directorate General of Post and Telecommunications (*Direction Générale des Postes et des Télécommunications*, DGPT) was in charge of governing the sector (article 34), and La Poste had to provide information to the ministry concerning its financial situation, its managerial structure and its fulfilment of public service requirements. Ministerial responsibility has changed over time, reducing the visibility of post and telecoms as a specific ministerial responsibility. Paul Quillès (1988–91) was the last PTT minister, and his successors were dedicated 'postal' ministers until 1995. Since then postal affairs have been one of the areas covered by subsequent ministers of industry and economy.

Under the 1990 regime a National Council for Post and Telecommunications (article 37 of the 1990 Act), headed by the minister and composed of parliamentarians as well as members representing the state, user associations, local entities and trade unions provided policy advice to the ministry, alongside a Higher Commission on Public Services in Telecoms and the Postal Sector (CSSPpt). The Council was abolished in 2004 together with other committees in an effort to simplify the administrative landscape (ordinance 2004–637). The CSSPpt (article 35 1990 Act) exists until today and constitutes the link between La Poste and the two chambers of Parliament. It is headed by an MP and composed of parliamentarians, alongside experts designated by the ministry. Under the current regime the CSSPpt also provides advice to ARCEP (article 4.2 2010 Act). The 1990 Act linked the ministerial and corporate arena through the establishment of administrative councils governing the postal and telecoms incumbent (article 10 of the 1990 Act). These councils were composed of 21 members representing the state, the trade unions and experts, the latter notably selected among user organisations. Over time, the composition has been subject to change in line with further reform steps: article 4 of the 2005 Act adds selection of experts representing local entities as a requirement; article 7 of the 2010 Act adds further precision on selection procedures and composition, limiting the number of members from user associations and local entities in order to include shareholder representation. Following the capital increase after privatisation, the public banking group Caisse des Dépôts as a new shareholder is furthermore entitled to hold three seats in the Council.

The 2010 reform was the most drastic change, two decades after La Poste had been established (1990) as an industrial and commercial public corporation (*établissement public à caractère industriel et commercial*, epic), which is a specific category of a public undertaking under French corporate law. In the European context La Poste's status formed an exception given that most operators had been transformed into limited companies even where the state continued to be the sole owner. The only meaningful change after the 2005 Act was the introduction of a state aid regime in 2006 (amended finance law no. 2006–1771) to secure financing of La Poste's pension scheme. The incumbent was released from all financial obligations against an exceptional payment of €2 billion. The amount of this payment has given rise to controversy, and has sometimes been referred to as one of the factors that contributed to the incumbent's financial difficulty in the years that followed (Michel, 2008a).

The financial and commercial situation of La Poste did not improve in the aftermath of the 2005 reforms, and management urged for further change. La Poste lobbied heavily for a change of its statute, generating evidence with the help of external expertise provided by the commercial bank Rothschild and the law firm Baker & McKenzie (Michel, 2008a). The final report by the Ailleret commission, published in December 2008, put forward three key motives for change: it stressed that La Poste would lack the commercial freedom and flexibility to secure the funds it needed and to respond to business challenges; also, in a longer-term perspective, the state was prevented from reducing its financial engagement and cutting back the sovereign debt; finally, the status of a public corporation appeared incompatible with European state aid rules and had been viewed with a suspicious eye by the European Commission (Commission sur le développement de La Poste, 2008: 32).

The report did, however, also reflect internal disagreement within the Commission as to whether corporatisation would lead to privatisation as in previous cases, such as Gaz de France or France Télécom, and took note of the fact that some members of the Commission were opposed to privatisation (Commission sur le développement de La Poste, 2008: 33–4). However, the minister in charge, Christian Estrosi, made a strong case for change, highlighting that the alternatives were either to increase La Poste's debt, attaining a level of close to €6 billion in 2009, or to ask for state aid, the latter being incompatible with European competition law. The only way out, Estrosi concluded, was to transform La Poste into a limited company and to generate new capital from the public bank *Caisse des Dépôts* (Estrosi, 2009). Indeed, the financial situation of the incumbent had deteriorated significantly ever since 2008, when La Poste, for the first time, paid a dividend to the state of €141 million for the financial year 2007 (Michel, 2008b). The 2010 Act constituted a compromise in order to secure the incumbent's financial viability, while maintaining public ownership, foreseeing that a majority of shares would be held by the state, and some other shares by public-law corporations and employees.

During two decades from 1990 to 2010, the state managed its relations with public corporations through the instrument of contractual plans (article 9 of the Act 90–568, changed by Act 2010–123). Details on the negotiation of the plans and overall objectives have been laid down by decrees (e.g. decree 90–1214), without specifying concrete policy expectations and goals which would be addressed in the contractual plans (Campbell, 2002: 250–1). The ministry in charge of postal policy, alongside the economic and finance ministry, drafted these plans and negotiated the managerial priorities and the financial framework for a period of three to four years with La Poste. A first contractual plan was signed in October 1994 for the period 1995–97 (La Poste, 1995), and subsequent agreements followed for 1998–2001 (La Poste, 1998), 2003–7 (La Poste, 2003) and 2008–12 (L'État et La Poste, 2008). With the 2010 Postal Act the planning instrument has been re-named (contrat d'entreprise, article 10) and significantly reduced in scope, in order to focus on issues directly related to the public service and the general interest mission of the incumbent. These changes in the legal framework had in practice already been anticipated throughout the planning period 2008–12, when a public service contract was complemented by a plan dedicated to the corporate strategy for the coming years (La Poste, 2008). This dualism has been interpreted as a disengagement of the state by critics, notably among trade unions (Interview, FO-COM). The corporate strategy for 2013–18 (La Poste, 2013) as well as the contractual plan 2013–17 (L'État et La Poste, 2013) have been laid down in a difficult context, combining the effects of an economic downturn, falling mail volumes and tense industrial relations. The gloomy outlook for La Poste's future has been one of the reasons CEO Bailly stepped down prematurely in order to allow for new leadership (Michel, 2013a). In August 2013 the Administrative Council chose Philippe Wahl as his successor (Pietralunga, 2013). Wahl, head of the Postal Bank, has a reputation of cultivating close links to the political left and thus appeared as an opportune choice to the Socialist government (Michel, 2013b). As he is a member of the liberal-minded economic think tank *Institut Montaigne* (Schaub, 2013) he is, however, seen with a suspicious eye by leftist trade unions such as SUD (SUD-PTT, 2013).

The move towards independent regulation in France has occurred with significant delay and has been limited in scope, in view of the persisting relevance of political intervention. As mentioned previously, the French abstained from delegating regulatory powers with the first transposition of European law in 1999, although the need to do so had been emphasised by right-wing Senators (Larcher, 1999: 7, 71). Thus, until the 2005 Act postal regulation in France *was* political regulation, that is, the ministry would define regulatory details. France eventually opted for an institutional model of annexation (OPEL, 2006: 75) by attributing postal regulation to the pre-existing and well-established telecoms authority

(ART). The telecoms regulator ART had been created by the Act no. 96–659 on telecoms regulation, and took up its function in January 1997. ART's composition, functioning, resources, its role in the policy process and its competencies had been laid down in article L 36 of the Postal Code (section 1, L 36.1–14). With the expansion of regulatory activities towards the postal sector, these provisions in the Code were amended by the 2005 Postal Act (L 130–4), creating the Authority for the Regulation of Electronic Communications and Postal Services (ARCEP). The agency has the status of an independent administrative agency which, according to French administrative law, disposes of a high degree of formal independence, notably through appointment rules and the collegial structure of the authority's board (Bougrab, 2004: 53). ARCEP has to fulfil information requirements, presenting an annual report for information to both the government and the Parliament (article L 135 Postal Code), but cannot be subject to ministerial instructions so that decisions taken by the regulator can only be overturned by the courts (Postal Code articles L 5–3 and 5–6). According to the Act (article 2), ARCEP is in charge of supervising the liberalisation and proper functioning of the postal market as well as ensuring the financing and protection of the universal service. The regulator, furthermore, monitors the operators' compliance with rules concerning accounting or authorisation requirements. The regulator is also in charge of tariff setting, with the exception of press distribution. The authority has put in place a price-cap regime since 2006 which replaced the previous regime of negotiated tariffs between La Poste and the government (*Le Point*, 2012: 85). The regulator operates within a framework laid down by law and ministerial decrees, the latter defining detailed implementation measures (e.g. decree no. 2006–507 on authorisations). ARCEP has no powers in the realm of competition law, but can refer matters to the French Competition Council (Postal Code article L 5–8).

In conclusion, the institutional framework governing the sector has changed considerably over time, yet state influence remains important. The institutional framework has been transformed with the move to independent regulation and corporatisation, but channels for political influence persist and public ownership is being maintained for the foreseeable future.

Between fragmentation and contestation: the politics of French union power

> En gros, on ne veut pas tomber dans le syndrome du plombier polonais. (Interview, CFTC)
>
> ('We have to avoid the trap of the Polish plumber syndrome', translated by author)

Industrial relations in the state-led regime are puzzling to the extent that these have to be understood as a tension between organisational weakness through fragmentation and political power through contestation. When focusing on patterns of coordination and state capacity, the state-led regime appears to be disconnected and insulated from societal demands that are weakly organised. French trade unions, especially, are referred to as 'policy community outsiders' (Hayward, 1986: 56–67). Very different from other countries where in particular social democratic parties have historically been close to trade unions, French political parties, with the exception of the Communist party, are clearly disconnected from workers' organisation (Howell, 2009: 234). In the absence of such established links, political actors cannot simply impose policies on resistant social groups. Rather, they have to gather support for their positions, which they want to be perceived of as being in the public interest (Hall, 1986: 164–5). What Howell has described as virtual unionism (Howell, 1998) functions as an important source of legitimacy in this respect: in the French context trade unions represent the labour interest at a political level, rather than representing employees' interests at an organisational level. Thus French unions are influential in the macro-political arena, and much less so in collective bargaining (Gumbrell-McCormick and Hyman, 2006: 483). The organisational weakness of the French unions has to some extent been offset by embedding them into the administrative and political structure (Bouin et al., 2010), while the state can rely on trade unions in order to legitimise policies that are socially costly.

When apprehending trade unionism from a longitudinal perspective, some major reforms can be noted, yet these did not unsettle the broad patterns characterising French industrial relations. Weak firm-level industrial relations, a high level of class conflict and deeply interventionist forms of regulation had been the credentials of the French trade union landscape until 1968, when a massive strike wave struck France (Reynaud and Dassa et al., 1971). As a response to this destabilising crisis, the state expanded *dirigisme* beyond state-planning into the realm of labour markets, and pursued a policy aiming at building up firm-level negotiation capacity from the 1970s (discussed in detail by Howell, 2006). This endeavour gained new momentum under the Mitterand government with the so-called Auroux laws which strengthened workplace participation (detailed documentation by Coffineau, 1993; for a critical discussion see Gumbrell-McCormick and Hyman, 2006: 483–85; Moss, 1988). In essence, these policies were regulatory in nature, as they sought to impose 'legal obligations inside the firm' (Howell, 2006: 166) to offset the lack of organisational capacity among the social partners. Trade unions are declared as being representative and must be involved in the negotiation of collective agreements at national level by ministerial order. The last order dated 30 May 2013 lists the same five trade unions as a previous order dated 31 March 1966, namely the CGT, the CFDT, the FO, the CFE-CGC and the CFTC. In order to be representative, social partners have to fulfil several criteria defined in the law (law no. 2008–789), such as achieving a minimum threshold of 8 per cent of the votes during professional elections.

As illustrated in table 5.1, La Poste has, for decades, been a major employer in the French national economy. The incumbent has employed 2–300,000 people since the late 1990s, with a rather moderate decrease over time. La Poste is historically one of the biggest employers in the country, with a share of population employed above 1 per cent, and persistently higher than in other European countries. In 2004, a percentage share of 1.14 was reported, which decreased to 0.9 per cent until 2010 (Eurostat, 2012; Lumio and Fickinger, 2007). The recruitment of employees with civil servant status ended comparatively late, in 2003 (Commission sur le développement de La Poste, 2008: 25), which explains a persisting high share of civil servants. By 2012, 50 per cent of La Poste employees had civil service status.

The union density in the French postal sector for 2009 has been estimated at around 8 per cent, while average union density in the country would also be below 10 per cent (Copenhagen Economics, 2010: 161; Ramboll, 2002: 207). In this context it is important to note that in practical and financial terms French unions do not depend on membership, given that they receive significant financial support for their role in state labour market and welfare institutions, and workplace representatives enjoy generous release from work (Gumbrell-McCormick and Hyman, 2006: 482).

The history of trade unionism in the postal sector reads much like a general history of national trade unionism. In the early decades of the eighteenth century, two rather leftist unions were dominant, representing the class conflict between labour and capital (Interview, CGT-PTT): the General Confederation of Labour CGT created in 1902 and back then closely linked to the Communist Party (Dreyfus, 1995; Thibault, 2002); and the CFTC created in 1919 (Mouriaux, 2010: 43–5). The CGT initially

Table 5.1: Employment in the French postal sector (La Poste)

	1998	2000	2002	2004	2006	2008	2009	2012
FTE (1000s)	306.6	322.5	312.9	309.3	303.4	296	248.6	266.18
% civil servants	77.1	70.9	67.2	61.5	56.6	51.5	57.6	50.4
% labour cost	69.6	66.2	64.2	63.5	66.8	63.2	64	60.5

FTE: full-time equivalents (ITA Consulting and WIK-Consult, 2009; Copenhagen Economics, 2010; WIK-Consult, 2013a)

was the 'big guy' in French industrial relations, until the Second World War, whereas the CFTC was rather small. Both unions experienced several schisms throughout their history which led to the emergence of another four unions, while the creation in 1947 of the French General Confederation of Executives (CGC) took place independently of these two main branches (Mouriaux, 2010: 45–52). The standing of the CGT was considerably weakened post-war by the creation, under American influence (Kantrowitz, 1978), of the more moderate General Confederation of Labour-Workers' Force CGT-FO in 1948 which appealed to reformist spirits within the CGT (Bergounioux, 1975; Mouriaux, 2010: 35–7; Pernot, 2010: 192–209).

Over time, the CGT-FO was perceived as being too accommodating, which re-strengthened not only the CGT, but also gave rise to another spin-off in 1993 with the creation of the National Union of the Autonomous Labour Unions (UNSA). In 1964, when part of its more radically oriented adherents organised within the CFDT, the CFTC experienced a first schism (Mouriaux, 2010: 44). Given that the CFDT moved more and more towards the political centre over time, following a philosophy of social partnership, the discontented extreme wing joined the union movement Solidarity, Unity and Democracy-PTT (SUD) from 1989 onwards (Pernot, 2010: 255). While SUD is quite close to the CGT in its leftist position, expressing itself in a general mistrust vis-à-vis the political and economic elites, it pursues a different organisational philosophy and strategy of mobilisation. SUD perceives the organisation of the CGT as top-down and hierarchical, and instead seeks to foster participation of its members and internal democracy through bottom-up decision making processes; furthermore, it privileges street-level activism and mobilisation over negotiation (Interview, SUD-PTT). Among these seven unions present in the sector, SUD and UNSA are not legally recognised as being representative confederations, given that they have not achieved the 8 per cent threshold during professional elections for the Administrative Council. Since the body was created in 1990 five elections were held in 1991, 1995, 2000, 2005 and 2010. The CGT persistently gained more than

30 per cent of the votes, with a relative decrease from 39 per cent in 1995 to 32 per cent in 2010. SUD has obtained over 20 per cent throughout time, with a slight decrease (26 per cent in 1991 to 21 per cent in 2010), while the share of the CFDT dropped significantly (from 26 per cent in 1991 to 18 per cent in 2010). In the Councils elected in 2005 and 2010 the CGT disposed of three, SUD of two and CFDT and FO of one member, respectively (La Poste, 2006: 33, 2011: 16;).

The size of the workforce and the number of jobs at stake have made postal reform a highly contested issue and raised the profile of the many trade unions mobilising in the sector throughout the reform process. Also, French governments and trade unions alike, despite different political orientations, opposed the European liberalisation agenda during several rounds of EU-level negotiations and, at least externally, could speak with a unified voice. This only changed more recently when the French conservative government agreed to full liberalisation, introduced by the third directive. Domestically, however, there has been considerable disagreement and disunity among trade unions, and subsequent governments have had a hard time securing their alignment in order to legitimise change. The seven trade unions, with very different political orientation, have found it difficult to reach a common stance on domestic reform, with some of them being geared towards protest and mobilisation, and others with a more moderate outlook being oriented towards negotiation and compromise. The CGT and SUD, in particular, adopted more radical positions and were not willing to be signatories of agreements.

In 1990 the CGT was the only union opposing the change of La Poste's statute, while the other unions were willing to negotiate. The key manoeuvre of minister Quillès in the negotiations was to dissociate the question about the corporation's statute and the question about the employees' status. The unions eventually accepted that La Poste would become a public corporation, but in exchange succeeded in securing civil servant status for sector employees (Interview, CGT-PTT). The CGT also opposed the 2005 reform on the grounds that it wanted to safeguard the status quo and, notably, civil servant status for all sector employees. In the view of CGT members collective bargaining practices constituted a second best option, legitimising reduced benefits and privileges for employees through negotiation (Interview, CGT-PTT). The CFTC and CFDT, on the contrary, were willing to accept change on condition that social guarantees would be introduced. In particular, they welcomed the legal obligation to negotiate a collective agreement as a great achievement by the unions in the bargaining process (Interview, CFDT; Interview, CFTC; Interview, CGT-PTT).

Disagreement transformed into agreement when the European Commission put its proposal for full liberalisation on the table, a proposition univocally opposed by all French trade unions. On 14 November 2006, a day of protest against the third directive and ongoing restructuring within La Poste was organised by the CGT, SUD, FO, the CFDT, the CFTC and the CFE-CGC (*Le Monde*, 2006). Similarly, the same unions with the exception of the CFE-CGC joined forces when plans to privatise La Poste became public, signing a joint declaration in July (CGT-FAPT, 2009: 59) and organising a national strike in September 2008 (*Le Figaro*, 2008). Furthermore, trade unions participated in a national committee against the privatisation of La Poste composed of several associations and parties of the political left, which organised a national vote calling for a referendum on the future of postal services in October 2009. According to press coverage, more than two million people participated in the vote, with particularly high levels of participation in rural and underprivileged urban areas (*Le Monde*, 2008e). Trade unions were therefore highly critical of the 2010 law, and pressed hard to obtain social guarantees regarding pensions and health insurance. Trade union representatives also reported that the social climate and industrial relations had deteriorated within La Poste (Interview, CGT-PTT; Interview, SUD-PTT). Such assessment resonates with press coverage regarding increased stress levels in the workplace and incidents of suicides committed by employees (Bartnik, 2010; Michel, 2007). The unions also share a negative assessment of structural reforms within La Poste and what they call a disengagement of the state which they see materialising in an altered role of strategic and contractual plans. Elected members of the unions in the Administrative Council, for instance, rejected the contractual plan 2013–17 voted in a session in April 2013 (CGT-FAPT, 2013).

While union mobilisation proved strong in the political arena, with social partners seeking to influence political regulation, the track record is rather mixed in the realm of industrial relations. The remuneration and social security schemes of civil servants are defined within the framework governing the civil service, and all other employees are covered by collective agreements. As stated earlier, the state has sought to shape industrial relations in the sector, mainly by introducing binding legal requirements on the social partners. A general minimum wage has existed in France since 1950. Sector-specific rules for the postal and telecoms sectors have been laid down by a joint collective agreement following the separation between La Poste and France Télécom in 1992. In addition, the 2005 law imposed the negotiation of a collective agreement that should apply to employees at La Poste without civil servant status and to all employees of licensed postal service operators (section 26, law no. 2005–516). To this end, the law prescribes the creation of a committee consisting of delegates from nationally representative union organisations of employees and employers. Postal operators including La Poste created the Association of Postal Operators (SOP) in 2006. The composition of SOP has varied over time, and some operators have left the association so that not all licensed postal operators engage in negotiations. La Poste, Swiss Post International France SAS, Adrexo, DHL Global Mail (France) SAS, IMX France SAS and G3 Worldwide (France) SAS were the six founding members of the association. Another six players subsequently joined, namely Let, Stamper's, Pro Courrier, Courrier Plus, Alternative Post and Press'tissimo. In 2013 Adrexo, Spring, DHL Global Mail, bpost, 3L DistriPlis, FamilyPro Courrier and the *Groupe* La Poste constituted the SOP. The employees' side is represented by the CGT, the CGC, the CFDT, the CFTC, FO and SUD.

Negotiations started in April 2007, but so far have not been concluded due to persistent disagreement between the social partners (CFTC, 2013; CGT-FAPT, 2012). Both the substance and scope of a potential agreement gave rise to controversy. Trade unions feared that a new agreement would water down the provisions set in the existing joint collective agreement, and insisted that the standards set by the latter should be regarded as the starting point for further negotiations (Interview, CGT-PTT). Concerning the scope of the agreement, a discussion arose about whether licensed postal operators whose core business is not in the postal sector should be subject to the agreement (Commission sur le développement de La Poste, 2008: 27). During the formulation of the 2010 Act the SOP thus suggested an amendment to the law, which would allow for arrangements where several collective agreements would apply to a single employee, a proposal fervently rejected by trade unions (Tellier, 2010). The track record of a similar agreement covering direct mailing activities is rather discouraging: it took the social partners fifteen years of lengthy negotiations before the agreement entered into force in 2006 (agreement no. 2372). According to trade union representatives (Interview, CFTC; CFDT), operators had opted for a delaying strategy in order to save labour costs. What is more, ever since the collective agreement on direct mailing came into effect, compliance has posed serious difficulties. Salaries paid could vary to up to 30 per cent, one interviewee estimated, yet monitoring was difficult in a situation where trade unions were hardly present within new operators (Interview, CFDT). The French regulator, ARCEP, has no legal role in monitoring compliance with such collective agreements and does not endorse a role as a social regulator. Interview partners at ARCEP argued that the social partners, disposing of the required information and expertise, would be in a far better position to report non-compliance to the Labour Inspection Office (Interview, ARCEP). Trade union representatives, on the contrary, suggested that authorisations should be made conditional on the adherence to the SOP to increase the coverage of the agreement (CFTC, 2013). Among trade unions, the CGT has been most reluctant to sign agreements – the union has not endorsed any of the deals struck by the SOP and other unions, and repeatedly did not sign wage agreements for employees at La Poste (e.g. the agreement for 2012, rf.La Poste, 2012).

In accordance with diverging negotiation positions, the social climate within La Poste has been assessed very differently. The Ailleret report (Commission sur le développement de La Poste, 2008: 26–7) came to the conclusion that the social dialogue is working, given that major crises have been prevented and numerous agreements have been signed (referring to 41 national, and 650 local agreements between 2003–7). Representatives from the leftist unions CGT and SUD, on the contrary, argued that industrial relations have deteriorated and are in bad shape (Interview, CGT-PTT; Interview, SUD-PTT).

Postal services in the state-led model

> Donc ça n'est pas n'importe quoi, le service public... les fonctionnaires sont recrutés, ils ont une qualification, un rôle, une mission de service public à remplir, en toute indépendance, ce qu'on leur demande c'est de faire leur travail, de bien faire leur travail, de prêter serment, d'assurer la continuité du service public... c'était la confidentialité, la sécurité, les lettres arrivent, elles ne se perdent pas en France. Maintenant ça commence à devenir n'importe quoi. Parce que n'importe quel privé prend le truc et... ça se perd, ça arrive parterre, dans la boîte aux lettres à côté, chez celle du voisin. (Interview, CGT-PTT)
>
> ('The public service mission is not trivial ... the civil servants were recruited following certain procedures, they were qualified, they had a role, a public service mission to accomplish, in total independence; what was asked from them was to do their job, to do it well, to swear an oath, to guarantee the continuity of the public service ... there was confidentiality, security, mail items reached their destination, they did not get lost in France ... today, it starts to become trivial. Any private operator can transport the mail ... items get lost, they fall on the ground, they get posted into the letter box next-door, of the neighbour', translated by author)
>
> Vous n'êtes pas n'importe quelle entreprise. En termes de présence, de service, nous devons refaire de La Poste une référence, un exemple. (François Hollande, 27 March 2012)
>
> ('You are not just any other business. We need to re-establish La Poste as a point of reference, as a role model in terms of presence and service', translated by author)

The French context, more than the situation in any other country, is characterised by its state-centred public service paradigm (Brachet, 1999; Chevallier, 2003; Delfau, 1999; Savary, 2005). The French *service public* forms part of the welfare obligations of the Republican state to serve the general interest (Ambrosius, 2000; Schweitzer, 2001) and constitutes both a 'legitimizing myth for state power and a social and institutional reality' (Clark, 2000: 164). In fact, the notion is at the very basis of the French administrative and political system and its operational principles, laying down the duties of the civil servants (Cole, 2000). It dates back to a 1946 general statute which defined the requirements for a civil servant career, the terms and conditions of services as well as the ethics and responsibilities of the civil servants (Cole and Jones, 2005: 569). In the postal sector the public service mission attributed to La Poste is broad and goes well beyond the more narrowly defined universal service (Chevallier, 2003: 101). It comprises the area of banking services, press delivery and territorial cohesion. The distribution of press articles, for instance, is perceived as an important element of the postal public mission (Petel, 1996:34–5). The territorial presence of the postal network forms a key element in the French administrative and political system: the post office has often been the sole presence of the state in a centralised and dispersed territory and has played a role in social cohesion by fostering local economic development (Boldron et al., 2008: 57–8). In the banking sector, in particular, La Poste has traditionally provided critical social services through its presence in rural and newly urbanised areas facing social problems (Anderloni and Pilley, 2002: 15; Delfau, 1999). It, therefore, comes as no a surprise that trade union representatives opposing change have referred to this public service heritage, when defending the civil servant status and functions, as illustrated by the interview quoted above. In what follows, I first address policymaking arrangements in the French postal sector, and then discuss regulatory provisions and policy practice concerning mail delivery and the postal network.

French postal policy traditionally implemented policy goals through contractual planning. The reregulatory movement accompanying liberalisation, modernisation and corporatisation reforms has, however, required an upgrade of the legal framework in the sector strengthening political regulation, and a transition towards independent regulation. Throughout reform the state has also sought to reduce its financial involvement in service provision. While the 1990 reform broadly defined La Poste's and France Télécom's public service mission, it left further detail on issues such as affordability, quality of services or the density of the network to the schedule of conditions and the contractual plans. According to the law, mail delivery, the transport and distribution of press items and banking services formed part of La Poste's duties (article 2), which together with France Télécom also had a task in safeguarding public security (article 5) and territorial cohesion (article 6). The transposition of the first European directive, which introduced minimum standards for the USO to be laid down in national law, required more detail in French legal provisions (Anderloni and Pilley, 2002: 48; Rodrigues, 2002: 240). The 1999 Act therefore specified the scope and quality provisions for the universal service, attributed the USO to La Poste as the USP, and specified upper limits for the reserved area in accordance with the European directive. At the same time, legal provisions transgressed a narrow notion of a universal postal service very much in line with the French public service tradition, referring to equality, territorial and social cohesion as well as economic and social efficiency as leading principles of postal policy (article L 1 of law no. 99–533). To handle user complaints, a mediator was set up by decree in 2001 (no. 2001–1335). The 2005 reform has substantially altered the regulatory regime governing mail delivery and the postal network. Political regulation does, however, continue to play the predominant role through a combination of legislation, which sets the broad framework, and ministerial decrees, which specify regulatory detail. This did not change fundamentally with the last reform in 2010, although the latter attributes some additional competencies to ARCEP. In comparison to other European member states, the French agency is therefore narrowly circumscribed in its regulatory role, and operates within the boundaries of a politically defined framework (WIK-Consult, 2013b: 14).

The postal presence on the French territory has traditionally been secured through contractual planning. Such plans have been negotiated by the state, the Association of French Mayors and the incumbent. The move towards more detailed political regulation and a role for independent regulation is a recent development. The 1990 Postal Act provided that 90 per cent of the population in a department should have access to a post office that is no further than 5 km and in not more than a 20–minute drive by car. The decree on universal service provision (no. 2007–29, 5 January 2007) complementing the 2005 Postal Act specified that 95 per cent of the population should have access to a contact point at a maximum distance of 10 km. The 2010 Act, for the first time, laid down a specific number of postal outlets, requiring La Poste to operate some 17,000 contact points (article 3 law of the law no. 2010–123). The law did not, however, specify the nature of these contact points, nor did it require a minimum number of full-service post offices. As a consequence, contractual planning did not disappear, but recent reforms have provided for a more detailed legal and regulatory framework. Governmental regulation complementing the 2005 Postal Act provided guidance in this respect, such as the decree on La Poste's contribution to spatial planning (decree no. 2006–1239, 11 October 2006) and the decree governing a national postal fund for geographical equalisation (decree no. 2007–310, 5 March 2007).

In order to justify practices of state funding through objective and transparent measurement, the 2010 Act entrusted ARCEP with the task of evaluating the net cost of the territorial presence following a method defined by the State Council. In its first two assessments for the years 2010 and 2011, the agency evaluated the net cost at €269 million and €247 million, respectively (decision no. 2012–1311). State contribution in the same period amounted to €156 million and €171 million (L'État et La Poste, 2013: 17). La Poste is also receiving money from La Banque Postale, as the latter continues to use the postal counter and distribution network (Commission sur le développement de La Poste, 2008: 13–14). The state contributes to such compensation relating to banking services, yet has reduced the amount of annual payments, which went down from €280 million in 2009, to €210 million in 2014 (L'État et La Poste, 2013: 13–16). As table 5.2 illustrates, the number of outlets in relation to the size of the country and population density has been relatively stable over time. In comparison to other European countries France has a rather large and less densely populated territory. Population density in France is constant at around a hundred inhabitants per square km (WIK-Consult, 2013a: 38). In addition, there is considerable variation between densely populated urban areas and remote rural areas. The rate of urbanisation was already high in 2008 at a level of 77.3 per cent (ITA Consulting and WIK-Consult, 2009b: 43), and had significantly increased to 86 per cent by 2011 (WIK-Consult, 2013a: 34).

Despite these rather challenging preconditions, the density of the French postal network is high compared to other European countries. The average density of outlets across Europe in 2002 has been measured at a level of 2.38 outlets per 10,000 inhabitants, while France provided some 2.8 postal outlets (WIK-Consult, 2004: 165). As the data reported below illustrates, the number of outlets has been maintained at a level of around 17,000 contact points, which corresponds to the minimum density laid down in the 2010 Postal Act. Until then the actual density of the French network went far beyond minimum legal requirements. In fact, compliance with the law was already secured where La Poste provided at least 14,500 contact points (Commission sur le développement de La Poste, 2008: 20). This density, which in rural areas surpasses the accessibility of other proximity services, has been justified with spill-over effects and positive demand externalities for commercial services (Boldron et al., 2008: 57–8) – that is, positive side-effects of the postal presence on the local business environment. While maintaining its postal presence,

Table 5.2: Postal outlets in France (La Poste)

	1999	2000	2002	2004	2006	2007	2010	2012
outlets	17,080	17,065	17,048	16,947	17,041	17,066	17,079	17,041
% POs	82.7	82.5	83.3	81.0	73.2	70	59.8	57.6
outlets inh.[1]	2.8	2.8	2.8	2.7	2.7	2.7	2.64	2.61
Area/outlet[2]	32.6	33	32.4	32.5	32.4	32.3	32.3	32.4

[1] outlets per 10,000 inhabitants
[2] average area in sq km covered by an outlet
(ITA Consulting and WIK-Consult, 2009; WIK-Consult, 2004; UPU, 2012; WIK-Consult, 2013a)

La Poste has also engaged in cost-cutting by transforming the type of postal outlets. During the period from 1999 to 2012, La Poste reduced the share of in-house branches by some 25 per cent from over 80 to below 60 per cent. Launching the so-called *Terrain* project, La Poste committed to provide a minimum of one in-house branch per geographical unit (terrain), which would be complemented by at least one or more other outlets. The central office secures the governance of the other outlets in matters such as reporting and management. The transformation project aims at increasing the share of partnerships, as these are far less costly for La Poste and presumably better fitted to customer needs with more flexible opening hours (Commission sur le développement de La Poste, 2008: 20; ECORYS, 2005: 164). In 2007 La Poste operated some 12,000 branches, of which 3,600 local post offices were located in town halls, and 1,400 postal agencies operated as partnerships with local retailers (Commission sur le développement de La Poste, 2008: 20).

With respect to mail delivery the legal framework identifies minimum requirements regarding the scope and quality of the USO as well as the frequency of mail deliveries and collections. Provisions on the universal service require that basic letter mail is to be provided at a uniform tariff at no more than one euro and that home delivery to all households is guaranteed six days a week. The 2005 Act also introduced a compensation fund to be activated where the universal service provider could not cover its costs. France has maintained a ubiquitous USO which in terms of services covered ranks top in the EU 27 (Campbell Jr et al., 2008: 198; ECORYS, 2008: 47–8; WIK-Consult, 2013b: 129). The French USO includes addressed direct mail and bulk mail, newspapers, periodicals, catalogues, printed matter and parcels. Services delivered within the scope of the USO have been exempt from VAT, which is also laid down in the decree on universal service provision (decree no. 2007–29, 5 January 2007).

Furthermore, ministerial regulation has dealt with issues related to press distribution (decree no. 2007–787, 9 May 2007) and the quality of service (order, 22 July 2008). The specific mandate of La Poste to distribute press items is furthermore governed by tripartite agreements which are regularly being negotiated between the state, La Poste and the press organisations.

Given that volumes of items delivered are in decline, while the costs per item increase, there have regularly been tensions between La Poste and the publishing houses over quality and price issues (Campbell, 2002: 261). As with the other contractual agreements the state has reduced the level of financial compensation granted, going down from €242 million in 2009 to €180 million in 2015 (L'État et La Poste, 2013: 11–12). Independent regulation plays a key role in monitoring compliance with the USO and in regulating prices. ARCEP determines the multi-annual tariff framework of universal service provision, ensures compliance with the quality targets determined by ministerial order and is in charge of signalling a potential shortfall in financial coverage for the universal service provision (article L 5–2 of the Postal Code). The compensation fund foreseen in the law would thus be activated on the basis of a recommendation by the regulator. ARCEP also provides an opinion on funding for the provision of universal service press items, and in the past has approved tariff increases (e.g. opinion no. 2012–0575 approving an average increase of 4.3 per cent). The evolution of tariffs for mail items has become more stable since the introduction of a price-cap regime implemented by ARCEP. Previously negotiated contracts had been characterised by both instability caused by long periods of stagnating prices followed by sudden price changes and a lack of transparency as to the rationale underlying the price policy (*Le Point*, 2012: 85). As table 5.3 illustrates the price for a mail item of less than 20 grams was stable at €0.46 for a relatively long period, prior to a sharp increase to €0.50 in 2003, and to €0.53 in 2005. Between 2005 and 2010, increases were mostly incremental, but another sharp increase was introduced in 2011. In fact ARCEP had repeatedly approved tariff increases (e.g. an average increase of 2.6 per cent in the price of the universal service, ARCEP opinion 2012–1406), while the incumbent had not fully used the flexibility given by price-cap regulation. Rather than increasing the prices of single-piece mail items, La Poste has resorted to increases in bulk mail tariffs, in order to rebalance its accounts (*Le Point*, 2012: 97). The rate of next-day delivery has, overall, improved since 2005, and now is better than in the late 1990s.

In conclusion, postal reform in France provides for interesting findings regarding the expectations raised in Chapters 2 and 3. The transition towards the regulatory state in France did not make redistributive policies disappear, although the financial engagement of the state has been reduced

Table 5.3: Mail services in France (La Poste)

	1999	2003	2005	2007	2008	2010	2011
20g tariff FSC[1] in €	0.46	0.50	0.53	0.54	0.55	0.56	0.63
20g tariff EU letter FSC[1] in €	0.46	0.50	0.55	0.60	0.65	0.70	0.80
D+1 performance %	80.5	65.7	79	82.5	83	83.4	87.9

[1] Fastest Standard Category
(ITA Consulting and WIK-Consult, 2009; WIK-Consult, 2013a)

over time. The move to independent regulation remained narrowly circumscribed. The trade unions influenced the political debate, but were less effective in shaping industrial relations in the sector. Although legally empowered to do so, the social partners have not succeeded in negotiating a sector-specific collective agreement. From the perspective of comparative capitalism France exhibits a strong degree of path dependence in line with the SME model. Liberalisation and, more recently, privatisation have not led to the rollback of the state, but rather involved a redeployment of state capacity (Levy, 2005: 122) through new forms of public and independent regulation. There was not a decline of interest organisation, given that from the outset the situation in France was characterised by low levels of unionisation.

6

Negotiating change: postal reform in Germany

The reform path in the coordinated variant of capitalism can best be described as 'negotiated change', where societal input played a key role. Deutsche Post supported privatisation and liberalisation in view of its strategy of international expansion, while the state strengthened the growth of the incumbent firm without sheltering it from competition. This approach to postal policy has been described in the literature as a 'mercantile model' (Campbell, 2002). As discussed in Chapter 4, subsequent German governments have lent support to EU-wide liberalisation. Hence the transposition of European directives coincided with domestic reform steps, and at several instances Germany anticipated EU-induced change. Privatisation predated market opening, and the German post office is one of the few incumbents in the European context to have engaged in structural reorganisation and privatisation since the 1980s. Alongside the post office, a strongly organised trade union imposed itself as a key negotiation partner in the corporatist German system. As a result, social considerations regarding both service delivery and employment conditions have been taken into account throughout the process. There was, however, considerable controversy within the political arena about how the balance should be struck between economic and social objectives. In this context arm's length state-economy relations have helped to bring about a regulatory regime which prioritised market creation both in terms of legally stated objectives and in regulatory practice. The following sections will review the history of German postal reform, analyse the separation of operational and regulatory tasks, discuss the role of the social partners and examine how the provision of postal services has evolved.

Pace-setting privatisation and liberalisation reforms

> Die politische Diskussion hat sich zu Beginn der 1990er Jahre vor allem darauf fokussiert – und das war ein Beschleuniger der Privatisierung – dass

> die Telekomleute (Vorstände, aber auch die Mitarbeiter) immer gesagt haben, dass sie die Post mitsubventionieren müssen. Die Post ist nicht, hat keine eigenen Erträge, sie ruht sich auf der Zusage der Telekom aus, dass sie jährlich von der Telekom die Verluste ausgeglichen bekommt. (Interview, MP 1)
>
> ('At the beginning of the 1990s the key issue in political discussions – and this has been speeding up privatisation – was that telecoms people (CEOs, but also staff) kept saying that they had to subsidise the post office. The post office would not generate its own revenue, it would rely on the guarantee that the telecoms branch made up for the annual deficits', translated by author)

German postal history reflects German state-building history, given that the centralisation of the postal infrastructure has played a key role in unifying the territories in order to create a nation state. Prior to the establishment of a national postal system under the control of the state, the Thurn und Taxis family had built up a network under the patronage of the Habsburg emperors which covered most of Europe (North, 1995: 32–4; Novácek and Kopecký, 1989: 59–67). Unlike France and Britain, where efforts to centralise territorial organisation through an efficient postal system date back to the sixteenth century, in Germany regional postal schemes survived until the twentieth century. With the creation of the German Empire (1871–1918) a unified postal system was set up, and Prussia took over the Thurn und Taxis privileges (Novácek and Kopecký, 1989: 67). However, Bavaria and Wurttemberg kept their own postal administrations until 1920 (North, 1995: 54–5). Heinrich von Stephan, the general post director of the Empire, played a key role in administrative reorganisation and operational centralisation of the postal system. The 1871 law on the postal system was in force until 1970 (North, 1995: 56). During the Third Reich postal policy was instrumentalised in terms of the Nazi propaganda, and the privacy of correspondence, posts and telecommunications had been abolished. Following the Second World War the postal system was reconstructed with the establishment of the German Federal post office and the post office of the German Democratic Republic (GDR).

The above quote points to the fact that German postal reform launched in the early 1990s has been driven mainly by dynamics in the neighbouring telecommunications sector. While the possibility of privatising state enterprises had been debated since the 1960s, the idea of selling shares might have seemed appealing when an economic slowdown in the 1970s put public finance under pressure (Windisch, 1987). The post office, a loss-making and non-profitable business at the time, could have been an obvious candidate for privatisation (Arnaboldi and Bauer, 2002: 99–100), yet no actions were taken at this point in time. The climate for reform changed in the early 1980s, when an incoming government envisaged telecoms and postal reforms (Grande, 1989) in order to foster technological innovation and structural change (Bulmer et al., 2007: 369; Schneider, 2001: 63). The first postal reform (Poststrukturgesetz 8 June 1989, Federal Law Gazette I 1026) was part of a broader reform agenda aiming at privatising special estates of the Federation (Gramlich, 1990; Bulletin of the Federal Government no. 34 28 March 1985 p. 281 ff.). The 1989 law split the German Federal post office into three separate business units, dealing with postal, telecoms and banking services.

Postal reform was subsequently accelerated in the context of German reunification. The GDR post office with its particularly dense and antiquated network had accumulated a huge workforce and was a central element in the GDR's political system, particularly in the area of state security. Modernising the GDR's pre-existing communication system therefore was a major challenge that required an enormous amount of investment (Arnaboldi and Bauer, 2002: 120). In addition, the international reform movement in telecoms had started to raise concerns about the competitiveness of the German incumbent. Political negotiations to move ahead with privatisation kicked off in 1991. Given that public ownership of the postal and telecoms administration was laid down in the German Basic Law (article 87.1), change required consent by a two-thirds majority in both parliamentary chambers in order to amend the constitution. The reform bill was negotiated by a cross-party committee composed of representatives from the CDU, FDP and SPD (Interview, MP 1). The Social Democrats were initially opposed to the idea of transforming the post office into a limited company, but their support was secured in exchange for a commitment that postal employees would be covered by a collective agreement and that their civil servant status would remain untouched (Dörr, 1994: 35–6). The resulting law (dated 30 August 1994, Federal Law Gazette I 2245) came into effect in September 1994. The provision of postal and telecoms services could from now on be entrusted to private companies succeeding *Deutsche Bundespost* or other private operators, yet the Federation would have the duty to guarantee territorial coverage of service provision. Also, majority state ownership was mandatory for a transitional period of at least five years, and any further change would require a federal law with the consent of the Bundesrat. Stipulating that monopoly rights would only be granted for a provisional period until the end of 1997, a sunset clause was built into this reform step, preparing the ground for further change.

While the 1989 and 1994 reforms had been introduced under a conservative government, which held a majority in both chambers, the situation was fundamentally different for the third round of reform in the mid-1990s. The conservative government, consisting of a CDU/CSU-FDP coalition, had to cope with the SPD-dominated upper house, with the upcoming elections in 1998. The postal ministry had already announced its reform intentions in 1995 (Federal Ministry for Post and Telecommunications, 1995), and a government proposal was brought forward in March 1997 (Bundestag Printed Paper no. 13/7774, 30 May 1997). This proposal deviated substantially from a parliamentary motion that had been adopted by the SPD faction (Bundestag Printed Paper no. 13/4582, 8 May 1996). It turned out that at this stage there was no majority for total market opening. The 1997 Postal Act therefore still granted a statutory fixed-term exclusive licence to the post office (article 51). The government had initially suggested that letter mail items weighing more than 100 grams could be opened to competition (Bundestag Printed Paper no. 13/7774, 30 May 1997), but the compromise was to double this threshold to 200 grams, and to include addressed catalogues and mass mailings weighing less than 50 grams in the reserved sector.

Concerned about risking a race to the bottom of social standards in the labour intense sector, the Social Democrats initially wanted to impose a minimum wage which would be around 90 per cent of the wage levels paid by the incumbent (Interview, MP 2). In the course of negotiations the Social Democrats put forward less ambitious proposals in order to secure support from the other parties. These added social objectives, and in particular proposed to include licensing requirements related to working conditions (Bundestag Printed Paper no. 13/871, 8 October 1997). Although as a matter of principle the government was opposed to such social safeguards, arguing that these were an issue of social policymaking rather than of regulating a specific sector, it had to give in for the sake of compromise. The deal was struck in a last minute showdown shortly before existing legislation was due to expire at the end of December. Agreement was reached to insert article 6.3 stipulating that authorisations should only be granted to operators respecting the prevailing working conditions in the sector.

Once in power, the Social Democratic government led by Gerhard Schröder (1998–2005) again intervened as advocate of social interests in the sector. In 2001 the legal monopoly granted to the post office, due to end in 2002, was extended until 2007. The government argued that liberalisation should take place at equal pace across the EU, and that Germany should not unilaterally put jobs and working conditions in the sector at risk (FAZ, 2001; German Bundestag Printed Papers 14/6300:III; 15/1226:III; 15/5790: VII). Within the upper house several state governments were firmly opposed to further delaying full market opening, but they remained in the minority. Similarly, an initiative in the upper house launched in autumn 2004 by the Christian Democratic state governments of Hesse and Lower Saxony, seeking to overturn the monopoly extension, failed to secure sufficient support (FAZ, 2004, 2005).

The postal debate re-emerged during the mandate of the grand coalition government (2005–9), composed of the CDU/CSU and SPD, led by Angela Merkel. While German legislation stipulated market opening as of January 2008, further delay in EU-wide liberalisation had become a likely scenario (discussed in Chapter 4). The Social Democratic coalition partner therefore argued in favour of another extension of the legal monopoly rather than a pioneering role of Germany, raising concerns about practices of social dumping by private operators (Hulverscheidt, 2007). By 2006 and 2007 competitors in the German market had already gained a significant market share, and critics argued that their competitiveness was mainly attributable to low wage levels. CDU/CSU leadership was not ready to give up on the timetable, but secured support from the SPD in exchange for social guarantees. The Social Democrats agreed to liberalise the German market by 2007 on condition that a sector-specific minimum wage would be introduced (*Spiegel*, 2007a). The issue was, however, not settled for good since conflict persisted among the social partners resulting in two rival agreements negotiated by the incumbent's and competitors' side. The CDU-led ministry of economics was therefore reluctant to lend support to the agreement negotiated between Deutsche Post and ver.di. These reservations were substantiated by an economic rationale arguing that the wage level set would crowd out competitors (FAZ, 2007b; Hoffmann and Schneider, 2007). The SPD's discontent with this attitude was paramount, and put the stability of the coalition under threat (Fried, 2007). Chancellor Merkel therefore aligned her party so that both parliamentary chambers declared the legal validity of the agreement, taking effect as of January 2008 (Bundestag Minutes of plenary proceedings no. 16/134, 14 December 2007, Bundesrat Minutes of plenary proceedings no. 840, 20 December 2007).

Following complaints filed by private operators with administrative courts at several levels, the agreement was, however, invalidated by a court ruling (Berlin Administrative Court no. VG 4 A 439.07). After an episode of renewed disagreement within the grand coalition, existing legislation on the posting of workers and minimum working conditions was amended to address the concerns raised by the judiciary (*Spiegel*, 2008a). In particular, the legal priority of collective agreements (*Tarifvorrang*) over political regulation was reversed, so that the latter could invalidate pre-existing collective agreements (German Bundestag Plenary Protocol 16/200 dated 22 January 2009, 21718–21610; Bundesrat Plenary Protocol 854 dated 13

February 2009 3–10). By 2010, however, when the agreement in ongoing court proceedings was invalidated for formal reasons at the highest judicial level (ruling of the Federal Administrative Court dated 28.01.2010, BVerwG 8 C 19.09), the new coalition government composed of CDU/CSU and FDP chose not to use these legal prerogatives. Rather than by a sector-specific agreement, minimum wage levels for postal delivery will be governed by a general minimum wage, agreed in July 2014. A transition period allowing for lower wages until 2017 applies to newspaper delivery (*Spiegel*, 2014).

Economic regulation and the social challenges of reform

> Unserer Meinung nach hätte die Regulierungsagentur von Anfang an Informationen einholen müssen für die Umsetzung des Artikel 6.3, aber sie hat in die Richtung eben nichts unternommen – zumindest viele Jahre lang nicht, und sie hat's jetzt im letzten Jahr unter dem politischen Druck getan. Dass es möglich ist, und dass sie eigentlich verpflichtet wäre, ist ja damit bewiesen, dass sie es jetzt getan hat, unter einer unveränderten Gesetzeslage. (Interview, MP 2)
>
> ('We think that the regulatory agency should have collected the information needed to implement article 6.3 from the very beginning, but she has been inactive in this regard – at least for many years, and she has become active during the last year due to political pressure. That it is possible, and that she had a duty to do so is proven by the fact that the agency has now become active, while the legal framework is still the same.' Translated by author)

Prior to privatisation the post office constituted a special estate conducted as a matter of Federal administration with its own subordinate administrative structure. As such, the incumbent not only formed part of German public law in organisational terms, but was also granting services according to conditions set by public law (Möstl, 1999: 32). The organisational split-up between the postal, telecoms and banking branches introduced by the 1989 Act established separate accounting with a view to put an end to practices of cross-subsidising from the more profitable telecoms towards postal services (Braubach, 1992: 23; Federal Ministry of Economics and Technology, 2002; Plagemann, 1996: 53). In the 1980s the German post office was in a very bad condition, relying on an inefficient and costly bureaucracy that produced losses year after year. In 1990, for example, the deficit of the West German incumbent amounted to €320 million, with an additional €750 million of liabilities accumulated by its East German counterpart (Arnaboldi and Bauer, 2002).

As a result of the second reform in 1994 the business units were transformed into public limited companies by two legal acts (*Postneuordnungsgesetz* (PTneuOG), 14 September 1994 Federal Law Gazette I, 2325 and *Postumwandlungsgesetz* (PostUmwG), 14 September 1994, Federal Law Gazette I 2325, 2339). Practices of political oversight did not, however, disappear with reorganisation. In particular, the lead ministry could continue to control managerial decisions inasmuch as these were affecting territorial coverage of services provided (Möstl, 1999: 32). At the same time the new regime gave the companies greater commercial flexibility in adapting to competitive pressures and in securing the required financial funds. This appeared particularly relevant in telecoms, but it was also anticipated that the postal incumbent would be exposed to increasing competition in the context of the envisaged European legislation launching gradual market opening (see the government's proposal and justification, Bundestag Printed Paper no. 12/6718, 75–76). This strategy of anticipating reform proved successful, and by the end of the 1990s Deutsche Post was in much better shape than a decade before. The company had completed internal restructuring and aimed at using its position as 'Europe's largest postal company as a springboard to becoming the world's leading letter services and logistics group' (DPWN, 1999: 3). In view of such substantial change in corporate strategy, the rather slow pace of the liberalisation process evoked criticism by legal experts. The very idea of granting an exclusive licence was found to be in contradiction to the principle of market-driven competition (Gramlich, 1998: 868–9). From a competition law perspective the legal monopoly, in combination with comparatively high postage rates, would facilitate unwelcome practices of cross-subsidies from the reserved area to the competitive sector (Schweitzer, 2001: 306). Competition law experts also were highly critical about the social objectives formulated in the postal law, which they considered to be an anomaly in the context of economic administrative law, opening the door wide to political instrumentalisation (Schweitzer, 2001: 302).

Privatisation helped in securing the required financial flexibility to engage in an expansionist strategy. Deutsche Post shares were first traded on the stock market in November 2000. As a first step 49.9 per cent of the shares were issued to the bank KfW (*Kreditanstalt für Wiederaufbau*) and the German states to prepare the IPO (DPWN, 2001: 36). KfW is a public law institution partly owned by the Federal Republic of Germany (80 per cent) and the federal states (20 per cent), which is why the state has (indirect) financial interest as long as the bank holds shares. The DPAG had a free float of around 29 per cent at the end of financial year 2000, while 50 per cent plus 26 shares were in the possession of the Federal

Republic of Germany and 21 per cent held by the KfW (DPWN, 2001: 37). DPAG was obliged by law to guarantee that the Federal Republic of Germany would remain the main shareholder until 2002. Once these legal restrictions were lifted, the state in November 2003 sold around 30 per cent of the shares to the KfW banking group, and by 2005 no longer directly held shares. The state does, however, continue to have an indirect interest in Deutsche Post through the state-owned bank KfW, which by 2013 held 21 per cent of shares (Deutsche Post DHL, 2013: 83).

Once the state stepped back and adopted an arm's length approach, the incumbent enjoyed higher commercial flexibility. Disposing of the required funds, Deutsche Post engaged in a strategy of targeted acquisitions, investments and partnering agreements as well as steady expansion through integrated services. One important step in this direction was the acquisition of the US logistics company DHL International. Deutsche Post had acquired a minority interest in 1998 which it expanded subsequently to finally become a wholly owned subsidiary in 2002 (DPWN, 2003: 25). Diversification of business activities meant that the domestic letter market became less important as a share of total revenue. Despite this decrease the letter business continued to be an attractive segment with relatively high profit margins. The incumbent had an interest in consolidating its business at home, given that expansion strategies abroad proved to be risky. During the first decade of the new millennium, for instance, Deutsche Post struggled with high losses resulting from expansion strategies in the US market (Grabitz, 2006). While striving for international expansion, Deutsche Post sought to protect established privileges and market power at home. Close links to politics and competent leadership helped the incumbent in achieving this goal. Klaus Zumwinkel, director of Deutsche Post between 1990 and 1994 and CEO of DPAG between 1995 and 2008, was an efficient networker and lobbyist who enjoyed high standing among politicians (Meck, 2007; Wanner et al., 2007). Zumwinkel was regarded as a role model among leading German managers (Machatschke, 2003) until 2007–8, when the company's expansionist strategy turned out to be a financial failure (Meck and Siedenbiedel, 2007) and when a tax evasion scandal ruined his personal reputation (Schmid, 2008).

In general, Deutsche Post maintained close links to the Social Democrats and trade unions. Putting the leading SPD politician and trade unionist Monika Wulf-Mathies in charge of public relations tasks was thus an emblematic choice in this respect. Wulf-Mathies, who had a leading position during Willy Brandt's chancellorship, and in 1982 was the first woman to be elected head of one of the major unions (Public Services and Transport Union, ÖTV), headed the DPAG department for politics and sustainability between 2001 and 2008 (Granzow, 2009). During her mandate Deutsche Post launched a huge public relations campaign to raise the company's stakes in the course of political discussions on whether or not to engage in liberalisation by 2007.

The transition towards the regulatory state in the German postal sector has come much earlier than in other European countries. Postal and telecoms regulation had been attributed to a newly created Regulatory Agency for Telecommunications and Postal Services (RegTP) in 1996 and 1997 by the telecommunications and postal acts, respectively. The telecoms and postal ministry was dissolved and remaining sovereign functions such as the issuing of postage stamps were taken over by the finance ministry. The creation of a regulatory agency was not uncontroversial when the 1996 Telecoms Act was negotiated. Entrusting the Federal Cartel Office (BKartA) with telecoms regulation was discussed as an option that would mirror established practice in the energy sector (Döhler, 2001: 108–9; Gassner, 2001: 231), and which gained strong support from the German Monopolies Commission (Special Report no. 24, 1996). Yet this option to expand the competencies of the existing competition authority was not chosen. Instead, an new authority for the regulation of telecoms and postal services was created. Here the controversy was about its legal status. Given the constitutional requirement (article 87f) that state tasks relating to the postal and telecoms sector have to be performed by the federal administration (Badura et al., 2004: 892) the choice was limited to creating either a Supreme, or a Higher Federal Authority. The ministerial draft bill suggested the establishment of a Supreme Federal Authority (Bundestag Printed Papers no. 13/3609), thus giving the new authority a status which, so far, had only been granted to the Federal Audit Court and the German Central Bank.

This proposal was, however, dropped on the grounds that the degree of independence granted to such an authority would have been out of proportion to constitutional constraints set in article 87. As a consequence the postal regulator, as a Higher Federal Authority, remains within the reach of ministerial oversight. It is subject to service, expert and legal supervision of the next higher Federal Authority, the economics ministry (Wissmann, 2003: 998). Most importantly, the agency is bound by ministerial instructions which can target any regulatory activity, given that formulating exceptions to ministerial oversight would have been in contradiction to the German Basic Law (Geppert et al., 2006: 1899). The statute and function of the regulator had first been defined in the relevant section of the Telecoms Act, to which article 44 of the Postal Act referred. With the expansion of the regulator to other sectors in 2005 and its renaming as Federal Network Agency (BNetzA), the applicable statutory provisions were codified in a new law (7 July 2005, Federal

Law Gazette I 1970). At least in formal terms, independence has been strengthened with the new Act which, unlike previous laws (Scheurle and Mayen, 2002: 868; Wissmann, 2003: 997), now explicitly referred to the authority's independence. In practice, the ministry in 2000 issued an instruction which should prevent the regulator from lowering the incumbent's basic tariffs (Federal Law Gazette no. 69 of 7 April 2000, p. 6374).

Internally, this episode contributed to the discontent and departure of the regulator's president who had the reputation of following a pro-competitive stance (Wendel, 2000). Given these close links to the executive, institutional safeguards were introduced into the legal framework to secure parliamentary involvement (Bender, 2001: 508). According to the 1997 Postal Act the agency has a legal duty to submit a report to Parliament, at an interval of two years (article 47.1 PostG). Reporting activities are supposed to pay particular attention to aspects of service provision, such as the definition and the scope of the universal service, and the requirement to maintain an exclusive licence. Besides reporting duties, parliamentarians sit in the agency's Advisory Council. The Council was established at the request of the *Länder* governments who were keen to voice their interests on postal matters (Badura et al., 2004: 893; Scheurle and Mayen, 2002: 879). While the RegTP Advisory Council was composed of eighteen members equally representing parliamentarians from both chambers chambers according to the Telecommunications Act (article 67 TKG, *Telekommunikationsgesetz*), the BNetzA Advisory Council comprises thirty-two representatives in view of the broader cross-sectoral mandate of the Federal Network Agency according to the law governing the agency (article 5 BEGTPG, *Gesetz über die Bundesnetzagentur für Elektrizität, Gas, Telekommunikation, Post und Eisenbahnen*). The Council has a number of prerogatives: it is involved in the appointment procedure of the agency's president and vice-presidents; members can request measures to implement the regulatory aims and to ensure universal service; they have the right to obtain information upon request; the Council provides advice to the regulator's activity report and to decision making processes within the agency's ruling chambers. The postal regulator has primary responsibility to enforce competition law, yet it cooperates closely in this matter with the Federal Cartel Office.

The German network regulator operates under the aegis of the economics ministry and for reasons of organisational history is a well-resourced agency that appears overstaffed in comparison to other regulators (Federal Audit Court, 2004: 121–2). Through its practice, and in close cooperation with the competition authority, the agency took a pro-competitive stance and played a decisive role in opening up the German letter mail market. By contrast, the authority was more reluctant to realise social objectives and thus operated as an economic regulator rather than a social regulator. In particular, the regulator's authorisation practice reveals how it proactively used legal provisions to engage in regulation for competition, while it did not make use of the social clause (article 6.3 of the Postal Act) to intervene in the realm of working conditions. This is in line with expectations formulated in Chapter 3, according to which independent regulation is more pronounced in economic, compared to social, regulation, and that in the latter field an independent agency is likely to engage in a strategy of deference. German postal law excludes several types of postal activity from the monopoly right by means of article 5.1, among them mass mailings and 'services distinct from universal services, having special features and higher quality'. The regulator applied these legal provisions through its licencing practice by issuing a special authorisation for value-added services. This category fuelled substantial market entry ahead of full liberalisation. In 2002, for example, about half of the new entrants' market share was in the realm of value-added services (RegTP, 2004: 88). The lawfulness of this licence type had been challenged by the incumbent before the courts through numerous complaints, yet none of these were successful (BNetzA, 2008: 138). The incumbent must in general have been suspicious about the agency being biased towards market entrants, as a delicate episode reported in the media illustrates: in 2001 Deutsche Post hired a private detective to find out whether RegTP would keep its neutrality in the dealings with potential market entrants (Kietzmann and Stadler, 2001).

While such incidents may still be attributed to the day-to-day tensions between regulators and regulated firms learning to play the game (Coen, 2005a), a major political controversy arose in the context of the minimum wage discussions. The debate unfolded over the question whether or not the agency should have intervened in line with its legal mandate. The 1998 Postal Act had introduced a licensing regime (chapter II, articles 5–10), which required the regulator to consider social objectives in its authorisation practice, and opened the possibility of adding collateral clauses ex post (article 6.2, Postal Act). According to the law (article 6.3) a licence can be denied if an operator lacks the required efficiency and reliability, if there are concerns over public safety, or if the prevailing working conditions are not being respected. The agency was attacked from 2007 onwards by trade unions and Social Democrats for having facilitated practices of social dumping through its regulatory practice, which critics found to be in contradiction to the spirit of the Postal Law (Barthel, 2007; ver.di, 2007). The proponents of a minimum wage argued that the agency should have intervened on the basis of article 6.3 (Interview, MP 2).

In response to such criticism, agency head Matthias Kurth intervened publicly in February 2007 (*Wirtschaftswoche*, 2007a). When assessing the working conditions in the letter mail market, Kurth said, one should keep in mind that new entrants were still operating with relatively small mail volumes and thus could not take advantage of economies of scale. Taking the wage levels paid by quasi-monopolist DPAG as the sole benchmark was therefore erroneous, he argued. The regulator's head announced that BNetzA had commissioned a study and a legal opinion. The regulator further launched an inquiry into the working conditions of letter mail providers, issuing a questionnaire to all licensees. The fact that the agency could gather such information within its legal mandate was subsequently used by the proponents of a minimum wage as an argument in favour of a stronger social monitoring and regulatory role for BNetzA (Interview, MP 2). Seeking to avoid disclosure of information on their working conditions, several private operators had initially appealed to the Cologne Administrative Court to allow their objections. The Court allowed the appeals, yet the Münster Higher Administrative Court overturned the decision. The Higher Administrative Court ruled that the information requested was necessary for the Agency to fulfil its regulatory functions (BNetzA, 2008: 138–9).

The results of the expert studies were published in May 2007. While the legal opinion authored by a Berlin-based law professor sought to explicate the substance of 'prevailing working conditions' as stipulated in the law (Säcker, 2007), the WIK study (WIK-Consult, 2007) aimed at assessing the actual working conditions in the sector. Analysing working conditions in comparable sectors such as forwarding companies, cab drivers and the retail industry, the authors concluded that the level of wages paid by DPAG were unusually high. Also, wages paid would differ substantially across regions, so that imposing a uniform minimum wage would shake the cost structure of low-wage regions. The study, furthermore, emphasised the detrimental effect of the minimum wage level on competition, estimating that costs for new operators would rise by around 30 per cent, with cost increases ranging from 7 per cent to 58 per cent in different states in Germany (Dieke and Wojtek, 2008: 292). Such evidence resonated with market developments immediately following the introduction of the minimum wage: the regulator reported a market share in the letter markets in terms of revenue of competitors of 8.5 per cent for 2008, while market shares were still at a level of 11.3 per cent in 2007. By 2012 the market share of competitors was at 11.3 per cent, which led the agency to conclude that full market opening had no significant effect on competition (BNetzA, 2009b: 126–7, 2013: 33).

From the regulator's perspective, the findings of the studies and the immediate decrease in market share after the introduction of the minimum wage backed up its regulatory practice. From the perspective of DPAG and ver.di, the study findings and the conclusions drawn by the regulator revealed the latter's dubious working practices (FAZ, 2007a; *Spiegel*, 2007c). The situation did not change when the results of the sector inquiry became available at the end of 2007. According to the regulator, the findings and results were very much in line with the conclusions drawn by the WIK study (BNetzA, 2007). Thus, the agency did not intervene when court decisions were pending over the validity of the minimum wage, although the agreement had become binding as of 1 January 2008. Supporters of the agreement urged the regulator to finally take action against non-complying operators by suspending existing licences or refusing to issue new licences to companies that were in breach of the minimum wage levels (Barthel, 2008). Yet the agency opted to maintain the status quo arguing that regulatory intervention would distort competition without being based on the required legal certainty (Interview, BNetzA 2). The regulator backed this stance with further evidence from a second sector enquiry (BNetzA, 2009a).

The transition towards the regulatory state has thus materialised in a regulatory regime which fuelled end-to-end competition in the letter market ahead of full market opening. The new sector regulator perceived its role mainly as an economic regulator and was reluctant to take on board social objectives in the realm of working conditions.

The decline of postal corporatism

> Wir müssen Schluss damit machen, dass einige Unternehmer sich ihre Dumpinglöhne durch den Steuerzahler auch noch bezahlen lassen. (Franz Müntefering, Minister for Employment and Social Affairs, Tagesspiegel, 25 September 2007)
>
> ('We have to end a situation where some firms make tax payers pay for their dumping wages', translated by author)
>
> Neue Gewerkschaften gegen Mindestlohn (tabloid *Bild*, 11 October 2007)
>
> ('New trade unions oppose minimum wage', translated by author)

Industrial relations in the postal sector are emblematic of broader trends in the German economy. The coordinated market economy stands out in comparison to other capitalist types with its dense patterns of interest organisation (Hancké et al., 2009: 290–3), and the postal sector is no exception to this rule. The major trade union ver.di is one of the largest in

Table 6.1: Employment in the German postal sector (Deutsche Post)

	1998	2000	2002	2003	2004	2006	2008	2009	2012
FTE (1000s)	263.3	320	375.9	375.1	381.5	597.6	535.4	436.6	428.1
% civil serv.	37.1	26.9	19.5	18.7	17.7	12.3	11.8	10.2	9
% labour cost	71.2	36.3	36.4	36.0	34.5	32.8	28.8	47	32.3

(ITA Consulting and WIK-Consult, 2009b; Copenhagen Economics, 2010; WIK-Consult, 2013a)

the world, relies on a strong organisational basis. It resulted from a merger of five pre-existing unions in 2001, covering public and private service providers and aimed at making trade union representation in these sectors more effective (Annesley, 2006; Keller, 2005). Yet as in other sectors levels of unionisation are in decline, and old mechanisms of collective bargaining have come under threat.

As table 6.1 illustrates, Deutsche Post employs an impressive number of staff. In 2012 it employed more than 400,000 people. Historically, the incumbent was among the biggest employers, and in the mid-1990s the share of postal employees as a percentage of the active population was still close to 1 per cent. It subsequently went down to around 0.5 per cent in 2004 and 0.4 per cent in 2010 (Eurostat, 2008, 2012; Lumio and Fickinger, 2007). In order to reduce costs in the labour-intense sector, Deutsche Post has started to rationalise its workforce by cutting jobs and phasing out civil service employment schemes early on. Data on domestic, rather than total employment within Deutsche Post points to a downward trend, from close to 400,000 employees in 1990 to around 190,000 employees in 2004 (PricewaterhouseCoopers, 2006: 62–3). The share of civil servants has been reduced significantly, from around 40 per cent in the late 1990s to below 10 per cent in the second decade of the new millennium. As a result of these measures, the share of labour cost has gone down by some 40 per cent during the same period.

Union density in the postal sector, at around 80 per cent in 2009, is high compared to the estimated average union density in the country at a level of 20 per cent (Copenhagen Economics, 2010: 161). Until 2001 the biggest share of employees was organised within the German Postal Workers' Union (DPG). The DPG dates back to 1949 and formed part of the Confederation of the German Trade Unions (*Deutscher Gewerkschaftsbund*, DGB). By the end of 1999, DPG was composed of more than 450,000 members in all three branches of Deutsche Post (Keller, 2005: 213), of which 285,675 were postal employees. DPG was influential on policy makers and also had a major impact on reform outcomes in the telecoms sector (S.K. Schmidt, 2005: 158). Already, then, the union density in the postal sector was substantially higher than average density which in 1998 was been estimated at around 30 per cent (Ramboll, 2002: 207). DPG experienced a first spin-off when liberalisation reforms were on the political agenda.

From 1997 onwards, some of the employees in the postal and telecoms sectors started to become organised within the newly created German Postal Association Communication Workers' Union (DPVKOM). DPVKOM is a member of the German Civil Service Federation (*Deutscher Beamtenbund*, DBB). A third player is the Christian Union for Postal Services and Telecommunications (CGPT). In 2001 the DPG joined the cross-sector Unified Service Sector Union (ver.di). Ver.di is the major player representing more than 60 per cent of the incumbents' employees, followed by DPVKOM, which represents another 10 per cent, while the much smaller CGPT is not seen as a significant player (Vogel et al., 2008). Overall, DPVKOM takes more radical positions than ver.di, with the latter being the major actor in negotiating collective agreements. CGPT, by contrast, rather seeks to accommodate employers' interests in order to gain ground as a negotiation partner (Interview, ver.di).

Over time, the representativeness of established organisational structures has been challenged with the emergence of private operators. In particular, the minimum wage controversy which came up in the context of full liberalisation in 2007 involved the creation of new organisational structures. The major organisations representing the interests of the incumbent and its subsidies, ver.di on the employees' side and a newly created Employer's Association of Postal Services (AGV) on the employers' side, were competing with new organisations created by market entrants: employees within the Trade Union of New Postal and Delivery Services (GNBZ), and operators within the Employers' Association of the New Postal and Delivery Services (AGV-NBZ). Both sides challenged the representativeness of the other side. The private operators claimed that ver.di had been heavily involved in launching the employers' association AGV (FAZ, 2008), while ver.di objected that the creation of the GNBZ had been steered and sponsored by the PIN Group AG and TNT, and was, by no means, a body representing the employees bottom-up (*Spiegel*, 2008b). The trade union further suspected that employees had been forced to go onto the streets and demonstrate against the minimum wage (Röhm and Voigt, 2007: 29–37). Thus the divide between the two camps on the postal delivery market translated into two antagonistic organisational structures of labour interests.

Evolving organisational structures were also reflected in the lobbying efforts of industry and labour interests in the sector throughout the political reform process. Organised interests had a major impact on reform outcomes in the coordinated variety of capitalism. Although privatisation and liberalisation reforms were controversially discussed and at times heavily contested, negotiated change in Germany was possible because a sufficient level of responsiveness to social concerns could be secured. Initially, the trade union fervently opposed privatisation and the respective constitutional amendments. In the course of negotiation, when voices were being raised during the 1992 political summer break in favour of abolishing the civil servant status of postal employees, the issue reached the top of the political agenda. In order not to risk an agreement on privatisation, the Chancellor issued a clear statement reassuring employees that their status would remain untouched in the course of reform (Interview, MP 1). As a result the 1994 reform guaranteed the civil servant status of employees when being transferred to the newly created companies (article 143b). The privatisation laws were furthermore complemented by measures aimed at safeguarding the social service functions in the course of the privatisation process. To that end a public-law institution for postal services and telecommunications (*Bundesanstalt für Post und Telekommunikation*, BanstPT), subordinated to the finance ministry and provided with public funds, was created by a dedicated Act in 1994 (*Bundesanstaltpostgesetz*, BAPostG, Federal Law Gazette I 2325, 14 September 1994). The institution took over social service functions that the *Bundespost* had previously provided to its employees, as well as the administration of the social benefits of former civil servants.

Following the privatisation of the state monopolies introduced by the first and second postal reform, the next step to be taken was liberalisation. When discussions were ongoing by the mid-1990s, a major outbreak of union protest was the response to governmental liberalisation plans. In the run-up to the third postal reform, the German postal workers' union in 1996 and 1997 mobilised strongly and organised strikes and demonstrations (Interview, MP 1; FAZ, 1996, 1997). The postal union DPG opposed liberalisation and pressed for the introduction of minimum social standards (FAZ, 1996; FAZ, 1997; *Zeit*, 1997). As discussed previously the Social Democrats were responsive to the employees' concerns, and the 1997 Postal Act contained a number of social guarantees. Time and again, such social regulation was complemented by financial support provided by public funds to compensate reform losers. Such compensation helped to avoid major protests during the merger of the GDR post office with the West German post office and the ensuing reduction of the existing workforce. Deutsche Post was able to grant generous dismissal wages to former GDR post office clerks. The state also granted substantial financial support to enable the incumbent to shoulder the financial burden resulting from the rather generous pension scheme. In 2012 the European Commission (IP/12/45) ruled that such measures involved incompatible state aid in the range of 500 million to one billion euros. The Commission argued that the combination of high regulated prices and pension relief subsidies was incompatible with European competition law. In November 2013 the Commission referred Germany to court for failure to recover this incompatible aid (IP/13/1127).

Trade union pressure also played a role in subsequent extensions of the monopoly. Here ver.di joined forces with Deutsche Post to lobby for the extension of the legal monopoly in 2001 and again in 2007 (FAZ, 2001; Storn, 2007; *Welt*, 2000). In the run up to full liberalisation in January 2008, Deutsche Post announced that liberalisation would cost 32,000 out of the 160,000 jobs in letter mail delivery (*Sueddeutsche*, 2007a). In order to generate supporting evidence, ver.di had commissioned a study examining the working conditions within the new operators. The study found that wages paid by competitors were on average around 50 per cent lower compared to starting salaries paid by Deutsche Post (input consulting, 2006: 51). The study further argued that over 60 per cent of employment relations within the new mail delivery services were in marginal employment, which would stand in sharp contrast with the situation in other, comparable sectors (input consulting, 2006: 44). Input consulting thus concluded that the business model implemented by the entrants would rely on combined wages where employees receive social security benefits on top of their salaries to make a living.

Once the extension of the monopoly was off the table, Deutsche Post and trade unions started to lobby for the introduction of a minimum wage. Here the social partners exerted pressure in favour of political regulation to avoid the free-riding problem in a sector characterised by declining organisational density. In the course of this debate on market opening and corrective actions the competitors also voiced their interests effectively. In their view the minimum wage agreement was mainly a manoeuvre of the incumbent to disadvantage the private operators by introducing wage levels that they could not comply with. Since fair and equal competition on the letter market was not possible under these conditions, a minimum wage set at the level of wages paid by the incumbent would trigger bankruptcies and job losses with the competitors, they argued. At this stage market entrants were in an extraordinarily good position to make headlines in the media since the major private competitors were owned by big German publishing houses, mainly Springer (Röhm and Voigt, 2007). In the course of the debate, direct rivalry developed between Deutsche Post and Springer. In particular, the most widely read German tabloid *Bild*, published by Springer, engaged in an aggressive campaign against the minimum wage

(*Bild*, 2007a, 2007b), and later in the course of events *Bild* took the lead in denouncing Deutsche Post CEO Klaus Zumwinkel for tax evasion (*Bild*, 2008a, 2008b). In response, Deutsche Post withdrew advertising from Springer publications and envisaged producing and distributing its own newspaper free of charge (*Spiegel*, 2007d; *Wirtschaftswoche*, 2007b).

While the incumbent and the major trade union mostly joined forces in their lobbying efforts to influence political decisions, their interests often conflicted with respect to managerial decisions and internal measures. Still, compared to the situation in France or Britain, industrial relations in the German postal sector functioned reasonably well and with much less conflict. The social partners managed to settle conflict by negotiating collective agreements, which took into account employees' concerns when engaging in structural reforms. When new entrants had acquired significant shares of the letter market at around 10 per cent by 2006 and 2007 (BNetzA, 2008: 131), the industrial relations landscape changed substantially and collective agreements covering the whole sector no longer existed. The minimum wage controversy had led to a situation where the two camps had independently negotiated agreements with very different outcomes: Deutsche Post and affiliates agreed with ver.di to fix the minimum wage at a level of €9 in East Germany and €9.80 in West Germany. The new entrants and their associations, by contrast, had agreed to fix the wage level at €6.50 in East Germany and €7.50 in West Germany.

The resulting conflict fuelled practices of adversarial legalism since all parties involved made use of judicial review. In December 2007 the PIN Group AG took legal action with the Federal Cartel Office against the minimum wage negotiated between Deutsche Post and ver.di (*Spiegel*, 2007b; *Sueddeutsche*, 2007b). The Group called for accelerated proceedings in view of the fact that the envisaged wage regulation would distort competition on the letter market. In March 2008 ver.di pressed criminal charges against the new entrants' trade union GNBZ at the Public Attorney's Office Cologne, suspecting corruptibility and defalcation (*Spiegel*, 2008b). The trade union took further action at the Labour Court Cologne challenging the fact that the GNBZ could lawfully negotiate collective agreements in accordance with the Collective Bargaining Agreements Act. With its judgment dated 30 October 2008 (no. 14 BV 324/08) the court ruled that the GNBZ was, indeed, not in a position to lawfully negotiate collective agreements, given that it lacked the required impartiality. The competitors appealed against the decision, yet the Higher Labour Court Cologne in May 2009 confirmed the stance taken previously (decision dated 20 May 2009, no. 9 TaBV 105/08).

Judicial battles continued once the political arena had endorsed the minimum wage agreement negotiated by ver.di and Deutsche Post. Competitors filed several complaints with administrative courts against the minimum wage ordinance in the first months of 2008. In a judgment dated 7 March 2008 (no. VG 4 A 439.07), the Berlin Administrative Court ruled that the ministerial order was unlawful since only employees outside the scope of a collective agreement could be subject to a minimum wage. Therefore the labour ministry would have transgressed the realm of its legally attributed competence. The government appealed against this ruling, yet with a decision dated 18 December 2008 (no. 1 B 13.08) the Berlin Higher Administrative Court rejected this appeal and thus confirmed the ruling in first instance. The court stipulated that the order would infringe the priority of law, that is, that its regulatory content should be provided for by a law instead of an order. The labour ministry took the case to the next instance (i.e. the Federal Administrative Court). As mentioned, the judgment declared the agreement null and void for procedural reasons. The situation resulting from such legal disputes can best be described as competitive corporatism where social partners compete over legitimately representing the sector.

Postal services in the coordinated model

> Schließungen. Post ohne Filialen (Kanning, 2008)
>
> ('Closures. Post without branches', translated by author)

Compared to France, where the *service public* has a long tradition in French public law, no such unifying legal concept exists in Germany (Ambrosius, 2000: 18–19). The term *Daseinsvorsorge*, referring to the state's mission to provide fundamental services to its citizens, was developed to describe actual policy practice, rather than being an enforceable legal concept. Ernst Forsthoff coined the term in the 1930s to capture and conceptually underpin the expanding role of the German state in providing services, making explicit reference to the older French concept *service public* (Ambrosius, 2000: 19–20). Forsthoff argued that the state was supposed to counterbalance the growing importance of the market sphere politically, where private interests and profit-seeking behaviour would otherwise prevail. Since the concept justifies an expansive logic of state intervention in the general interest, it has been heavily criticised in the economic and legal literature (Schweitzer, 2001: 74–8). Despite, or probably thanks to, its fuzziness the term has become an influential point of reference in relevant academic, judicial and policy debates. In the postal sector the state's task to provide *Daseinsvorsorge* has been strategically used to intervene into the national political economy, for example as an instrument of fiscal policy or employment and stabilisation policy (Knauth and Dommermuth, 1996: 44). Throughout the decades unprofitable infrastructure services had been financed from national budget funds in both parts of Germany, and provision of a universal service under competitive conditions (i.e. liberalisation), appeared unrealistic. The decision to privatise and liberalise postal services alongside the more profitable telecoms services thus constituted a fundamental change to established political practice.

Legally speaking, the German Basic Law identified those services of general interest where the public administration was supposed to play a central role either at the federal level, which was the case for postal services or railways, or at the state level, which applied to education and broadcasting. The privatisation of postal and telecoms therefore required changes at constitutional level in order to allow private companies to deliver these services. The newly added article 87f which abolished the state monopoly formulated the task to 'ensure the availability of adequate and appropriate postal and telecommunications services throughout the federal territory'. The second major innovation was to introduce competition as the mechanism through which the universal service should be provided. The paradigm change in the German postal sector was thus more fundamental than in other countries, where service provision in the legal hierarchy was often prioritised over competition.

The postal universal service in Germany is defined mainly through political regulation. According to the legal hierarchy stipulated in the 1997 law, the promotion of competition (article 1) has become the prior objective of postal policy (Elsenbast and Smit, 2000, for a legal discussion rf.: 29; Schwarz-Schilling, 2001: 10). The USO is regulated in the 1997 Postal Act (section 3), which also provides for a definition of the universal service obligation (article 11.1). The German USO comprises counter services, newspapers, magazines and money orders. Given that the definition of the USO provided in German law is more precise than the rather wide definition to be found in the 1997 EC directive, competition lawyers have assessed the German legal framework positively, as it makes political instrumentalisation pursuing industrial or social policy objectives more difficult (Schweitzer, 2001: 302).

Further regulatory detail concerning the scope and quality of the USO was laid down in the 1999 ordinance on the postal universal service (PUDLV, 15 December 1999 BGBl. I. p. 2418). PUDLV is a governmental decree which required the consent of both chambers in the parliament. Lengthy political negotiations caused the time gap between adoption of the postal law in 1997 and the adoption of the ordinance in 1999. The ordinance was reviewed and amended in 2002 and 2005, specifying requirements regarding the postal presence and adapting the obligations imposed on Deutsche Post to the extended duration of its monopoly. In the German regime governing the universal postal service political actors have therefore retained their policymaking authority, as all relevant decisions are taken either by the legislator or the government (WIK-Consult, 2013b: 14). Thus with regards to service provision the regulatory agency has a role in implementing, rather than in shaping, policies.

The ordinance PUDLV formulates detailed requirements for the density of the network: at least 12,000 contact points out of which 5,000 had to remain in-house until the end of 2007; at least one contact for communities with 2,000 inhabitants; in communities with more than 4,000 inhabitants a contact point within a distance of 2 km; a contact point each 80 square km per administrative district; letterboxes at a distance of 1 km or less. The preconditions on German territory are not as challenging as in some countries in Europe and elsewhere around the world. Germany, with a surface of 357,104 square km, is rather densely populated with around 230 inhabitants per square km, and a rate of urbanisation at 74 per cent in 2011 (WIK-Consult, 2013a: 42). As a result, the number of postal outlets per 10,000 inhabitants is substantially below the EU-average (2.38 in 2004) with around 1.5 postal outlets reported for the same year (WIK-Consult, 2004: 165). As illustrated by table 6.2, the total number of outlets, which complies with the minimum number of 12,000 outlets, as well as the density and accessibility of the network, has been relatively stable.

Maintaining access to the postal infrastructure has been a sensitive issue in Germany, and when the number of outlets were reduced to a value closer to the minimum threshold in 2002, a political discussion about the deterioration of service provision unfolded. In response to such public pressure, and fearing that the legal requirements for universal service provision could be tightened, the incumbent in 2004 voluntarily committed to standards which went beyond the minimum requirements formulated in the law (German Bundestag Printed Papers 15/3186 dated 25 May 2004). The data reported in the table illustrates that Deutsche Post has upheld a relatively dense network during the duration of its legal monopoly. Until 2007 the monopolist was required to maintain 5,000 out of 12,000 branches in-house, which amounts to a share of around 42 per cent and very much corresponds to the levels reported between 1999 and 2007. Since then, however, Deutsche Post has massively outsourced the operation of branches. The incumbent had already started to adapt its network in 2005, when it launched a first pilot project with the introduction of 300 postal agencies (Hennemann, 2005). Another innovation was the introduction

Table 6.2: Postal outlets in Germany (Deutsche Post)

	1999	2000	2002	2004	2007	2008	2010	2012
outlets	13,948	13,663	12,683	13,019	13,526	13,445	14,050	13,000
% POs	42.7	40.9	39.7	41.3	43.4	*	0.1	0.1
outlets/ inh.[1]	1.7	1.7	1.5	1.6	1.5	1.5	4.47	3.33
outlet/ area[2]	25.5	26.4	28.2	27.4	26.4	26.6	27.4	27.5

[1] outlets per 10,000 inhabitants
[2] average area in sq km covered by an outlet (UPU)
(ITA Consulting and WIK-Consult, 2009b; WIK-Consult, 2004; UPU, 2012; WIK-Consult, 2013a)
* year not reported

of so-called Postpoints, which are contact points offering basic services in retail shops (Siedenbiedel, 2007).

Such change was accompanied by a programme that involved the successive closure of hundreds of in-house branches each year (Goldschmitt, 2007). In 2008 Deutsche Post announced plans to fully phase out in-house branches by the end of 2011 (Kanning, 2008; Kranz, 2011). Following the separation of the entities, Deutsche Postbank had acquired some 750 postal outlets by 2005 (Hamburger Abendblatt, 2005). In 2012 Postbank operated 1,100 own branches and 4,500 partner branches (Postbank, 2013: 12). Within Deutsche Post the number of agencies increased sharply to the extent that the share of post offices reported for 2010 and 2012 decreased to 0.1 per cent (WIK-Consult, 2013a: 44). These changes to the postal network have at the same time meant an increase in access. According to the data reported by WIK in 2010 and 2012 the postal network provided an average of more than three to four outlets per 10,000 inhabitants (WIK-Consult, 2013a: 44), which compares to a significantly lower average between one and two in the period 1999–2008 (ITA Consulting and WIK-Consult, 2009b: 52). The regulator's assessment has been positive throughout the process, as it took into account the total number of outlets irrespective of their type (in-house branch, postal agency, contact point) and partner (Deutsche Post or competitors). For the period 2010–12, for instance, the regulator reports a total number of postal outlets of more than 366,000 (BNetzA, 2013a: 74).

In terms of mail delivery German regulation requires delivery of at least 80 per cent of letters the next working day and 95 per cent by the second working day, and a minimum one delivery per working day. The USO was imposed on Deutsche Post during the duration of its legal monopoly until the end of 2007 (article 15 of the Postal Act). Since then the provision of an adequate service level is perceived as being the task of all market participants collectively. Unlike in other European member states, the USO is therefore no longer mandated on the incumbent operator. Only where the market would fail to deliver an adequate level of services could the regulator impose the USO on a specific operator or, alternatively, activate public procurement procedures. This fall-back option would follow a rather complex procedure defined in the law (articles 12–17 of the Postal Act). According to regulation experts, it is neither likely that there will be a need to apply these provisions, nor would the procedures be workable to address such market failure (Interview, BNetzA 1). The law also foresees a safeguard mechanism for a situation where service provision could not be financed through market dynamics. In this case a service provider on which the USO has been imposed would need to apply for compensation with the regulator, demonstrating that the long-term costs of providing the universal service exceed the income generated from the service. The law does not prescribe a specified procedure according to which the regulator would be supposed to calculate the cost of the USO, but does provide some general guidance in this regard.

As in other countries, the regulatory agency has the task of implementing the legal framework. In practice, this means that the agency has developed procedures to measure and monitor the operators' compliance with universal service standards. The regulator reports on the fulfilment of network density requirements and, to this end, engages in detailed calculations concerning the location of postal outlets and letter mail boxes (Interview, BNetzA 1). Until 2004 the agency also conducted measurements of delivery times in-house, but this practice was ended by the Federal Audit Court for reasons of cost. Since then the regulator relies on data provided by Deutsche Post, but has expressed its concerns as to whether the data on which such performance measurement is based complies with international standards (BNetzA, 2009c: 98–9). The German agency, furthermore, regulates and approves tariffs, which in accordance with the universal service ordinance (article 6) requires an assessment of affordability in terms of real prices relating to the price level in 1997. Finally, the regulator is entrusted with the task of advising the government on the adequacy of the USO (article 47.1 of the Postal Act). The agency has thus far not recommended a revision of the ordinance. In its 2012–13 report it did, however, announce the commissioning of a study by WIK on consumer needs (BNetzA, 2013a: 55).

In practice, Deutsche Post continues to be the USP without being mandated as the USP. Legally speaking this takes the form of a voluntary commitment of Deutsche Post vis-à-vis the Federal Central Tax Office to comply with the USO, which in return allows for the exemption of such services from VAT. In the past this tax exemption was limited to the services provided by the incumbent operator, and thus constituted a

Table 6.3: Mail services in Germany (Deutsche Post)

	1999	2003	2006	2013	2014
20g tariff FSC[1] in €	0.56	0.55	0.55	0.58	0.60
20g tariff EU letter FSC[1] in €	*	0.55	0.70	0.75	0.75
D+1 performance %	94.6	94.5	95.9	92.3[2]	*

[1] Fastest Standard Category
[2] 2012 value
(ITA Consulting and WIK-Consult, 2009b; WIK-Consult, 2013a; BNetzA, 2013a)
* years not reported

comparative price advantage for Deutsche Post (ECORYS, 2008 country sheet summaries: 45). In response to European pressure (IP/07/1664) Germany has, however, opened up the possibility for tax exemption to all operators providing the universal service. Supposing that the market failed to deliver the universal service, Deutsche Post would currently be the only market player fulfilling the eligibility criteria for the imposition of the USO in accordance with the law (BNetzA, 2013a: 59). Deutsche Post delivers mail six days a week, and thus goes beyond the minimum legal requirement of five-day delivery. The possibility of reducing delivery to five days a week has come up in the context of full liberalisation, but has proven highly unpopular and has so far not been realised (FAZ, 2007c; Fokus, 2010). Compared to France, the share of private correspondence in total mail volumes is rather low, at a level of 10 per cent in 2008 (ITA Consulting and WIK-Consult, 2009a: 93). It decreased from a level of about 1,600 items in 2001 to below 1,400 items in 2007, while the number of items sent by business customers is relatively stable at around 8,000 items (WIK-Consult, 2009a: 6–7). Thus, in economic terms, there would clearly be an incentive to cut back services for private customers.

According to the data provided by Deutsche Post, compliance with quality standards on delivery times was secured. The regulator did, however, express reservations as to the reliability of the incumbent's measurements, as did journalists on the basis of test sampling (Nienhaus and Siedenbiedel, 2009). Table 6.3 indicates that nominal stamp prices have increased over time. According to the regulator, however, the real prices (adjusted for inflation) have decreased by more than 20 per cent since 1998, and in comparison within Europe, were at a comparatively low level when seen in relation with average costs of living (BNetzA, 2013: 43–6). The price for a standard letter within Europe was the same level as for domestic mail in 2003, but was increased to a higher level in 2006.

In conclusion, the transition towards the regulatory state in Germany did not lead to a rollback of the state in the area of redistributive policies, independent regulation has not taken on board employment related social goals, while the decline of postal corporatism has triggered political controversies over social regulation. On the German letter market we have seen a relatively high degree of de facto market opening compared to other countries. Competitors gained a market share of around 10 per cent, which might appear as a rather modest share, but is quite considerable in the context of international postal liberalisation where few markets have seen similar levels of competition. Hence the German case posed new issues related to fair competition, as well as to viable working conditions in the labour intense sector.

7

Liberalising through the back door: postal reform in Britain

Postal reform stands in sharp contrast with change in other British public utilities. From the 1980s onwards key sectors such as telecoms, electricity or rail underwent privatisation, and subsequently liberalisation. In the postal sector, Britain figures as a latecomer rather than a pioneer, in Europe and internationally. Privatising and liberalising the Post Office was off limits during a considerable period of time. It was in the wake of the new millennium that the British eventually embraced gradual liberalisation. Interestingly, full market opening was achieved through the back door by regulatory intervention rather than political determination. It took Britain another decade to launch the privatisation of the publicly owned incumbent. Postal sector reform therefore did not only come late, it also came in reverse order: liberalisation occurred in a market dominated by a public firm, followed by privatisation as a recent development. This chapter reviews the history of reform, then analyses the transition towards the regulatory state, discussing the role of industrial relations, and summing up with findings about service delivery in the British postal sector.

Hands off a sacred cow! The long way to liberalisation and privatisation

> I am not ready to have the head of the Queen privatised (attributed to Prime Minister Margaret Thatcher)

> The intellectual arguments for introducing private capital into the Royal Mail are overwhelming; the only arguments the other way are social and political. I made it clear that the Government would have liked to proceed with privatisation, but that a small number of supporters on the Conservative Back Benches were not prepared to do so. (Michael Heseltine, President of the Board of Trade, HC Deb 21 November 1994 c 352)

For decades the Post Office has been 'the most important' (Foster, 1992b: 76) state enterprise in Britain. The history of postal services dates back to 1516 when Henry VII started to organise postal carriage, while in 1635 Charles I made postal services available to the public (Postal Heritage Trust, 2005). A public monopoly was defined by the Post Office Management Act in 1837, attributing an exclusive privilege to the Post Office (Daunton, 1985: 10, 50; The Monopolies and Mergers Commission, 1980: 3). Innovations introduced under Rowland Hill in 1840, known as the 'Penny Post', are widely held as the foundation of modern postal administration (Coase, 1939, 1947; Daunton, 1985: 3–35). Under the uniform penny postage scheme, rates were based on weight regardless of distance. For decades the Post Office functioned as a government department, until the Post Office Act in 1969 created a publicly owned corporation.

Despite this kick-start, further reform did not follow easily. Throughout the 1980s, several attempts to bring the postal sector onto the vanguard of privatisation failed. When Margaret Thatcher came to power in 1979, the Conservative government launched a massive privatisation programme. Such change had already been envisaged in the Ridley report prepared for the shadow cabinet in 1977 (Economic Reconstruction Group, 1977). Privatisation appeared as an effective means for government to keep debt and interest payments off the public budget (Starr, 1990: 44). Change had also been promoted in the postal sector, notably by two reports published by the Monopolies and Mergers Commission in 1980 and 1984 (The Monopolies and Mergers Commission, 1980; 1984), but no action followed. Prime Minister Thatcher was not ready to tackle the Post Office, a promise which she reiterated during her 1987 election campaign. Besides the politics involved, there was also no economic rationale for privatising the Post Office at the time. In the 1980s the British incumbent was making a profit and contributed significantly to the Exchequer (Walsh, 2012: 29, 2013: 322). By contrast, the case for reforming British telecoms, with its shortages in supply, was far more obvious at the time (Thatcher, 1999, chapters 7 and 8; Thatcher, 2007b; Vogel, 1996: 71). Thus the organisational separation between postal and telecoms in 1989 was actually used to exclude the postal incumbent from the privatisation process. The only meaningful change that the 1989 British Telecoms Act introduced was a reduction of the postal monopoly to items costing below £1, which meant opening up the courier services segment to competition. Furthermore, in 1986 three distinct business units were set up within the Post Office Group – Royal Mail, Royal Mail Parcels (rebranded as Parcelforce in 1990) and Post Office Counters (Postal Heritage Trust, 2005).

The reform debate gained momentum towards the end of the 1980s, but reform proposals were time and again put on hold due to disagreements within subsequent governments, concerns of the governing parties to cut back services in their constituencies, and an effective anti-privatisation campaign led by trade unions (McGowan, 2002: 336). By 1991, postal reform was envisaged in the context of the 'Citizen's Charter' initiative for public service reform. The government suggested improving the quality, efficiency and choice of services, to reduce the Post Office's letter monopoly and to introduce an independent regulator, in charge of monitoring compliance with performance standards and complaints handling (The Prime Minister, 1991: 30–1). In 1994, the Trade and Industry Committee issued a report in support of privatisation and urged the government to stop using the Post Office as a revenue generator (Trade and Industry Committee, 1994). This parliamentary report was followed by the government's Green Paper, 'The Future of Postal Services', favouring partial liberalisation and privatisation, but also emphasised the need to maintain a link between the government and the Post Office (Campbell, 2002; Department of Trade and Industry, 1994; discussed by Dnes, 1997). Owing to the controversy these suggestions triggered in Parliament and elsewhere (HC Deb. 12 July 1994 cc835–934; Hillyard, 2000: 10), they were not included in the parliamentary programme. The union representing Post Office Workers, the Communication Workers Union (CWU), sought to provide counter-evidence commissioning a report from London Economics, that is a consultancy firm associated with reforms of the previous decade. Drawing on economic comparison of the Post Office's performance with privatised companies, the report concluded that the transaction costs involved in privatisation would outweigh the gains obtained, and thus recommended that public ownership be maintained (London Economics, 1994). An anti-privatisation campaign 'Protecting Postal Services' proved highly successful (Campbell, 2002: 340), and Conservative backbenchers from rural constituencies effectively blocked reform (HC Deb 21 November 1994 c 352).

The change of government in 1997 did not amount to a U-turn on privatisation policy, given that the Labour party had never univocally opposed the reform programme of the Conservative government, nor had the Conservative party ever univocally supported the government's stance (Abromeit, 1988: 72, 74). Generally speaking, New Labour was in favour of liberalisation and privatisation, but there was a considerable degree of disagreement within the party concerning the specific case of the Post Office. The same is true for New Labour's attitude vis-à-vis the unions: on the one hand, the party was eager to create some distance in order to appeal to a more centrist electorate; on the other hand, the party internally needed to rely on long-standing ties with the unions in order to rally support for policy decisions (Faucher-King and Le Galès et al., 2010: 91–2). In its election manifesto, the party had announced that a Labour government would grant the Post Office 'greater commercial freedom to make the most of new opportunities', but that it would not engage in a sale of postal shares (Labour Party, 1997: 62–8). In a public appearance together with the, then, CWU Secretary General, the newly elected party leader Tony Blair had indeed announced early on that he was opposed to postal privatisation (Campbell, 2002: 341).

Once in office, the Labour government commissioned a two-stage process of sector review (Hillyard, 2000: 13–15). During a first, consultative, stage more of those who might be called 'Old Labour' had a say, whereas the second, internal, stage involved the 'New Labour' party elite (Campbell, 2002: 341). The first phase triggered controversial discussions among stakeholders and in Parliament (Trade and Industry Committee, 1998), to the effect that during the second phase certain options had already been precluded. Nevertheless, a fervent interdepartmental disagreement had to be settled before Peter Mandelson, then Secretary of State and Industry, could present the government's reform package in December 1998 (MacIntyre, 2000: 474–8). Gordon Brown, Chancellor of the Exchequer, was keen to preserve the Treasury's interest in the revenue generated by the Post Office and thus sought to impose severe restrictions on the incumbent's borrowing powers. Mandelson, himself a supporter of privatisation, ultimately rallied support from the Prime Minister in order to grant greater commercial freedom to the Post Office. His announcement of the government package was followed by the White Paper on Post Office reform (Department of Trade and Industry, 1999) and the Postal Services Bill published in 1999 (for a detailed discussion see Hillyard, 2000). The fact that EU law imposed a minimum degree of change towards the end of the 1990s has certainly fuelled domestic reform. The publication of domestic reform proposals thus coincided with the transposition of the 1997 EU directive, which was secured by the 1999 Postal Services Regulation. Acknowledging that Europe is generally not considered as a legitimate justification for domestic change by the British (Hay and Rosamond, 2002: 158–9), it is hardly surprising that the European impact has not been voiced publicly in the British debate (Thatcher, 2007b: 236).

The 1999 Regulation launched partial market opening in line with the directive and established the Postal Services Commission (Postcomm) as a consultative body within the Department of Trade and Industry. The 2000 Postal Services Act introduced two important institutional innovations: transforming Postcomm into an independent regulatory agency, and creating the Shareholder Executive (SHEX). The Act maintained public ownership and emphasised that there would be no disposal of shares without further primary legislation. It enshrined the USO and the uniform tariff for the first time in law. Postcomm as the new regulator was put in charge of setting the threshold rate for the monopoly area. Commentators have considered the substance of this regulatory framework to be 'hybrid' or 'transitional' (Campbell, 2002: 331), failing to get the incentives right for an effective transformation (Walsh, 2013). The Act has, however, triggered full liberalisation, given that Postcomm in 2006 used its legal prerogatives and fully opened the letter market to competition.

The next step to finally privatise the Post Office was taken under Conservative lead in 2011, while preparatory work had already been done by the preceding Labour government. Independent reviews and reports played a crucial role in framing the ideas underpinning this last round of postal reform. In their reports published in 2006 and 2009, the National Audit Office analysed the implementation of the quality of service regime by Postcomm and Royal Mail (National Audit Office, 2006) and the implementation of the network change programme by the ministerial department and Postwatch (National Audit Office, 2009). These reports pointed to a need to improve the regulator–regulatee working relations in the area of price control and highlighted the difficulties in putting into place a more cost-effective, but viable postal network. Highly visible was the impact of the so-called Hooper reports (Hooper, 2010; Hooper et al., 2008), which became a point of reference for the stakeholders in the sector (Interviews, BIS; Ofcom), but have also been viewed very critically by privatisation opponents (Interview, CWU 1; Compass, 2009; Lawson, 2009). Richard Hooper, the former deputy chairman of Ofcom (2002–5) holding a varied background in the public and private sectors (Cave, 2010), chaired the independent review panel making the case for privatisation. Key elements of the 2011 Postal Act follow the recommendations made in these reports (Eccles, 2008: 21): the need to reform the regulatory framework, especially in the area of downstream access, the introduction of Ofcom as the postal sector regulator and the influx of new capital through privatisation (Hooper, 2010: 31–42; Hooper et al., 2008: 71–86, 87–103).

In February 2009 the government presented a draft bill (Postal Services HL Bill 24), which envisaged the privatisation of Royal Mail. A few months later, in July 2009, the reform was put on hold due to domestic opposition, the economic downturn and resulting government uncertainties (Wintour and Webb, 2009). In 2010 and 2011, however, the reform was brought back onto the agenda and was successfully concluded by the incoming coalition government of Liberal Democrats and Conservatives (HM Government, 2010). The Postal Services Act 2011 (HMSO, 2011; for a detailed analysis see Eccles, 2013) launched privatisation and legally separated the operation of the network (Post Office) from delivery services (Royal Mail). It removed the restrictions on ownership of Royal Mail, yet maintained public ownership of the Post Office and considered mutualisation as an option for mixed ownership. To ease privatisation, it enabled the transfer of Royal Mail's historic pension liabilities to the government. The Act further introduced important regulatory reforms and designated Ofcom as the new sector regulator. It also sought to rally public support through social safeguards, such as granting employees' shares in Royal Mail. In September 2011 a consultation process on ownership options was launched by the Liberal-Democratic led ministry, and in early summer 2013 the sale of Royal Mail was put on track with the designation of coordinators and book-runners (Neate, 2013). Finally, in October 2013 Royal Mail shares were traded on the London Stock Exchange. It was thus three decades later that a British government went 'where Thatcher feared to tread' (*Guardian*, 2013) and ended century-old public ownership of the Post Office.

Moving at double speed: the transition towards the regulatory state

> Under the reforms, for the first time, we will create an arm's length relationship with Government, based on a five-year strategic plan, giving the Post Office greater freedoms to develop new products and services; to price commercially; and to borrow for growth investments. For the first time, we will introduce a tough, new independent regulator, the Postal Services Commission, to promote and protect customer interests, set high quality standards, regulate prices, and promote competition and innovation.
> (Minister Alan Johnson, HC Deb 17 January 2000 c 620)

Granting commercial freedom to incumbent operators and introducing independent regulation are two cornerstones in the transitional process towards the regulatory state. Lifting state influence in practice requires the separation between operational and regulatory tasks, which ultimately need to be left with the operators and the regulators, respectively. In the British postal sector, this transition has come with delay. Once on track, Britain has moved at double speed when compared to the more incremental processes of change observed in France and Germany. The following sections illustrate the evolution towards the postal regulatory state with regards to operational and regulatory issues.

Time and again throughout the reform process, the incumbent's lack of commercial freedom has been raised as an argument in favour of privatisation. But just as Margaret Thatcher did, all incoming governments failed to tackle the Post Office. One of the reasons may be that conventional wisdom behind privatisation appeared to be at odds with evidence in

Britain. Evidence did rather speak in favour of, than against, strong state intervention, at least as long as intervening governments got the incentives right: while during the 1970s interventionism combined with financial instability, during the 1980s increased interventionism combined with commercial success. Although on paper the 1969 Postal Act stipulated an arm's length approach, governmental oversight had been tightened considerably by the incoming Conservative government after 1979. Thus in the postal sector the widely acclaimed rollback of the state under Conservative capitalism was a myth rather than a reality, as the power of the state had expanded substantially (Graham, 1997: 119, 122). Rather, the Conservative revolution implied a rollback of governance, which would be replaced by more interventionist, 'hand-bagging' government (Richardson, 2012: 315–16) and a form of statist centralisation that mobilised a new set of instruments (Le Galès, 2004).

Tight financial controls and performance requirements were conducive to a situation where the Post Office regularly outperformed government finance targets throughout the 1980s until the early 2000s (McGowan, 2002: 336; Walsh, 2012: 2). As Walsh put it, this may best 'be described, positively, as the "good chap" theory of incentivisation. Royal Mail's senior leadership did not wish to displease ministers; an ethos of duty, service and accountability predominated' (Walsh, 2012: 2). Through this interventionist strategy which at least temporarily proved successful, the Conservative governments, without intending to do so, had undermined the case for privatisation (Campbell, 2002: 340). In the long run, however, Britain missed the chance to undergo a structural process of modernisation in the golden age of the 1980s, characterised by growing mail volumes and financial stability, rather than in the later phases of decline (Cave, 2010). By the end of the 1990s, the absence of commercial discipline, combined with continued political interference, had aggravated the incumbent's financial situation, which due to falling mail volumes and a fast-growing pension deficit was not in a good shape (Walsh, 2012: 26).

Governments did not ignore this evolution and suggested changes at several instances: granting a greater degree of commercial freedom was a cornerstone of the 1994 Consultation Paper published by the ministry (Department of Trade and Industry, 1994). Acknowledging that 'many people would prefer a closer link between the Government and Royal Mail than this option [a 100 per cent share sale] would provide' (ibid.: 16), the ministry sought to suggest measures to increase 'commercial freedom within the public sector' (ibid.: 14–16). This approach resonates with the stance adopted in the report commissioned by the CWU, which discarded a rationale for privatisation, but made a strong case for granting more commercial freedom (London Economics, 1994: ix, 50–75, 79).

The proposals made by the incoming Labour government from 1997 onwards also took into account widespread opposition to full privatisation, emphasising that it was 'committed to the Post Office remaining in the public sector', but at the same time would seek to grant 'greater commercial freedom to enable it to compete effectively in Britain and overseas', and to this end would consider 'a range of options for partnership with the private sector (such as joint ventures) and for the involvement of employees and customers' (HC Deb 6 April 1998 c 64W). The Labour government stressed that 'the relationship between the Post Office and Government has to change' and that 'the Government's role in the Post Office will be restricted to the strategic level' (HC Deb 7 December 1998 cc 21–39). As noted earlier, however, there was internal division between the departments for trade and industry and finance, and due to budgetary interests the reform was again at risk of being unable to grant greater financial and managerial freedom to the Post Office.

The outcome of reform with the Postal Services Act 2000 was to introduce only limited change. The Act transformed the Post Office from a statutory corporation into a public limited company (effectively from March 2001) with the British government as the sole shareholder. With the creation of the SHEX, the government's shareholder interests were represented from within the lead ministry. SHEX was put in charge of monitoring the financial viability and profitability of the incumbent to thus 'mimick the role of capital markets' (Walsh, 2013: 323), yet it was probably too keen on guarding its neutrality at the expense of having a real influence (ibid.). The role of SHEX is thus much weaker than the one played by the KfW banking group in Germany, where the KfW sits on the board of Deutsche Post and has had an influential voice as a majority shareholder.

As a public limited company, the Post Office was from now on allowed to retain a considerable share of its profits for investment, and to borrow funds from the government at a commercial rate to finance acquisitions and joint ventures. The period following the implementation of the Act was indeed characterised by a new strategic orientation of the incumbent operator, which has been assessed by some commentators in rather critical terms (Walsh, 2012: 26). In 2001 the Post Office was rebranded as 'Consignia', seeking to signal a modified business orientation as an operator competing at regional, national and international scale (McGowan, 2002: 344). Consignia engaged in a strategy of international expansion through a series of acquisitions, yet at the same time failed to effectively put into practice measures of modernisation and rationalisation (McGowan, 2002: 344). The 'Consignia' episode was short-lived, and coincided with considerable financial deterioration. In June 2002 the newly appointed chairman

Allan Leighton announced that the incumbent should rebrand as 'Royal Mail', an element of his renewal plan that 'proved almost universally popular' (Peston, 2008: 318). This rebranding clearly sought to invoke the incumbent's century-old royal heritage, rather than renewal and change (Stewart, 2011; Verdin, 2002). Under the new management the financial performance of Royal Mail improved, moving from a deficit in 2001–2 to an operating profit of £355 million in 2005–6. This has been seen by some as a 'financial turnaround in the face of great odds' (Peston, 2008: 322), but is at least partly due to the fact that in 2001–2 it was convenient to exaggerate losses in order to justify restructuring, while later on there was a need to prove success (Peston, 2008: 323).

During the first decade of the new millennium, however, Royal Mail's financial situation deteriorated again, particularly when its pension scheme ran into deficit (BERR, 2009: 2–3). By 2006 Royal Mail's pension deficit was estimated at £5.6 billion. The responsibility for this imbalance goes back to previous Post Office directors, ministers and actuaries 'who consistently underestimated the liabilities of the scheme and overstated the likely returns to be made from its assets' (Peston, 2008: 323). Based on the Post Office's bad track record throughout the early 2000s, a case could be made that corporate renewal was deemed to fail in the absence of access to 'corporate experience' of private sector companies and additional capital influx (Hooper and Hutton et al., 2008: 13). The Hooper reports provided strong evidence in support of privatisation: selling Royal Mail would be a means to ensure new capital influx and allow for more financial freedom outside the rigid state aid regime which applies to public companies (referred to in Interview, BIS; Hooper, 2010: 31–2; Hooper et al., 2008: 77). The IPO of Royal Mail shares in October 2013 thus marked an endpoint to a long and tedious journey towards postal privatisation in Britain. The way in which privatisation has been implemented proved highly controversial given that the share price for Royal Mail increased rapidly following the IPO. The National Audit Office, in an assessment published in April 2014, came to the conclusion that the costs for the approach taken by the government in the sale has ultimately been born by the tax payer (NAO, 2014). The latter has thus been considered as the 'loser in this Royal Mail privatisation' (Jenkins, 2014)

A hands-off approach on operational issues usually goes hand in hand with the delegation of regulatory tasks to an independent body. In line with expectations formulated in the conceptual chapters, independent regulation should constitute the best match with LMEs and thus constitute the predominant mode of rulemaking in the liberal version of capitalism. In the postal sector, regulation has been delegated towards a nonmajoritarian institution since 2000, and thus considerably later than in the British telecoms and energy sectors (Vogel, 1996: 132). As in the case of privatisation, however, several attempts had failed. The government's proposals on the 'Future of Postal Services' (Department of Trade and Industry, 1994) made the case for a director general, appointed by ministers, with independent powers. The incoming Labour government in 1998 also included institutional innovation in its reform proposals, announcing the creation of an independent regulator (HC Deb 7 December 1998 cc 21–39).

In practice, a postal regulator (Postcomm) was first introduced by the 1999 Postal Regulation as a consultative body within the Department of Trade and Industry. The Act subsequently reconstituted Postcomm as an independent agency with proper regulatory competencies, but not entrusted with the enforcement of competition law (section 15 of the 2000 Postal Services Act). The government had originally envisaged granting powers concurrent with those of the Office of Fair Trading (Department of Trade and Industry, 1999: 6), but such provisions were excluded in the final text of the 2000 Postal Act. The remit of the authority is limited to the delivery branch of the postal business, while oversight of the Post Office has remained in the ministerial realm. The regulator can recommend changes to the scope of the reserved area, subject to approval by a resolution of both houses of Parliament (section 8 of the 2000 Postal Services Act). Based on encompassing consultation with stakeholders, Postcomm in February 2005 announced its intention to abolish Royal Mail's legal monopoly by 1 January 2006 (Postcomm, 2005). The move towards full liberalisation in the LME was thus driven by independent regulation rather than political determination. Postcomm also played a proactive role in increasing the level of competition in the letter mail business by allowing downstream access to Royal Mail's infrastructure (Dudley et al., 2009; Rodriguez, 2013; Walsh, 2013). The licence which Postcomm granted to Royal Mail stipulated that prices for access services should include a discount known as the headroom (i.e. a differential between the prices for corresponding retail and access service), in order to avoid any practices of margin squeeze. Regulatory experts have argued that through such practice Postcomm, not disposing of competition law enforcement powers, sought to combat a specific type of anti-competitive practice through ex ante regulatory control (Eccles, 2008: 349–53). The extent to which this access regime put the incumbent into a position to recover its actual costs has been controversial and gave rise to continued disagreement between Royal Mail and Postcomm (Walsh, 2012: 16–21, 2013: 325–7). The 2008 Hooper report was particularly critical about Postcomm's approach to the headroom and urged for change (Hooper et al., 2008: 97–100).

The regulator–regulatee relationship was in bad shape in the wake of the last British postal reform. Postcomm and Royal Mail disagreed on several key issues, such as the definition of the postal market or the size and distribution of Royal Mail's costs. From a Royal Mail perspective, the regulator's practice was unbalanced, charging Postcomm with being 'too focused on the introduction of competition, at the expense of the regulator's primary duty to protect the universal service' (Hooper et al., 2008: 58). The working relationship between Postcomm and the incumbent had thus continued to deteriorate and came to a point where it appeared unviable (Walsh, 2012: 13–15, 2013: 324–5): the regulator did not trust the data provided by the incumbent and opted for strict regulatory controls, while the incumbent felt deprived of the commercial freedom it aimed to achieve. Postcomm thus appeared to be part of the problem when the reform debate took off. The direct relationship between Postcomm and Royal Mail as a 'single firm regulator' (Walsh, 2012: 14) and Postcomm's lack of competition law enforcement powers were often referred to as major shortcomings in the institutional arrangements. The specific case of Postcomm thus matched the broader British reform agenda to streamline and consolidate regulatory activity. To that end, the scope of individual institutions had been reorganised and broadened, such as in the case of Ofcom which was established by the Office of Communications Act 2002 as the regulator for British communications industries, merging several pre-existing regulatory bodies.

With the Postal Services Act 2011 (Part 2 on postal regulation) Ofcom took on board the postal sector and was entrusted with far-reaching regulatory and competition law enforcement powers. The regulator operates under a legal regime which is considerably less burdensome than the previous one when it comes to regulating downstream access, prices and universal service provision (Eccles, 2013: 20). More specifically, Ofcom has been put in charge of: adopting a 'universal postal service order' which describes the services and relevant standards; reviewing minimum standards formulated in the law; designating the USP and imposing conditions; reviewing the costs of universal service provision and recommending necessary action (Part 3 of the 2011 Postal Services Act, section 29–47). Assessing the rather short period of Ofcom's activity in the sector, policy insiders have argued that the regulator–regulatee relationship has improved considerably (Interview, CF; BIS, 2010; Interview, Ofcom). In line with the 2011 Postal Services Act, Ofcom has relaxed the regime providing downstream access, and seeks to adopt a more balanced approach on competition and universal service provision. This last episode thus appears to introduce a phase of normalisation into British postal regulation to the extent that the existing regime is well in line with the well-established Anglo-Saxon tradition of independent rulemaking.

Long live the union! Industrial relations in the postal sector

> What started in Whitley Council days as a very proper policy of extending and formalising consultation with staff at all levels about postal operations and policy has gradually developed into a situation in which any management decision is a matter for negotiation with the UPW, and where failing agreement in such negotiation, management is reluctant to act for fear of disruption of postal business. (The Monopolies and Mergers Commission, 1980: 84)

> I have quite a hard message for the union, which is not to take industrial action; to negotiate, not to walk away from meetings. I have the same hard message for management: don't bounce the union, give them plenty of time, give them information, allow them to make a contribution. (Lord Sawyer, CWU, 2002)

The continued erosion of British neo-corporatism (Gospel and Edwards, 2012), which in the 1980s was accelerated by legislation dismantling union power under Margaret Thatcher (Blanchflower and Freeman, 1994; Towers, 1989), has been a key element in Britain's evolution towards a LME. Thatcherism constituted a significant break in a political economy where trade unions at the beginning of the early twentieth century, according to the National Insurance Act 1911, had played a double role in industrial relations and the administration of the national system of pensions and social insurance (Crouch, 1999). In the early post-war period the situation in British industrial relations very much resembled a CME with voluntarist, nation-wide multi-employer bargaining (Gospel and Edwards, 2012: 1233). Thus, in a system where the law did not play the same role in governance as in many other countries, corporatism was a key element in industrial relations.

Discontinuity should not, however, be overrated, since the erosion of British neo-corporatism predated Thatcherism (Gospel and Edwards, 2012). The organisational and legal foundations of corporatist arrangements were weak, given the limited scope of national agreements and discrepancies between formal national rules and informal workplace practices, in particular in the private sector (Gospel and Edwards, 2012: 1233). By the mid-1970s an incoming Labour government sought to counterbalance this trend through the introduction of new legislation, yet these decentralisation reforms, paired with centralised income policies, had paradoxical effects and eventually increased industrial conflict (Howell, 2006: 149–50). When Margaret Thatcher was elected Prime Minister in 1979, following the famous 'Winter of Discontent', it appeared legitimate to dismantle the trade unions for the sake of economic reform. In order to move 'from crisis to a new set of institutions designed to manage crisis' (Howell, 2006: 147), the existing legal framework was overhauled substantially. The 1980, 1982, 1984 and 1988 Employment Acts introduced by the incoming Conservative government circumscribed the scope and the legal validity of collective bargaining, and thus significantly weakened union power (Blanchflower and Freeman, 1994; Towers, 1989). Contemporary observers of reform expected that 'its bark was worse than its bite will be' (Todd, 1980: 275) and, in any case, the decline in union membership Britain experienced during the period following the Thatcher reform cannot exclusively be attributed to government intervention, given that the economic context as well as the occupational structure had also been subject to change (Towers, 1989).

When New Labour came to power in 1997, after eighteen years of Conservative administrations, the change in government did not amount to a reversal in industrial relations politics. The Labour party, which had left its close links with trade unions behind, maintained most of the legislation introduced by previous governments (Faucher-King et al., 2010: 42, 90–3; Howell, 2006: 164). New Labour sought to limit the power of public sector unions, and, in particular, the incoming Prime Minister Tony Blair had reservations vis-à-vis the trade unions, while Gordon Brown was more accommodating (Faucher-King et al., 2010: 32–3 and 44). The party elite was, however, keen to preserve flexible labour markets seen as a competitive advantage, and would rather seek to cushion their negative effects through redistributive policies as well as through an additional layer of regulation (Howell, 2006: 162, 164; Faucher-King et al., 2010: 33). Also, a minimum wage was introduced in order to fulfil one of the major electoral promises, but at a rather low level and in a depoliticised institutional setting where a newly created independent body (Low Pay Commission), rather than trade unions, would take the lead (Faucher-King et al., 2010: 33; Mabbett, 2011: 218).

In this context the situation in the British postal sector appears anachronistic. In the period 1979–87 following the Thatcher reform the major union in the sector, the Union of Communication Workers (UCW), initially lost only 2.8 per cent of its members and towards the end of the period in 1986–87 even experienced an increase of 3 per cent (Towers, 1989: 176). By way of comparison, the Electrical, Electronic, Telecommunications & Plumbing Union lost 21.4 per cent of its membership during the same period (ibid.). The resilience of workplace unionism in the postal sector has thus attracted attention (Darlington, 1993), and poses a puzzle to macrolevel generalisation within the VoC framework. The following sections briefly describe the evolution of organisational patterns in the British postal sector, assess the role of trade unions as a stakeholder, voicing its interests throughout the reform process, and examine industrial relations.

As table 7.1 illustrates, Royal Mail continues to be an important employer, and the share of labour cost, out of total cost, remains stable at a relatively high level. Until 1922 the British Post Office was the largest employer in the country, with some 249,696 employees reported for the period 1913/1914 (Daunton, 1985: 193). Although the share of persons employed in the domestic postal sector as a proportion of total employment has decreased over time, it is still significant: in 2010, the number amounted to almost 0.6 per cent (Eurostat, 2012), while in 2004 it was at a rate of 0.69 per cent (Lumio and Fickinger, 2007). Labour intensiveness is also documented by the fact that the related costs have amounted to a significant share of total cost in the sector. Historically, this share had risen from 35.4 per cent in 1870/71 to 67 per cent by the First World War (ibid.). As table 7.1 illustrates, labour costs still amounted to around 60 per cent within Royal Mail during the period 1998 to 2012. Therefore determining wage levels continues to be of vital importance for the postal operator.

The debate about the underlying economic rationale, and the comparison with wage levels in similar sectors, dates back to the early days of the Post Office. In line with Rowland Hill's belief that wages shall be determined by market forces, in 1855 the Department and Treasury agreed that remuneration could vary geographically according to local wage levels and labour supply (Daunton, 1985: 222). When employees started to articulate their concerns over wage levels and working conditions, this resulted in a wave of unionisation in the late 1880s (Daunton, 1985: 226–7): in 1887 the British Postal Clerks Association was founded by provincial Post Office clerks, in 1889 the Postmen's Union, and in 1890 London sorters formed the Fawcett Association. Throughout the nineteenth century, however, the ministerial department did not tolerate unionisation as it expected employees to be obedient in the established hierarchy, and any behaviour contrary to these principles involved disciplinary measures and dismissal (Daunton, 1985: 259–65). As a result, trade unions were not recognised and had no role in negotiating wages. The situation changed when an incoming Liberal government gave privileged legal status to unions and the Post Office became less convinced about the advantages of excluding unions. This resulted in a U-turn with the recognition of unions within the Post Office in the early twentieth century (Daunton, 1985: 260–7).

In the period following the First World War a decision was taken to implement Whitleyism in government departments, and the so-called Whitley report provided for the principles governing the relations between employers and employees. In 1920 the Union of Post Office Workers (UPW)

Table 7.1: Employment in the British postal sector (Royal Mail)

	1998	2000	2002	2003	2004	2006	2008	2009	2011/2
FTE (1000s)	*	210.7	*	227.2	218.6	211.5	199	*	176.2
% labour cost	62.5	55.8	56.1	56.1	57.8	68.8	65.2	64	62

[1] value 2005
[2] value 2010
(ITA Consulting and WIK-Consult, 2009; Copenhagen Economics, 2010; WIK-Consult, 2013)
* years not reported

was established, while as from 1921 employees in the telecoms sector organised within the National Federation of Postal and Telegraph Clerks, and engineers within the Post Office Engineering Union (POEU). The POEU took a different stance on industrial action compared to the UPW, considering strikes to be contrary to public service duty. Similarly, postal sorters had organised separately, which caused disputes around representation. As a reaction to such union unrest and the ensuing General Strike, civil service unions in 1927 were forbidden from engaging in political action, and the Post Office closely cooperated with the UPW rather than with secessionist movements (Daunton, 1985: 267, 349). When the Post Office had been transformed into a corporation, the Whitley Council system was replaced by a Council of Post Office Unions as the official forum for consultation (The Monopolies and Mergers Commission, 1980: 75). In 1980, the UPW became the Union of Communication Workers (UCW). In 1985, POEU merged with the Postal and Telecommunications Group of the Civil and Public Services Association to form the National Communications Union (NCU). In January 1995, the UCW and the NCU merged to form the Communication Workers Union (CWU).

Despite various secessionist movements, the CWU and its predecessor UCW have represented the biggest share of employees throughout decades, and have acquired 'genuine postal intelligence' and 'a sophisticated understanding of postal developments' (Campbell, 2002: 331). In the 2000s, the CWU continued to represent around 80 per cent within Royal Mail, with lower rates among managerial staff where the Communications Managers Association (CMA) comprises the second union in the sector. The CMA in 1958 replaced the Post Office Management Staffs Association representing supervisors and junior management. The number of union members in the sector reported by Newell (in 2008) amounted to 160,000 employees organised within the CWU and 11,500 persons within the CMA. Total membership within the CWU rose from 196,426 in 1983 to 279,679 in 2002 (Gall, 2003: Appendix C) and according to CWU figures numbered 203,500 members in 2012. Within the Post Office, CWU covers only employees working at Crown Post Offices, which constitute a small share of the total workforce, while the National Federation of SubPostmasters represents the lion's share of Post Office employees at all the other branches (National Federation of SubPostmasters, 2012: 2).

Throughout the decades of building up and reforming the postal administration, politicians have sought to circumscribe the influence of an organised workforce on the politics of reform and change. In 1925 unions were prohibited from engaging in political action, and again in 1982 the Employment Act sought to draw a line between industrial and political action. According to related case law industrial action against privatisation was unlawful (Towers, 1989: 170). The largest strike in the sector occurred in 1971 when employees feared the loss of public service privileges in the course of corporatisation (Daunton, 1985: 351–2). UPW members walked out for more than six weeks, yet failed to gain their wage demands. This episode, followed by a period of industrial unrest in the 1970s, marked industrial relations in the sector by putting an end to the post-war period of quiescence (Gall, 2003). The battles fought by the trade union were related to liberalisation and privatisation attempts in the postal sector. In the 1990s the CWU, together with other unions and organisations, effectively intervened against the reform initiatives of the Major government. They provided counter-experience and input (London Economics, 1994; UCW, 1993) and organised a robust campaign raising concerns related to service quality and social cohesion (PPS, 1994; UCW, 1994).

The union also provided input when the Labour party started to consult on postal reform in the mid-1990s and voiced their concerns in the run-up to the 2000 Postal Services Act (CWU, 1997, 1998, 1999). The CWU consistently argued against unfair competition, which would erode the public service and the Post Office's financial viability. In this context the CWU organised a ballot to boycott downstream access (CWU, 2013). The union was also vocal in the political debates on privatisation. The CWU organised a wide range of action against privatisation, such as the campaign 'Keep the Post Public', 'Save our Royal Mail' and 'The Future of the Post Office'. It also provided policy input during consultation (CWU, 2008a, 2008b), and sought to provide counter-evidence to the Hooper report (CWU, 2009), aligning with leftist think tanks (Compass, 2009).

While the Post Office was one of the earliest testing grounds for innovations in industrial relations such as the Whitley committees, observers have described industrial relations in the sector as being 'poor' (The Monopolies and Mergers Commission, 1980: 80), 'traditional, brutal and unimaginative' (Campbell, 2002: 336), 'extremely difficult' (Hooper et al., 2008), and 'enormously damaging to Royal Mail' (Lord Sawyer et al., 2001: 13).

Union activities by postal workers have been studied as evidence of 'militancy' characterised by strong reliance on mobilisation and the frequent threat, or use, of industrial action (Gall, 2003: 12). The union has indeed made use of its capacity for disruption, which has increased owing to processes of rationalisation and modernisation. The latter involve a higher degree of centralisation of the workforce such as in the large mail sorting centre in London and thus increase the vulnerability of operations (Interview, CWU 2). Throughout the 1980s, the level of conflict was considerable, as highlighted in two reports by the Monopolies and Mergers Commission (1980; 1984). The 1980 report pointed to a 'situation in which any management decision is a matter for negotiation with the UPW, and where failing agreement in such negotiation, management is reluctant to act for fear of disruption of postal business' (The Monopolies and Mergers Commission, 1980: 84). It concluded that the consultation practice which had been introduced under the Whitley Council procedure was no longer appropriate and should be abolished (The Monopolies and Mergers Commission, 1980: 83–4). Industrial relations became increasingly tense, resulting in further national postal strikes from the mid-1980s onwards (Gall, 2003: covered in chapters 5 and 6).

A major strike in 1988 comprised official and unofficial industrial action triggered by disputes over a wage supplement to be paid in difficult recruitment areas which was perceived as threatening nation-wide collective bargaining practices. A second national postal strike in 1996 and 1997 turned out to be the largest strike in the national economy throughout the 1990s in terms of days lost and employees involved. This time postal workers resisted the introduction of team working practices, and Royal Mail had to acknowledge the need to find new ways of securing cooperation and loyalty from employees (Gall, 2003: 100).

Continuing difficulties led Royal Mail and the CWU to jointly commission an independent review which was published in 2001 (Lord Sawyer et al.). The assessments made in the so-called 'Sawyer Report' was overtly negative regarding the attitude of managers, the role of the union and the industrial relations culture: the employee relations culture in failing Mail Centres was described as being outdated and confrontational; the authors reported how the CWU blocked several Royal Mail initiatives to increase workplace effectiveness through the introduction of team working and bonus schemes throughout the 1980s and 1990s; how the CWU avoided liability through unofficial industrial action; how the knock-on effect of industrial action disrupted the operation of Mail Centres; how the national leadership of the CWU was not sufficiently connecting to and communicating with its membership, and how it showed indifference or inertia in its strategic involvement in corporate change. The report recommended a new partnership approach as well as a moratorium on industrial action. Although progress in this area was assessed positively (CWU, 2002; Priestman, 2003), this did not bring to an end industrial conflict. In 2007 industrial action peaked at over 627,000 employee days lost, accounting for 60 per cent of days lost to strikes across the country (Hooper et al., 2008: 55), and coming close to the 811,000 days lost during the national strike in 1996 and 1997 (Gall, 2003: 55).

Disproportional levels of industrial activism should, however, not obscure the fact that unions played a key role in negotiating collective agreements. In the 1980s the UPW was the only union to have a closed shop agreement with the Post Office (The Monopolies and Mergers Commission, 1980: 12), and today both the CWU and the CMA conclude collective agreements. At present, bargaining coverage within Royal Mail is estimated at an approximate minimum level of 63 per cent (Newell, 2008). For a considerable period, relatively low wage levels were compensated by working overtime and receiving additional payment (Campbell, 2002: 361).

The extent to which postal workers benefited from a wage premium gave rise to controversy. Employment in the Post Office was traditionally attractive due to job security, opportunities for advancement and promotion, and a wide range of extra benefits such as a pension scheme, which was introduced as of 1859 (Daunton, 1985: 237, 246, 248). Another source of extra benefits were overtime and additional payments on top of the normal salary, so that a 1980 review prepared by the Monopolies and Mergers Commission found that wage levels were 'substantially in excess of basic wages' (The Monopolies and Mergers Commission, 1980: 11). Wachter and Perloff (1991), engaging in a comparative analysis of wage levels in British and US postal sectors, argued that in 1989 there was a negative postal premium of less than 1 per cent, and that the British Post Office premium was 'small' in comparison to wage premiums paid by the United States Postal Service. Taking into account the beneficial effect of job security, and the fact that there were no reported difficulties in hiring workers outside London and southeast, they did, however, make the case that there was a small wage premium in Britain, which was zero in London and in the southeast, and small in other regions. The CWU rejected the argument about a wage premium paid to Royal Mail staff and pointed out that weekly earnings were significantly below British average pay (CWU, 2008a: 12).

Agreements to settle questions regarding payment and working conditions were at the core of collective bargaining. A major deal between the CWU and Royal Mail following the 1996 dispute was struck in 1999 with the 'Way Forward' package, which included pay settlement and an agreement on new working methods, and received a high level of approval during the union's ballot in 2000 (Campbell, 2002; CWU, 2000: 361). In view of the unsatisfactory performance during the Consignia episode, the incoming Chairman Allan Leighton sought to rationalise the workforce. The result was a drop of 6 per cent of Royal Mail's bill for wages and salaries from £4.8 billion in 2001 to £4.5 billion in 2005–6 (Peston, 2008: 322). In 2004 another ballot was organised on a 'National Agreement on pay and major change' between the CWU and Royal Mail (CWU, 2004). Recent agreements include the 'National Industrial Relations Framework Agreement' (CWU, 2010b) as well as an agreement between the Post Office, Royal Mail and the CWU in connection with the separation introduced by the 2011 Postal Act and the resulting transfer of employees (CWU, 2012). Within Royal Mail industrial relations have improved with the more accommodating style introduced by the CEO Moya Greene (Interview, CWU 2). The agreement 'Business Transformation 2010 and Beyond' (CWU, 2010a) reflects the new focus on the negotiation of change. An important element in accommodating the latest postal reform in Britain was to solve the problem posed by Royal Mail's aggravating pension deficit. The CWU lobbied heavily in this process, and a deal struck was that the state would take over Royal Mail's £4.6 billion pension deficit. Pension payments are ensured by the establishment of a new fund, the Royal Mail Statutory Pension Scheme, an outcome welcomed by the union (Interview, CWU 1). The European Commission has authorised this state aid regime in spring 2012 (rf. IP/12/260).

Postal services in the liberal model

> It is a glorious mission [...]. We're the only company in the land allowed to use Her Majesty's livery on everything. We go to 29 million addresses six days a week. (Moya Greene, CEO of Royal Mail, McKinsey & Company, 2012)

The USO in the British postal sector goes back to a long tradition and 'has been integrated intimately into the social fabric of the nation' (Campbell, 2002: 350). The inventions introduced under Rowland Hill with the Penny Post system, the Queen's image on the stamp, and a profoundly embedded policy belief that a public monopoly on letter delivery was required to preserve the universal service (London Economics, 1994: 27; The Monopolies and Mergers Commission, 1980: 88–9) have contributed to the delay in British postal reform. The 1981 Telecoms Act still highlighted that the Post Office would need to serve the social, industrial and commercial needs of the nation (s. 59 (2b) Telecoms Act). Rather than formulating detailed legal requirements in this regard, postal governance relied on close coordination between the Post Office and the government. Maintaining the reserved area, which goes back to the Post Office Management Act in 1837, was seen as a sufficient legal guarantee for preserving the universal service. The 2000 Postal Services Act was, therefore, a landmark change in the British postal regime as for the first time it set down in detail the scope and requirements of the USO, and attributed monitoring and implementing tasks to an independent regulator. The Act stipulated the protection of the universal service as the regulator's prior duty, while regulation for competition comes second (section 5 of 2000 Postal Services Act, discussed by Eccles, 2008: 341; McGowan, 2002: 340, 349; Prosser, 2005: 72).

This priority has not been subject to change with the 2011 Postal Services Act (section 29). The latest reform has, however, strengthened the prerogatives of the regulator in the area of universal service provision, and has thus inscribed into the law a further shift towards independent regulation. Such a high degree of depoliticisation was not intended with the 2000 Act under the New Labour government, which at the time had emphasised statutory guidance regarding social and environmental objectives (Department of Trade and Industry, 1998: 20; s. 61 of 2011 Postal Services Act). In the postal sector such guidance was issued in 2001, highlighting the regulator's duty to implement the social objectives of the Act, such as safeguarding the interests of vulnerable groups, reiterating the priority to be attributed to the provision of a universal service, urging the regulator to ensure access to public post offices particularly in rural and urban deprived areas (Department of Trade and Industry). Social objectives and user complaints in the British postal sector have also been addressed by dedicated consumer bodies predating the sector regulator. Already the 1969 Act (section 14) introduced the Post Office Users National Council (POUNC), which was replaced, with the 2000 Act, by a Consumer Council for Postal Services (section 2) known as Postwatch. Following criticism of its performance (House of Commons, 2005) and in an effort to streamline the consumer body landscape and reduce costs, the 2007 Consumer, Estate Agents and Redress Act abolished Postwatch and Energywatch and reallocated related tasks within the newly created Consumer Focus (Interview, CF). A separation between consumer advocacy and complaint handling was, furthermore, institutionalised with the creation of a Postal Redress Scheme in 2008 (Interview, POSTRS). In 2013 Consumer Focus was integrated into Citizens Advice. In the British postal sector there is therefore a clear trend towards independent bodies and depoliticisation, even in the realm of consumer protection.

Table 7.2: Postal outlets in Britain (Post Office)

	1999	2000	2002	2004	2006	2008	2010	2012
outlets	18,341	18,393	17,243	14,609	14,219	11,952	11,820	11,818
% POs	3.2	3.3	3.3	3.7	3.2	3.0	3.1	3.2
outlets/ inh.[1]	3.2	3.1	2.9	2.4	2.4	2.2	1.92	1.88
outlet/ area[2]	13.2	*	14	16.6	17	20.3	20.6	20.6[3]

[1] outlets per 10,000 inhabitants
[2] average area in sq km covered by an outlet
[3] value for 2011
(ITA Consulting and WIK-Consult, 2009; WIK-Consult, 2004; UPU, 2012; WIK-Consult, 2013)
* year not reported

Counter services provided through the Post Office are politically even more sensitive than the delivery branch, and policy decisions have been retained in the ministerial realm (Interview, BIS). According to the law the government, as the shareholder, has the responsibility to safeguard the public interest and to ensure a nation-wide post office network, and in fulfilling this task can ask the regulator for advice (section 42 of the 2000 Postal Services Act). The density of the network does not form part of the USO and is not specified in the law. With around 250 inhabitants per square km density is at a similar level to that in Germany, and higher than in France, but hilly and scarcely populated areas also pose specific geographical challenges. As table 7.2 illustrates, the postal presence was reduced by some 7,000 outlets between the late 1990s and 2012. More striking is the constantly low percentage share of in-house branches at around 3 per cent. This low number of genuine post offices is due to the fact that the British network is composed of two types of branches: the bigger Crown Offices, directly owned by the Post Office, and other outlets operated by private business people, the so-called subpostmasters. The number of Crown Offices has continued to reduce, going down from 1,339 in 1989–90 to 373 in 2012, while the total number of branches has been reduced less dramatically from 20,615 post offices between 1989 and 1990 to 11,818 in 2012 (BIS, 2010; Campbell, 2002: 360; The Post Office, 2013: 15). In 2002 the number of postal outlets per 10,000 inhabitants was still well above the EU-average (2.38 outlets) with around 2.8 outlets – that is the same level as in France (WIK-Consult, 2004: 165). However, the number of outlets had already been reduced between 1998 and 2003 by around 10 per cent (WIK-Consult, 2004: 164).

Downsizing was governed by successive closure programmes with the objective of improving the financial outlook of the Post Office, which had been making a loss since 2000 (National Audit Office, 2009: 5; PIU, 2000). The 'Post Office Network Change Programme', implemented between 2007 and 2009, involved 2,432 branch closures which were partially offset by the introduction of just over 500 new outreach services in rural areas (Postcomm, 2009: 1). Another round was launched with the Network Transformation Programme in 2010 (BIS, 2010), which will turn more than half of the existing branches (6,000 post offices) into two new operating models, Post Office Mains which are the bigger high street branches (4,000 post offices) and Post Office Locals (2,000 post offices) where post office services are offered as secondary retail services in existing retail businesses. The government is lending considerable financial support to this modernisation programme with £1.34 billion over a four-year period from 2011 to 2015 (BIS, 2010: 9).

These changes have been monitored by both the sector regulator and consumer bodies. Between 2001 and 2009 Postcomm issued nine annual post office network reports (Postcomm, 2001; Postcomm, 2009), and Postwatch was consulted, together with local authorities, by the Post Office prior to every single envisaged closure in order to assess the consequences for local communities (National Audit Office, 2009: 6). While in the past the Post Office's social significance was paramount as it provided essential services such as payment of pensions and social benefits, today the postal presence is limited to genuine postal product transactions which can be provided alongside other retail services. The British government is therefore seeking to enhance diversification in order to offer a broader range of government services through the network of postal branches (Interview, CF; Interview, BIS).

The 2000 Postal Services Act defined the universal service, requiring at least one delivery and collection per working day at affordable prices and in accordance with a uniform tariff within Britain, 'except in such geographical conditions or other circumstances as the Commission considers to be exceptional' (section 4). The 2011 Act (sections 29–47) furthermore provided Ofcom with a mandate to adopt a universal postal service order. This order was intended to describe the services and relevant standards, to review minimum standards formulated in the law, to designate the USP and to impose conditions, to review the costs of universal service provision and to recommend necessary action. Since no specified price limit for basic mail services has been defined in the law, the regulator had to come up with a working definition of affordability in its regulatory practice (Postcomm, 2011). The British regime exempted Royal Mail from paying VAT for all services provided. The scope of this tax exemption has been narrowed in response to competition law concerns raised by the European Commission (IP/07/1664) and since April

Table 7.3: Mail services in Britain (Royal Mail)

	1999	2001	2003	2006	2007	2009	2010	2011	2012	2014
20g tariff FSC[1] £	0.26	0.27	0.28	0.30	0.34	0.39	0.41	0.46	0.60	0.62
20g tariff EU FSC[1] £	0.30	0.37	0.38	0.42	0.48	0.50	*	*	*	0.97
D+1 performance %	91.1	89	91.7	91.4	94	85.2	91.4	*	92.2	*

[1] Fastest Standard Category (ITA Consulting and WIK-Consult, 2009; WIK-Consult, 2013)
* years not reported

2012 only applies to the universal service area. The Commission has, however, approved state aid at a level of £1,089 million to Royal Mail for granting access to its delivery network. Where the cost of providing the universal service would not be covered, the regulatory regime allows for the introduction of a compensation fund.

In policy practice the nature and social role of mail delivery has transformed substantially over time. In the early 1900s the Post Office operated up to eighteen collections and twelve deliveries in inner London (The Monopolies and Mergers Commission, 1980: 14), and until 2002 upheld two daily deliveries in urban areas (UCW, 1993: 3). The quality of the mail delivery service has varied over time. In its 1980 report, also referring to an earlier report prepared by the POUNC with similar conclusions, the Monopolies and Mergers Commission stated that the quality of mail delivery service, measured in terms of meeting delivery time targets, had declined owing to the inefficient use of both human and financial resources (The Monopolies and Mergers Commission, 1980: 14–21). Unsatisfactory performance continued throughout the 1980s despite attempts to introduce change, but significant improvements were achieved in the late 1980s thanks to a five-year service improvement programme launched by Royal Mail in 1988/89 (London Economics, 1994: 28–32). As the data in table 7.3 illustrates, delivery times have mostly been above 90 per cent since 1999. Letter mail prices have increased steadily once an independent regulator started to operate in 2000, and more significantly in 2012 under Ofcom. According to the findings of a study conducted by the regulator in 2013 postal services are, overall, affordable for a majority of consumers, with very limited exceptions (Ofcom, 2013a). The interesting question in the British context will be whether and how Ofcom will use its prerogatives in reviewing and potentially altering the USO. On the basis of a review published in 2013 (Ofcom, 2013b) Ofcom concluded that consumer needs were being met and that there was no need to propose changes to the scope of the universal service at this point in time.

In conclusion, British postal reform adds to the the findings of the previous chapters. The transition towards the regulatory state in Britain took place later, but at a faster pace, yet it did not make the need for financial compensation by public money disappear. State aid is still important in providing financial support to the Post Office, in securing territorial presence, and to Royal Mail for granting access to its delivery network. Put bluntly, the socialisation of cost has also been required in order to privatise profit when the state took over the historical pension burden of Royal Mail in the process of privatisation. When it comes to the process of depoliticisation, the British postal sector is a highly insightful case: although Postcomm was constrained in its regulatory practice by clearly defined policy objectives regarding the universal service, it was proactively opening up the mail delivery market to competition. The extent to which British postal policy has been delegated to an unelected body, even in the realm of social regulation, stands out in comparison to the other countries studied in this book.

8

Varieties of postal reform and regulation in a comparative perspective

This chapter compares the findings of the preceding chapters and widens the scope of analysis towards change in other sectors. It scrutinises the research questions formulated in the conceptual part of the book in the light of empirical evidence. The path, dynamics and scope of reforms are compared across the three countries, in order to assess whether varieties of capitalism have translated into varieties of postal reform. In order to avoid overgeneralisation from a single case study, evidence from the postal sector is situated in comparison to the reform record of France, Germany and Britain in other public utilities. The politics of reregulation in the postal sector are then examined to address how the emerging regulatory state has protected consumers and employees. Here the findings from the three countries are shown in a wider perspective of postal regulation across the member states of the EU.

Postal reform in France, Germany and Britain

In-depth analysis of postal reform processes in France, Germany and Britain has shown that the timing, dynamics and scope of postal reform were not always in line with the 'typical' patterns assumed for the three varieties of capitalism (see table 2.1). The reform record is particularly puzzling for the British case, as depicted in table 8.1: Britain was overall not a reform leader, and the privatisation of Royal Mail occurred some decades later than in other sectors. Germany, by contrast, was among the first European countries engaging in corporatisation and privatisation in the 1980s. Of the three countries studied, France constitutes the best match with SME-type expectations. Although cross-country variation relating to privatisation, liberalisation and regulatory reform is not always in line with expectations, the VoC typology is a valid approach where we integrate variation over time and across sectors.

Privatisation, where there is no direct impact by the EU on national

Table 8.1: Three types of postal reform

	France	Germany	Britain
Timing	**laggard**	**leader**	**hybrid**
privatisation	law 2010 no IPO yet	law 1994 IPO 2000	law 2011 IPO 2013
liberalisation	law 1999/2000 fully 2011	law 1997 fully 2008	law 1999/2000 fully 2006
reg. reform[1]	ARCEP 2005	RegTP 1998 BNetzA 2005	Postcomm 2000 Ofcom 2012
Dynamics	**state-driven**	**negotiated**	**state-driven**
privatisation	politically not opportune, blocked by trade unions, since 2007 driven by incumbent and government	driven by government & business community	politically not opportune, blocked by trade unions post-2007 driven by expert community
liberalisation	EU-driven	driven by business community under conservative governments, blocked by Social Democrats in response to trade unions and incumbent	initially EU-driven, full opening driven by regulator
reg. reform	EU-driven	government-driven	initially EU-driven further steps government-driven
Scope	**limited**	**comprehensive**	**comprehensive**
privatisation, structural reform	fully owned by government, high share civil servants and labour cost	no government share (KfW 21% in 2013), massive cut-backs civil servants and labour cost	government share 30% (following 2013 IPO), massive cut-backs civil servants, high share labour cost
liberalisation	de facto monopoly	end-to-end competition around 10%	upstream competition de facto last-mile monopoly
reg. reform	limited	considerable	limited initially, comprehensive over time

Information compiled by author

[1] The year indicates when the regulator started to operate

policy choices, is the most insightful component of reform from a comparative capitalist perspective. This is not to deny that a spill-over from liberalisation reforms frequently occurs where policy makers, often pressured by the incumbent operators, consider that a private company is better able to face competition. In the EU context market opening was imposed by supranational law on the member states, while they were free to decide about privatisation.

France is a useful example in this respect. The discussion of French postal reform history in Chapter 5 showed that privatising La Poste was, for a long time, off limits. A first attempt to alter the organisational structure of the post office was taken with the *projet Longuet* in the late 1980s, but it was effectively overthrown by massive strike action. Shortly afterwards Rocard's reform package sought to tackle postal reform, and this time industrial action by the lorry drivers in 1988 put an end to such plans. The only meaningful change during this period occurred as a spill-over from EU-induced telecoms reforms.

The Prévot report published in 1989 emphasised the need for structural reform, and legislation adopted in 1990 introduced a structural separation between the postal and telecoms branches. While the abolition of the PTT state administration constituted a landmark change, its effects were cushioned by social safeguards. In particular, the new scheme maintained the public service status of the employees, which explains why the number of public servants, until today, remains comparably high (see table 5.1). In the aftermath of the 1990 reform the political climate was not favourable towards taking further steps in the same direction: in 2000 a government proposal was opposed by the banking associations, who feared the loss of privileges, and by the trade unions. In 2005 the Villepin privatisation package did not even mention La Poste, nor did the 2005 Postal Act introduce any meaningful change in this respect. The situation changed with the perspective of EU-wide, total liberalisation. La Poste lobbied the government for greater commercial freedom in order to face future challenges, struggling with a surmounting debt and increasing mail volumes. The political arena proved responsive to such pressure, and the 2010 law transformed La Poste into a public limited company. At the time of writing La Poste was still fully state-owned, but it is probably only a question of time until an IPO is used by the government to alleviate some of its public deficit.

As discussed in Chapter 6, Germany was among the reform leaders in Europe. Germany had already engaged in corporatisation in the 1980s, and cleared the way for privatisation with a law and constitutional amendment in 1994. Such change has been driven by the incumbent's strategy for international expansion, a pronounced spill-over from dynamics in the telecoms sector, and political leadership. The first postal reform in 1989 was part of a broader policy package privatising special estates of the Federation, sponsored by a Conservative government holding a comfortable majority in both chambers. The second privatisation law, passed in 1994, has to be seen in the context of reunification, when a massive need to modernise the communications infrastructure in the new *Länder* was paired with concerns about Germany's competitiveness. Amending the German Basic Law, this reform required the consent of the Social Democrats, who were initially opposed to privatisation. Their support was secured by introducing social safeguards into the law, notably guaranteeing the civil servant status of the employees. Such guarantees did not prevent massive structural reform within Deutsche Post. The share of civil servants was drastically reduced to levels below 10 per cent, as was the share of spending on labour (at a level of 32.3 per cent in 2012, see table 6.1). The IPO of Deutsche Post took place in 2000, resulting in a selling off of all government shares by 2005. In sum, Germany has engaged in comprehensive change, and is one of the few countries in the world to have fully privatised their postal office (with the qualification that the state-owned bank KfW still holds above 20 per cent of the shares).

As discussed in Chapter 7, an economic argument for liberalising and privatising Royal Mail was lacking for a considerable period of time. Throughout the 1980s, Royal Mail was profit-making and considered a leader in the postal world (Walsh, 2012: 29; Walsh, 2013: 322), which is one of the reasons why the government decided to disentangle the postal business from the ongoing privatisation process in other utilities. If we consider privatisation alone, Britain is clearly a laggard just like France, introducing a privatisation law in 2011 almost two decades later than Germany. This is surprising given that the Post Office had already been transformed into a publicly owned corporation as early as 1969. Yet Thatcher, introducing an ambitious privatisation programme, shied away from tackling postal privatisation. Until Labour came to power in 1997, several attempts by Conservative governments to change the statute of the Post Office had failed. The only step taken was the establishment in 1986 of three distinct business units for the mail, parcel and counters. While Tony Blair had initially announced that he would hold off postal reform, he launched a reform debate in 1998. Legislation passed in 1999 and 2000 fell short of introducing any changes, other than the granting of greater commercial freedom. On the contrary, the 2000 Act maintained public ownership and stipulated that further primary legislation was required to dispose of shares.

Privatisation gained new ground once the British market had been fully liberalised. The decisive impulse was given by an independent report, prepared by experts maintaining strong ties to regulatory circles. The so-called Hooper report stressed that the financial viability of the incumbent, with its mounting deficit and pension debt in the face of falling mail volumes, was under threat. As discussed in detail in Chapter 7, Royal Mail has engaged in structural reform and rationalisation, which have led to a massive cut-back in the number of civil servants, yet the amount spent on labour is still considerable (above 60 per cent in 2012, see table 7.1). The 2011 Postal Act launched privatisation and legally separated the Post Office from Royal Mail. The IPO of Royal Mail in 2013 reduced government shares, with a single stroke, to some 30 per cent, yet the Post Office remained in public hands.

Different from privatisation, the EU member states could only delay, but not refrain from liberalising their national postal markets. The French fervently resisted tackling liberalisation of their post office in line with the predominant *service public* doctrine. For the French, the postal service embodies the very idea of their public service concept, and is cherished by policy makers and the population alike, for the contribution to socioeconomic and territorial cohesion. Therefore liberalisation was imposed externally, and France tried to resist and minimise the effect of such EU-induced change for a considerable period of time. The 1999 and 2000 legislation, transposing the first European directive, was introduced during the *cohabitation* of Chirac and Jospin, taking a cautious approach in order to secure the support of both chambers and appease social resistance. The outcome therefore amounted to a minimalistic transposition of European law, choosing the upper limits allowed for the reserved area and including as many services as possible within the scope of the USO. It is no coincidence that the first steps were in a law on spatial planning, given that political concerns about safeguarding territorial cohesion were paramount.

Political compromise was also the order of the day when the second directive was transposed in 2005, at a time when the French had just cast their no on the Draft Constitutional Treaty and were enraged by the neoliberal thrust of the controversial 'Bolkestein' directive. Compliance with minimum requirements was flanked by social guarantees aiming at safeguarding territorial cohesion, the universal service and viable working conditions. As discussed in Chapter 4, the negotiations of full market opening among the European heads of government were deadlocked due to French opposition in the run up to the 2007 presidential elections. The right-wing government under Villepin shied away from lending support to liberalisation in face of massive public resistance. In this context President Sarkozy came in as a deal maker for the internal postal market. While de jure France complied with full liberalisation, competition remained at insignificant levels, so that La Poste was in a position to maintain its domestic monopoly.

In Germany liberalisation was introduced virtually at the same time as the first European directive entered into force, and the market was fully opened to competition ahead of European schedule in 2008. Despite this pioneering role, liberalisation in the German context was a delicate balancing act between economic and social concerns. The third postal reform launching liberalisation, passed in 1997, was negotiated in a different political context. At this stage the conservative government had to cope with a SPD-dominated upper house. As a result, the 1997 reform took a cautious approach to liberalisation, introducing gradual market opening which was to result in full market opening by 2002. Under Social Democratic governments this timeline was postponed, extending the legal monopoly until the end of 2007. Exerting pressure as a partner in a grand coalition government, the SPD also achieved social safeguards in exchange for their support for full liberalisation in 2008, agreeing with the CDU/CSU that a sector-specific minimum wage would flank market opening. Already ahead of full liberalisation, end-to-end competition had emerged on the German mail delivery market at a level of around 10 per cent, which in comparative terms is a significant level for the letter mail business.

Liberalisation and regulatory reform in the British context were initially driven by requirements formulated at the European level, which is why their timing corresponds to the transposition of EU directives. Domestically, external pressure has been necessary in order to overcome political deadlock over postal reform, which can partly be explained by strong union power. The CWU has been a vocal actor throughout, assembling the majority of the postal workforce and lobbying the public against change. Market opening in the British postal market was only launched with the transposition of the first postal directive in 1999–2000. Before that, liberalisation appeared off limits for British policy makers, and the only step taken was to open the courier service to competition in the context of the 1989 British Telecoms Act. Once the market had been gradually opened up to competition, change came along rather quickly with anticipated full liberalisation in 2006. De facto competition in the British upstream market is considerable, while Royal Mail continues to dominate end-to-end delivery.

European legislation also laid down minimum requirements in the field of regulatory reform. Again, France can be singled out as a fervent reform opponent. French policy makers were keen to safeguard their decision making powers on postal policy. The 1990 law, for instance, helped to maintain political influence despite structural change, creating institutional structures such as the schedule of conditions, contractual planning and the administrative council. With the 1999 transposition of the first directive, postal policymaking was kept within the lead ministry, that is, France did not comply with the requirement to separate operational from regulatory tasks. Introducing some institutional reshuffling in response to European pressure, France sought to circumvent the creation of an independent regulatory agency. Only when the European Commission took France to court for continued non-compliance with the postal directive in 2003, did French policy makers eventually delegate regulatory powers to an independent agency. The policy prerogatives of the French regulator are, however, narrowly circumscribed by a detailed legal framework defined at the political level. In Germany an independent regulator for postal and telecoms had been introduced in 1998 (RegTP), and was transformed into a bigger cross-sector regulator (BNetzA) in 2005. The legal framework governing the regulatory powers is well balanced between economic and social goals, yet in practice the regulator has mainly ascertained its role as an economic regulator. The British track record of regulatory reform resembles the pattern observed with respect to liberalisation, going from initial resistance to rapid change. Postcomm, established by the 1999 Postal Regulation as a consultative body, became a fully fledged regulatory authority with the 2000 Postal Act, and in practice ascertained its role with determination. The agency used its legal prerogatives, and provided the decisive impulse for full liberalisation in 2006. Postal regulation was transferred to the communications regulator Ofcom following the 2011 Postal Act.

The timing of postal reform has deviated from predicted patterns in Germany and Britain, while the dynamics and scope of reform are more in line with expectations. Thus, it is important to consider change in national economies over longer periods of time, in order to put into perspective deviations at any given moment. Initially, the British situation resembled the French case, where societal opposition prevailed and the government lacked the capacity to simply impose change. In both countries external empowerment was needed to overcome the deadlock. By contrast, change in Germany was possible thanks to the political capacity to successfully negotiate change and accommodate the needs of various stakeholders. Major reform moves have been driven by the business community securing support mostly of conservative governments. This holds for the early privatisation reforms and the 1997 reform introducing liberalisation. Later on there was some stop-and-go concerning the pace of market opening, which was due to the fact that the Social Democrats proved responsive to the concerns raised by the sector trade unions and the incumbent. The trajectory of German postal reform therefore conforms to mainstream assumptions about a left–right divide on economic policy. The conservative and liberal parties pursued a pro-competitive stance and sought to reduce state involvement in the public sectors. The Social Democrats intervened time and again to protect the interests of employees in the sector, given the party's close links with the trade union ver.di. To be sure, the Social Democrats never held a governmental majority when the major reform deals were struck in 1997 and 2007. In 1997 they had a blocking majority in the upper chamber, and in 2007 the party's consent was required as a partner in the grand coalition government. This may have helped the Social Democrats to adopt more radical positions, compared to a situation where as a party in government they would have been part of the EU-level negotiation process.

In France and Britain major reform moves were undertaken under left-wing leadership, which raises the 'party paradox' discussed in the literature (Cioffi and Höpner, 2006). In the SME and LME context, however, left-wing governments may be in a better position to legitimise change, notably in seeking to marry economic objectives with social obligations. In doing so national government have been empowered by EU-level requirements, yet as discussed in Chapter 4 they also had the freedom to flank liberalisation with social safeguards measures.

The politics of reform in a cross-sector perspective

To what extent do the politics of postal reform vary from processes of change in other sectors? This question draws our attention towards variation within national capitalism, and thus relates to debates on the adequacy of a macrolevel typology. Examining processes in other public utilities also helps with making more substantial judgements about the timing of reform in view of the specific socioeconomic context in a given country. From that angle the British puzzle posed by postal reform persists, while French postal reform appears rather 'typical', and the German reform record varies across sectors.

Postal reform in France is a representative case for a wider pattern in the public utilities, where the predominant *service public* doctrine has hampered change (Schmidt, 2002: 81, 102). Part of the reform deadlock is due to the French 'capitalism without labour' (Schmidt, 2002: 187) which has precluded concerns raised by the trade unions mobilising against reforms. Unlike their European counterparts, French Socialists do not cultivate partisan links with the unions (Howell, 2009: 234), which is why the social partners have only limited involvement in the policymaking process. Unlike the reform record in the public utilities, other parts of the French economy were subject to significant transformation. In 1982, when the Socialists came to power after a long period of right-wing governments, the government initially engaged in nationalisation reforms (Levy, 2008: 421). Increasing difficulties in sustaining the French model of *dirigisme* did, however, trigger a U-turn in the economic and monetary policymaking of the Socialist government by 1983 (Levy, 2002: 322–5; Levy, 2008: 422–3). During the following years France experienced a wave of privatisation and liberalisation in key economic sectors. What had begun under the socialist government of Fabius (1984–86) was continued under Chirac as a prime minister during the first *cohabitation* (1986–88). The privatisation agenda, which comprised banks, insurance companies, firms in the audio-visual sector and major industrial groups such as Suez, fundamentally altered the French political economy (Levy, 2002: 324–6).

A renewed phase of privatisation occurred under Balladur's government after 1993, comprising companies such as BNP or Elf-Acquitaine (privatisation law no. 923, discussed by Goldstein, 1996: 1316–17). The privatisation record of previous governments was, however, topped by the Socialist government under Lionel Jospin, which from 1997 to 2002 sold state companies at a value of more than 200 billion French francs. Yet this massive privatisation programme has not led to a disengagement of the state. Rather, privatisations have mostly been partial, retaining a controlling state interest and allowing for strategic reorientation and modernisation (Clift, 2001). At this stage public utilities became the target of privatisation, the first case being France Télécom in 1997, followed by Air France in 1999. Reform moves in the telecoms sector ended a phase of inertia that had characterised the period until the late 1980s. During that time, there was a widely shared consensus, underpinned by trade union opposition to change, in favour of maintaining the status quo for the *service public* (Schmidt, 2002: 96). Towards the end of the 1980s, the management of France Télécom succeeded in aligning support from the government to reverse this long-standing position, and comprehensive reforms were undertaken throughout the 1990s (for a detailed discussion see Bartle, 2005: 112–15; Thatcher, 2007a: 176–84).

Such change, provoking major opposition and strike action by trade unions (Thatcher, 2007a: 179–80), was unthinkable in the neighbouring postal sector at this time. The logic of incremental, state-driven change observed in telecoms does, however, resemble the approach taken to prepare the privatisation of La Poste some two decades later. Compared to telecoms, reform proved more difficult in the electricity sector. At the European level France opposed the very idea of energy market liberalisation, initially seeking to protect its national champion in electricity supply, *Electricité de France* (EdF) and its centralised energy system (Bartle, 2005: 115–19), and subsequently opposing the Commission's proposal of ownership unbundling (Eikeland, 2011). Once liberalisation and regulatory reform had been imposed by the EU as legal requirements to be implemented at the national level, France managed to do this along the lines of 'redeploying the state' (Levy, 2005) rather than engaging in a rollback of the state. Market opening served industrial policy interests, given that the French national champion EdF had an interest to sell its surplus production. At the same time, EdF's dominant market position continues to pose an enormous obstacle for genuine competition to emerge (European Commission, 2012c). An independent energy regulator, the Commission for Energy Regulation (*Commission de Régulation de l'Enérgie*, CRE) operating since 2003, continued to be dominated by established technocrat élites (Thatcher, 2007d). EdF was established as a publicly registered company in 2004 and was introduced on the stock market at the end of 2005, with a legal guarantee for government shares to be kept at a minimum level of 70 per cent (in 2014 the French government held 84.49 per cent). The scope of policy change in the French electricity sector proved limited, where the major player EdF still controlled the French market, and where the state continued to realise objectives of industrial policy (Bauby and Varone, 2007).

Germany, in line with its consensus-seeking political culture, engaged in negotiated change (Bartle, 2005: 121–4). The German state played an 'enabling role' (Schmidt, 2002: 166) for public service reform, yet this capacity diverged across sectors. Reforms in the telecoms sector were implemented at about the same time as these were being discussed at the European level, and Germany was seeking to shape European negotiation outcomes accordingly. Domestically, telecoms reform can be characterised as a 'slow, politically initiated, pragmatic, and consensus-focussed process' (Schmidt, 2002: 96), which took on board the concerns of both management and workers within *Deutsche Telekom*. There was clearly a reform spill-over from the telecoms to the postal sector, which is quite specific to the German case. The institutional legacy of having formed one single ministerial department cannot explain this linkage. This also applies to other countries where the postal sector has nevertheless been insulated from reforms in telecoms. The immediate need to modernise and rationalise the postal and telecoms infrastructure in the new German *Länder* following reunification has certainly facilitated an encompassing reform move, as has the expansionist strategy of the telecoms as well as the postal operator. Legislation to corporatise and privatise the telecoms and the postal incumbent was passed at about the same time, while actual privatisation, as well as liberalisation, were speedier in the telecoms sector. The stock market launch of *Deutsche Telekom* took place in three steps in 1996, 1999 and 2000. In 2014 the state held 14.5 per cent of the shares, and the state-owned bank KfW 17.4 per cent (Deutsche Telekom, 2014: 209). As of January 1998 the telecoms market in Germany was fully liberalised and the telecoms and postal regulator RegTP started to operate. In the absence of exogenous pressures, change in the electricity sector was more difficult, hampered by opposition from the sub-national level and powerful private operators (Bartle, 2005: 124–8).

While the pace of reform in postal and telecoms was largely in line with European legislation, Germany repeatedly sided with France in opposing European initiatives in the energy field. Germany tried to prevent the introduction of an independent regulator (Eberlein, 2001) and ownership unbundling (Eikeland, 2011). The reform record also differed in the field of regulation for reasons of sector-specific peculiarities. In the postal and the telecoms sector, the regulator and the competition authority had built up their policy practice at about the same time, while in the German energy sector the Federal Cartel Office and state-level cartel offices based their activities on a comprehensive experience of competition law enforcement (Interview, BKartA). When European policy makers envisaged the introduction of independent sector regulators, this led to opposition in Germany, where competition law enforcement both at federal and state level was seen as a functional substitute for sector-specific regulation (Eberlein, 2001; Gassner, 2001). It was not until 2005 that Germany delegated energy regulation powers to the independent regulatory agency, establishing the Federal Network Agency as a multi-sector regulator for the utilities. The scope of change has been limited in the German electricity sector where four large private operators maintain a market share of above 80 per cent with persisting patterns of regional dominance (European Commission, 2012d).

In a cross-sector perspective the real puzzle is posed by British postal reform, given that both in telecoms and energy the British were the frontrunners of change, uploading their domestic approach to the European level. Under Thatcher, Britain pioneered telecoms reform in Europe, much ahead of the EU's liberalisation agenda (Humphreys and Padgett, 2006: 395; Schneider, 2001: 63; Thatcher, 1999). UPW resistance to telecoms reforms in the 1980s was weakened by the fact that telecoms workers organised within POEU supported change. In the absence of a common position between the two major sector unions, it was easier for the government to proceed with reform (Vogel, 1996: 71). The British deregulated and privatised their telecoms sector by the mid-1980s already. In 1984, BT was sold and an independent regulator was set up, yet in this initial phase liberalisation did not occur. This changed from 1991 onwards with the publication of a government initiative to boost competition (Department of Trade and Industry, 2001b). Reforms in the electricity sector were launched with the 1989 Electricity Act, which separated generation from network ownership – the latter to be centralised within the operator National Grid – and introduced liberalisation. An independent regulatory agency, the Office of Electricity Supply (OFFER), was introduced in 1989, merged with the gas regulator into the Office of Gas and Electricity Markets (Ofgem) in 2000. Such sweeping change, in a sector riddled with vested interests and insulated from exogenous pressure, has been explained with inter-sector isomorphism in the British context (Thatcher, 2007a: 209). In sum, British postal reform is a puzzling outlier case from the perspective of comparative capitalism. British postal reform highlights how change does not equally spread across policy areas. For a considerable period of time, postal policy constituted an anomaly in the British context: a bastion of politics, union power and societal resentment to change. The fact that the US, a role model for British reform in the other utilities (Jamison, 2011), had not engaged in postal reform is regarded as one explanatory factor for the postal exception (Thatcher, 2007b). But as discussed in Chapter 7, there were also a number of domestic reasons for the delay in British postal reform.

Sweeping technological change and emerging international pressure has thus led to some convergence among different varieties of capitalism in telecoms (Bartle, 2002; Schneider, 2002; Thatcher, 2004a), as it helped to overcome domestic institutional inertia. This holds for all three countries examined in this book, where France and Germany engaged in considerable transformation of the sector, though with a time lag in comparison to the British reform leader. This was not the case for energy and postal reform, where national policy paths persisted to a greater extent, despite European pressure. Electricity reform was opposed by both Germany and France for various reasons, but persistently over time. France also opposed postal liberalisation, while Germany supported EU-driven reform in telecoms and postal services, embracing change at about the same time domestically. The British reform record served as a model for change in telecoms and electricity for European policy makers. By contrast, the British were initially opposed to EU-driven postal reform, and only fully supported change during the third round of European negotiations.

Three varieties of postal policy and regulation

The second question is about the politics of reregulation in the postal sector, asking how the emerging regulatory state has protected consumers and employees. As discussed in Chapter 3, it is expected that policymaking will vary first, when comparing aspects related to service provision and employment (see table 3.2); and second, when comparing varieties of capitalism (see table 3.3). The findings on postal policy and regulation in the three countries are summarised in table 8.2.

The number and density of postal outlets are governed by a mixture of political and independent regulation, underpinned by redistributive policies (see table 3.2). Yet policymaking patterns across countries vary. The peculiarity in the French context is the reliance on contractual planning, involving considerable amounts of state aid. In this framework La Poste receives financial compensation for maintaining its territorial presence through its network of postal outlets, and for letting the *Banque Postale* use the post office infrastructure. In terms of governance the major shift in France was towards political regulation. While in the past network related aspects such as the density and type of offices were subject to direct governmental intervention and contractual planning, these became enshrined in domestic law. The 2010 Act laid down a minimum level of 17,000 offices, and introduced a procedure for assessing the net cost of La Poste's territorial presence, to be implemented by ARCEP. Government decisions provide regulatory detail in many areas, for instance through a decree governing a national postal fund for geographical equalisation. As discussed in Chapter 5, the French postal network is particularly dense, and is for the most part still directly operated by La Poste (see table 5.2). Since the late 1990s, however, there have been efforts to increase cost effectiveness by reducing the number of in-house branches.

Unlike in France, German postal policy was already governed by a detailed legal and regulatory framework prior to Europeanisation. The so-called postal universal service ordinance (PUDLV) laid down a minimum number of 12,000 contact points, together with specified requirements in terms of density of the postal outlet network. Deutsche Post has received state aid for its compliance with the USO, which in the German regime also comprises the network of postal outlets. Compliance with these requirements is monitored by the independent regulator. As discussed in Chapter 6, the number of in-house branches was cut back drastically, with counter services in Germany operated mainly by agencies, while the total number of outlets remained relatively stable over time (see table 6.2).

Contrary to France and Germany, British postal policy makes a neat separation between counter services, provided by the Post Office, and mail

Table 8.2: Postal policy in France, Germany and Britain

	France	Germany	Britain
(Re)distribution	**important**	**limited**	**important**
postal outlets	state aid territorial presence and banking services	state aid USO	state aid network transformation
mail services	VAT exemption, state aid delivery of press items, compensation fund (not activated)	VAT exemption, state aid USO, compensation mechanism (not activated)	VAT exemption, state aid for providing access to delivery network, compensation fund (not activated)
employment	state takes over pension liabilities (2006)	state aid pension scheme	state takes over pension liabilities (2011)
Political regulation	**dominant**	**important**	**limited**
postal outlets	17,000 contact points (2010 Act)	12,000 contact points, specified requirements density (PUDLV)	governmental responsibility (no specified requirements)
mail services	ubiquitous USO, 6 days (2000 Act)	USO (PUDLV), 5 days, specified requirements speed	USO (2000 Act), 5 days
employment	collective agreement legal requirement	binding validity minimum wage agreement (not enforced)	–
Independent regulation	**limited**	**important**	**dominant**
postal outlets	evaluation of net cost	monitoring compliance network density	advisory role
mail delivery	monitoring compliance USO, regulating prices	monitoring compliance USO, regulating prices	monitoring compliance USO, regulating prices, universal service order (2011 Act)
employment	–	monitoring minimum working conditions	–
Corporatism	**limited**	**dominant**	**important**
employment	negotiating collective agreement (not concluded)	collective agreements, minimum wage agreements	collective agreements

services, provided by Royal Mail. Policymaking concerning the Post Office remains highly politicised, where the number and density of postal outlets is the sole responsibility of the government, while the regulator only holds an advisory role. As discussed in Chapter 7, the Post Office's network has been restructured considerably, involving a significant reduction in the number of outlets operated by the incumbent (only around 3 per cent of the outlets are operated by the Post Office, see table 7.2). The Post Office receives a network subsidy in order to maintain and modernise unprofitable postal outlets.

Mail service provision is the classic area of postal regulation, and at the core of the USO. The minimum requirements and scope of the USO are usually defined in national law, while implementation is left to the sector regulators (see table 3.2). Providing adequate financial compensation to the USP is a key issue in regulatory economics and policy practice alike. In France, service provision aspects had been addressed by direct state intervention and contractual planning, until European directives required an upgrade of relevant legal provisions. In the French regime the legal framework governing the USO was specified with the 2000 reform. Comparatively speaking, French requirements are particularly strict where the law imposes a guarantee of six days' delivery, and defines a wide range of services as part of the USO. The latter comprises addressed direct mail and bulk mail, newspapers, periodicals, catalogues, printed matter and parcels. The French state funds the incumbent's duty to transport and deliver press items, and La Poste is furthermore exempted from paying VAT on products within the scope of the USO. ARCEP oversees price regulation, as well as monitoring and enforcement tasks concerning the USO, and the regulator would recommend the activation of a compensation fund foreseen in the law where need occurs. The depoliticisation of rate regulation had an immediate effect on price levels (see table 5.3). The French regulator allowed several augmentations in basic postage rates in line with its assessment of the costs incurred.

In Germany the shift towards independent regulation was more pronounced than in France, and political regulation continued to play an important role. As mentioned, state funding was granted to Deutsche Post for its wider universal service mission. The 1997 postal law introduced a compensation mechanism to be activated where the cost of the USO would not be covered. In Germany services provided within the scope of the USO are exempt from VAT. The German agency is in charge of monitoring compliance with the USO, and of price regulation. Postage rates increased incrementally over time, in order to cover the cost involved (see table 6.3).

The move towards the political, and subsequently independent, regulation of mail service provision was strongest in the British case. As in France the transposition of European directives in Britain required an upgrade of legal provisions regarding the universal service. The USO was for the first time enshrined in law with the 2000 Postal Act, and Postcomm was entrusted with the task of monitoring and enforcing compliance with these rules, and regulating postage rates. The 2011 Act attributed postal regulation to the communications regulator Ofcom, including the prerogative to define the exact scope of the USO. In Britain it is therefore up to the independent regulator to alter the scope of the USO, while such policy shaping capacity has remained in the political arena in the other two countries. Postcomm moderately increased basic postage rates from 2005, and a more substantial increase occurred under Ofcom in 2012 (see table 7.3). Royal Mail is being compensated to provide alternative operators access to its delivery network. The law also foresees the possible introduction of a compensation fund to secure the universal service, but this fund has so far not been activated.

Employment related aspects were expected to be governed by corporatist arrangements, flanked by minimum requirements defined by political regulation (see table 3.2). The French situation is particular where it attributes a relatively central role to legislation in this area. In the past the working conditions and wage levels of civil servants at France Télécom and La Poste were governed by a joint collective agreement. To cover those employees at La Poste without civil servant status, and those working for competitors, the 2005 law imposed the negotiation of a collective agreement on the social partners. The latter had created the required organisational structures, and since 2007 engaged in negotiations, but at the time of writing had not yet succeeded.

Postal corporatism was most pronounced in Germany, but the industrial landscape changed once competitors had acquired significant market shares. The potential effect of liberalisation on working conditions in a labour intense business had been anticipated by lawmakers when a social clause was inscribed into the 1997 Postal Act. According to this clause authorisations granted should be conditional on respecting prevailing working conditions in the sector. The sector regulator did not, however, integrate this legal possibility into regulatory practice, which would have required a detailed evaluation of working conditions in the sector. In the absence of any political guidance to alter its authorisation practice, the regulator granted authorisations to new operators whenever their employment schemes were in compliance with general labour and social security law standards. When a political discussion emerged around the question whether the new operators, paying significantly lower wages than the incumbent, would engage in practices of social dumping, the regulator became the target of heavy criticism. The German regulator generated additional evidence to legitimise its policy approach ex post, and was relieved from public scrutiny once the attention had moved to the political arena where the need to introduce a sector-specific minimum wage was debated. A political deal was struck to introduce a minimum wage, yet when two competing agreements had been negotiated, and the courts had invalidated their lawfulness, the issue was not pursued any further. These findings show that an independent regulatory agency can hardly be expected to implement employment related social policy objectives, even if laid down in the law, where it conceives of its role mainly as an advocator of competition and consumer interests.

The density of interest organisation in the British postal sector is at odds with expectations for the LME. At a closer look, however, the role played by trade unions is not as much of an outlier. The CWU relies on a strong organisation, and represents more than 80 per cent of employees within Royal Mail, yet industrial relations are difficult with a high level of conflict. Collective agreements are the major mode of governance in the realm of employment regulation. Negotiations with the employer's side are difficult and lengthy, and industrial relations are highly conflicting.

In all three countries incumbents received some sort of financial compensation so that they could cope with historical pension liabilities. The French state did take over the incumbent's pension liabilities in the course of reform, when in 2006 La Poste was released from all financial obligations against a once off payment of €2 billion. Similarly, the British state took over Royal Mail's pension debt in the run up to full privatisation. The financial support Germany granted to Deutsche Post to cover its pension scheme was judged incompatible state aid by the European Commission (IP/13/1127).

To conclude, the shift towards independent regulation has been least pronounced in France, moderate in Germany and significant in Britain. The governance of the postal sector in France equates a redeployment of the state (Levy, 2005) through new instruments, that is, political and independent regulation. In Germany the biggest challenge was to marry the regulatory state with established postal corporatism, and this proved to be an unhappy marriage in which the social partners were ultimately left alone by the political actors. The 2011 reform in Britain ended the postal exception also from a governance perspective, empowering the independent agency in the area of social regulation to an unseen extent.

Postal policy and regulation across Europe

The European regulatory framework leaves ample leeway to the member states in shaping postal policy and regulation. Chapter 4 illustrated that this holds in the area of the universal service, where EU-wide minimum requirement exist, and even more so when it comes to wider general interest goals and employment related aspects. In their implementation of the directives, member states have made ample use of the discretion in postal policy and regulation, resulting in a 'persisting diversity of national postal traditions' (Campbell Jr et al., 2008: 195). Member states mostly complied with the minimum requirements imposed by European law, but at the same time retained much of their policy shaping capacity.

Divergence is particularly pronounced in the area of counter services, where the member states face very different preconditions in terms of geography and population density. The governance of related issues is, however, similar across countries. Minimum requirements for access to postal outlets are usually laid down by national law, which is why the density of the network has been kept at relatively constant levels across European countries. On average, 2.4 postal outlets per 10,000 inhabitants were reported for 2004 and 2009 (Copenhagen Economics, 2010: 50; WIK-Consult, 2004: 165). Most member states sought to cut the cost of territorial presence, and thus reduced the number of post offices. Between 1998 and 2007 reductions were most pronounced in Denmark, Britain and Finland, while Cyprus, Greece and Malta significantly increased the number of outlets (ITA Consulting and WIK-Consult, 2009a). A second trend is an increased use of postal agencies. In Cyprus, Ireland and Britain the share of such agencies was well above 90 per cent of the total number of postal outlets since the late 1990s, while other member states such as Denmark, Finland or Sweden followed this trend, and engaged in substitution. In some member states agencies emerged only recently, and are well below a 10 per cent share, for instance in Luxembourg, Bulgaria and Slovakia. In comparison, France is the biggest postal market where the share of agencies is still relatively low (ITA Consulting and WIK-Consult, 2009a: 126).

The European framework is more restrictive in the area of mail services, where member states have to comply with minimum requirements they cannot modify unilaterally. The delivery has to be guaranteed at least on five working days a week, with one clearance and one delivery per day (article 3 of directive 2008/6/EC). Beyond such minimum requirements, the text is full of subsidiarity, so that member states define the scope of services to be included in the universal service obligation very differently (WIK-Consult, 2013b: 130): seven member states opted for the broadest possible scope of the USO, for instance Belgium and Ireland; while a group of eleven countries (including Germany, Finland and Britain) adopted a minimalist definition. Over time most member states reduced the scope of the universal service by excluding bulk letters and direct mail. The leader in this movement was The Netherlands, followed by Britain, where in 2005 the regulator concluded that bulk mail should be considered as being outside the universal service (Campbell Jr et al., 2008: 198). While all member states are complying with the minimum requirement to provide delivery five days a week, some member states maintain delivery on six days, which in France and some other countries is a legal requirement (Copenhagen Economics, 2010: 127). Most European countries are facing a significant decrease in mail volumes due to electronic substitution, an effect aggravated by the economic and financial crisis since 2008 (Copenhagen Economics, 2010: 27–9). Private correspondence, constituting a rather small share of total mail volume, is more affected by electronic substitution than business correspondence (ITA Consulting and WIK-Consult, 2009a: 93). Since the resulting financial pressure on the incumbent operators makes the provision of a universal service more costly, it is likely that service levels would be reduced once some of the minimum standards that are currently imposed by European law were lifted.

Most member states granted financial compensation to their USPs for the services provided. The European Commission, in its role as a competition authority enforcing European state aid rules, was mostly agreeable to such policy practice. In 2012 the Commission approved state aid, by Greece, to Hellenic Post for modernising the infrastructure and improving public service. And in 2013 the Commission allowed Belgium to compensate bpost for the provision of services of general interest covering the distribution of press items, home delivery of pensions, basic pension services and the maintenance of a network of counters, given that a competitive tender had been organised for these services, and that their cost had been calculated in a transparent way (WIK-Consult, 2013b: 77–87). In 2012, however, the Commission ordered Belgium to recover €417 million of incompatible state aid from bpost, arguing that the yearly compensation the operator had received from 1992 to 2010 for public service missions had resulted in overcompensation (European Commission press release IP/12/45).

State aid granted by national governments to relieve their historical operators from pension liabilities were admitted by the European Commission in France, Britain and Belgium, where Belgian Post in 1997 received €3.8 billion, and in Germany, under the condition that incompatible aid in the range between €500 million and €1 billion would be recovered (European Commission MEMO/12/43). Most member states furthermore granted financial compensation to the USP through tax exemptions, permitted under the so-called VAT directive (article 135 of the Council directive 2006/112/EC). In 2004 a group of ten member states exempted all postal services provided by the USP from paying VAT, among them Belgium and Britain. Another group of nine countries (including Germany and France), exempted the universal postal service, while only few countries like Sweden did not grant any exceptions in taxing (WIK-Consult, 2004: 76). In 2007 the European Commission started infringement proceedings against Britain for exempting all services provided by Royal Mail, and against Germany for exempting most services provided by Deutsche Post, arguing that such practice would distort competition. The Commission, furthermore, opened a case against Sweden for not complying with the VAT directive in the absence of tax exemptions (IP/07/1164). In response to a ruling by the Court of Justice (press release no. 32/09), Britain, alongside other countries, had to reduce the scope of the VAT exemption to services provided under the USO.

As discussed in Chapter 4, the impact of liberalisation on employment conditions and industrial relations has been a peripheral aspect of European reregulation. A dedicated European Social Dialogue of the Postal Sector had been set up in 1998 to encourage and promote the social dialogue, and to advise the European Commission. The Social Dialogue Committee conducted several projects monitoring change in the sector, such as a 'Social Observatory of the Postal Sector' (European Social Dialogue Committee for the Postal Sector, 2007: 9). Employment related aspects were covered in various studies prepared for the European Commission (Copenhagen Economics, 2010, chapter 6; WIK-Consult, 2013b, chapter 3.4). These studies drew a panorama of sector-specific social regulation across member states. Such regulation can take various forms (WIK-Consult, 2013b: 273–80): general or sector-specific minimum wages; collective agreements at the level of the USPs, their subsidiaries or competitors; and legal requirements concerning labour conditions as a prerequisite for authorisation. Employment related conditions within the USPs are governed in most member states by collective agreements, while employees of their subsidiaries are covered by collective agreements in only a few countries (this is the case in Germany, Spain, Finland, Hungary, Ireland, Italy and Sweden). Countries where private operators have concluded collective agreements also constitute a minority – this holds only for Cyprus, Spain, Finland, The Netherlands, Sweden and Slovenia.

Besides general minimum wages, which existed in a majority of countries, Austria, Spain and Slovakia introduced a sector-specific minimum wage. In Germany and Denmark employees working for private operators are neither covered by a collective agreement, nor by a general minimum wage (WIK-Consult, 2013b: 276). Several member states integrated labour protection into their sector-specific regulatory regimes (WIK-Consult, 2013b: 277–8). As discussed previously, Germany introduced a social clause in its 1998 postal law. In Austria similar provisions were laid down with the Postal Market Act 2011 (article 27.2), according to which the issuance of an authorisation is conditional on respecting working conditions prevailing in the sector, as well as applying collective agreements. The respect of collective agreements is also a precondition in Belgium, where the law furthermore requires an 80 per cent share of employees to be employed under a labour contract. Similarly, provisions in Hungary and the Netherlands mainly relate to contractual aspects that aim at imposing lawful employment relationships. The impact of liberalisation on actual wage levels paid in the sector has been assessed as moderate by various studies prepared for the European Commission. In comparing Sweden, Britain, Germany and The Netherlands the consultancy Copenhagen Economics came to the conclusion that a decrease in wages was driven by the combination of pre-liberalisation wage premiums, increased automation, lower mail volume and increased competition from new operators (Copenhagen Economics, 2010: 163–87; Okholm and Möller, 2012).

Drawing a panorama of postal policymaking across Europe, it appears that independent regulation is on the rise, but its role remains limited. Compliance with European law made it necessary to secure separation between operational and regulatory tasks, meaning that member states had to create independent regulators. In its detailed review of the allocation of regulatory powers conducted in 2009, WIK found that the major policy issues continued to be addressed in the political realm by legislation or ministerial decisions, whereas the remit of sector regulators was limited to fulfilling administrative tasks (WIK-Consult, 2009b). A European group bringing together national postal regulators (EPRG) was only created in 2011, much later than similar bodies in other sectors, and so far has not had a significant effect in terms of regulatory harmonisation. For the time being, political regulation remains dominant given that most decisions are kept within the political arena, either through legislation or ministerial regulation, while in only a few countries, such as Britain, can regulators actually shape the regulatory framework (WIK-Consult, 2013b: 14).

9

Postal reform in the international political economy

This chapter situates postal reform in a broader international context, and thus widens the perspective of comparative capitalism beyond Europe. In doing so, it seeks to scrutinise the generalisability of the findings of the in-depth qualitative country studies. Can we observe systematic variation in postal reform in line with the varieties of capitalism typology across the globe? Is postal reform different in emerging and transition market economies? Two sections situate the puzzle raised by the delay of postal reform in the British LME in a wider context examining change in other liberal regimes. While some LMEs like New Zealand and Australia have been reform leaders, others like the United States and Canada have been reform laggards. This chapter then goes on to discuss postal reform in Asian countries, with a special focus on change in the CME in Japan and the SME in Singapore. A last section is dedicated to postal reform in Asian and Latin American emerging and transition market countries.

LME postal reform leaders

> The time is now to make the necessary decisions for the future. Every postal system around the world is facing similar challenges and they are beginning to act. We cannot stand still and simply hope the problems will go away [...] Not gaining flexibility will leave us with some challenging and unsustainable options – asking for taxpayer funded subsidies to prop up the letters business; operating the postal business at a loss which will degrade the business over time; or cross-subsidising from other parts of New Zealand Post, denying the business the opportunity to grow and invest. (New Zealand Post Group CEO Brian Roche, New Zealand Post, 2013a)

The postal reform record in LMEs is mixed and has been attributed to different postal models (Campbell, 2002). New Zealand, following the 'market model' in postal reform (Campbell, 2002, chapter 5), in the late 1980s was among the first countries worldwide to transform its postal administration into a corporation, and to engage in meaningful structural reform. Australia can also be considered a reform leader in terms of timing, yet change has been more moderate, which is why it has been characterised as a 'hybrid model' (Campbell, 2002, chapter 10).

New Zealand's 'highly successful experiment in commercialization' (Crew and Kleindoerfer, 2013a: 7) took place in a specific political context. Corporatisation in 1987 was part of several reform measures in response to an aggravating domestic economic crisis involving a significant public debt. In New Zealand the party paradox (Cioffi and Höpner, 2006) was at play given that reforms were undertaken under a Labour government which assumed power in 1984. This economic U-turn, which came to be known as 'Rogernomics' named after the then minister of finance Roger Douglas, involved many neoliberal reforms such as the introduction of free trade and the deregulation of labour and financial markets (Campbell, 2002: 182). From a comparative perspective reform moves by the New Zealand Labour government in the 1980s appeared 'upside down', 'more Thatcherite than Thatcher and more into Reaganomics than Reagan' (Steele, 1991: 283). In the historical context of international postal reform in the 1980s, the conclusion could be drawn that, along the lines of the party paradox argument, 'only socialist governments will be able to privatize postal services' (Steele, 1991: 283).

This held at the time at least for liberal market economies, where neither the United States nor Britain had tackled this sector despite sweeping reforms in other utilities. Indeed, the New Zealand Labour party succeeded in combating the power of trade unions in a situation of economic crisis very much like Thatcher did, in Britain. Taming the unions was a key element for successful postal reform which occurred in the absence of major strikes and contestation. The postal union had gone bankrupt and joined a bigger public sector union and thus was considerably weakened (Campbell, 2002: 185, 202–4). Despite significant staff reductions and attrition, no work days were lost throughout the process of corporatisation (Toime, 1991: 278). New Zealand Post lived up to its legal mandate to operate as any other private company, turning from a loss-making state administration into an innovative and profit-making corporation (Campbell, 2002: 204–7; Toime, 1991: 275). In 1997 the National/NZ First coalition passed a bill which abolished the postal monopoly and introduced a new regulatory regime for a competitive market. Responding to public opposition, the government did however not tackle privatisation, and a new Deed of Understanding, replacing the one negotiated during corporatisation, was introduced with the aim of maintaining service levels and the scope of the network (Campbell, 2002: 189, 194). New Zealand did not delegate regulatory tasks to an independent agency, maintaining postal policy within the Minister of Economic Development. Putting aside the emergence of some niche players, liberalisation did not lead to real competition in the market (ITA Consulting and WIK-Consult, 2009b: 107). The good performance of the incumbent has certainly contributed to this outcome, yet New Zealand's insulated geographic situation and low population density pose natural barriers to entry. This has become even more obvious in recent years, when falling mail volumes put the profitability of the incumbent under serious threat. By 2013 the situation proved no longer sustainable, and New Zealand Post requested the government to allow for drastic cuts to its USO (New Zealand Post, 2013b). Taking effect in June 2015, the New Deed of Understanding negotiated with the government will reduce the scope of the incumbent's service obligation, limiting delivery to three times per week in urban areas, and to five times a week in rural areas (Adams, 2013).

The reform record in Australia in many respects resembles New Zealand, which is certainly also due to geographic vicinity and similar preconditions. Following the example of its neighbour, Australia in 1989 engaged in corporatisation, replacing the Australian Postal Commission with the Australian Postal Corporation. Australia furthermore engaged in partial liberalisation in 1993, reducing the reserved area to correspondence and direct mail weighing no more than 250 grams (Castro, 1995). The reform preconditions and outcomes were similar to New Zealand's, with a Labour government pushing for change during economic crisis, and a well-performing and profitable state enterprise having undergone substantial structural change (Castro, 1995: 34–7). Although the level of consensus needed in federal and corporatist Australia was much higher than in New Zealand, the government succeeded in gaining support from the trade unions (Campbell, 2002: 370–3). Involving the unions in the modernisation process actually helped appease industrial relations which, prior to reform, were highly conflicting. Labour and management negotiated several Enterprise Bargaining Agreements which, following sweeping industrial relations reforms, constituted the new mode of decentralised, firm-level bargaining (Campbell, 2002: 392–4).

Seeking to secure the acceptance by organised stakeholders and the general public, the scope of change in the Australian postal sector did however prove limited. The government organised several polls in which the public was asked to give its opinion on postal reform, and the majority voiced its preference for maintaining a public post office providing a universal postal service (Campbell, 2002: 372). As a result, Australian governments did not dare engage in privatisation, and maintained the scope and level of service provision. In 2003, for instance, a bill aimed at converting Australia Post into a public company was withdrawn due to concerns over last-mile delivery issues. Instead, legislation was introduced that sought to improve delivery services provided by Australia Post. More recently Australia engaged in regulatory reform, delegating regulatory powers to the Australian Competition and Consumer Commission (Paterson, 2008: 394). Regarding the scope and level of services provided, the Australian Post is bound by a Community Service Obligation according to which Australia Post is required by law (section 27 of the 1989 Australian Postal Corporation Act) to provide a universal letter service that is reasonably accessible to all citizens, and a standard letter service throughout the territory at a uniform price. When the Australian government requested advice on the postal market from the National Competition Council (NCC) in 1998, a key recommendation referred to maintaining the onerous USO in the absence of a 'feasible alternative to delivering on the social benefits' (NCC, 1998: 137). As a response to the cut-backs in postal delivery in New Zealand, Australia Post initially announced that it would maintain five days delivery, despite falling letter volumes (Adams, 2013). Yet the company came under immediate financial pressure once rapidly growing losses in the shrinking mail business were less and less offset by the profits in the growing parcel business (Bartholomeusz, 2014). In the first half of 2014 massive job cuts of around 900 jobs were announced, and the company started to lobby the government to reduce its service obligation to three days delivery (Knotts, 2014). Privatisation has been put into perspective in the 2014 report by the National Commission of Audit, which recommended privatisation of Australia Post at some time after 2016 (National Commission of Audit, 2014).

New Zealand and Australia have been leaders in the international postal reform movement as these LMEs were among the first to engage in corporatisation. In a longer-term perspective, however, the scope of change was limited since neither country engaged in privatisation, nor did competition in the letter mail business emerge on these big and scarcely populated islands. Shrinking mail volumes have put the financial viability of the public post offices under threat, and it seems that once again New Zealand and Australia set an example in the international postal reform movement, this time by cutting down on service delivery.

LME postal reform laggards

> tens of thousands of uneconomical post offices, postal routes and services employ and/or service millions of votes [...] The lack of a strong executive (shareholder) champion, the dominance of reactionary congressional interests, and the self-interest of private postal players have combined to halt postal reform in the United States. (Campbell, 2001: 93)

In contrast to New Zealand and Australia, the United States and Canada left their postal administrations untouched for a considerable period of time. Both have been following the 'national model' in their postal sectors (Campbell, 2001: 91–3, 2002, chapter 8), keeping the post office public and upholding a last mile monopoly.

In the United States the postal sector is the odd one out in comparison to other sectors such as telecoms, electricity and gas which have experienced substantial reforms (Jamison, 2011). An important difference compared to the European PTT model was that the US telecoms provider AT&T was a private company separate from the postal business, so that in the US telecoms reform would not spill over to the neighbouring postal sector (Melody, 2011: 104, 114). This may appear surprising given that corporatisation dates back to 1970. With the Post Reorganisation Act the Post Office Department was transformed into the United States Postal Service (USPS). Unlike New Zealand the new regime did not entail the transition towards a profitable regime in a normal business environment. Rather, the incumbent's privileges as a public entity were being maintained: USPS is exempt from paying taxes, and it can borrow from the US Treasury (Crew and Kleindoerfer, 2013a: 8; Hudgins, 2000a: 1).

While this regime had remained unchanged for more than three decades by the new millennium, commentators had expected sweeping change (Hudgins, 2000b), yet the new legislation introduced in 2006 (Postal Accountability and Enhancement Act) relaxed some regulatory requirements but, other than that, maintained the status quo attributing limited commercial flexibility to the USPS. In particular the incumbent's inability to control labour cost has posed an impediment to its viability and has been widely discussed in the literature (Comarow, 2000; Froelke, 2000; Wachter et al., 2001). In 1981, for instance, labour costs within the US post office amounted to 76 per cent of total postal service costs, and over 80 per cent of labour costs were costs for employees entitled to collective wages (Wachter et al., 2001: 4). While the 1970 framework deregulated labour–management relations and removed direct government intervention, it imposed new external strains on the USPS. Besides voluntary collective bargaining between the social partners, it introduced an arbitration procedure as a last resort. In practice, however, arbitration became the rule rather than the exception where conflicting industrial relations substantially hindered negotiated agreements (Froelke, 2000). The overwhelming assessment of the terms and conditions resulting from collective bargaining and inherited obligations is that the levels of protection and wages paid are at the expense of the post office's commercial profitability. In comparison to activities in similar sectors, the wage premium paid to USPS staff has been estimated at a consistent level of above 20 per cent (Froelke, 2000: 93–9; Wachter et al., 2001: 8–16). Critics argued that the costs for such privileges were ultimately borne by the American taxpayer. Duesterberg, for instance, observed that the number of full-time employees increased by about 5 per cent from the mid-1990s to 2000, while the mail volume grew at about 1 per cent annually for first-class mail. At the same time, the nominal price of a first-class stamp went up by about 10 per cent in real terms, whereas the inflation-adjusted price of a long-distance call had declined by 88 per cent (Duesterberg, 2000: 140).

Rate increases alone, however, did not offset the aggravating financial situation of the USPS. Falling mail volumes combined with an economic downturn and inherited fiscal obligations caused the US post office surmounting losses which reached several billion dollars. One of the reasons put forward for this gloomy performance was the USPS requirement, introduced by the 2006 Congressional mandate, to pay U$5.5 billion annually into a health fund for future retirees (Nixon, 2013). In view of such evidence one could argue that the US postal experience constitutes an example for the capture of nationalised firms by politicians, bureaucrats and trade unions as described in the literature (Majone, 1996b: 18). Numerous reform proposals to tackle the US postal deadlock have been put forward in academic as well as political circles. There are arguments in favour of maintaining public ownership while engaging in structural reform very much along the lines of the New Zealand example (Panzar, 2012); changing the governance structure towards more flexible and depoliticised arrangements outside the political arena has been seen as a key to change (Campbell Jr, 2013); and, finally, privatisation (Crew and Kleindorfer, 2000) as well as competition (Cohen, 2000) have been promoted as options to secure the financial viability of operators. The US experience in the railroad industry has frequently been mentioned as a negative example that should not be repeated in the postal sector, implying an urgent need for cutting costs and adapting service levels (Levy and Field, 2011).

Comprehensive reform proposals involving cuts in service levels and relieving the USPS of some financial pressure became stuck in Congress in the course of 2013 (Katz, 2013). In spring 2014 the Republicans in Congress, and the White House, voiced similar views on key points such as avoiding post office closures, increasing diversification by offering more governmental services at post offices, providing some degree of prefunding for retirees' health care and eliminating Saturday mail delivery, yet continued opposition by Democrats and the Senate remained a likely scenario at the time of writing (Katz, 2014). In the meantime, the USPS has engaged in cost-cutting and modernisation measures, such as closing down mail sorting centres (Becker, 2014). A pilot project to sell postal products in Staples stores was ended in July 2014 in response to a protest organised by the American Postal Workers Union (Kumar, 2014).

Canadian postal policy resembles the experience of its neighbour in many respects. Like the US, Canada was among the pioneers transforming the USP into a corporation, and in the 1980s the Canadian experience was studied as a role model for postal reform (Campbell, 2002: 271). The Canada Post Corporation (CPC) was established in 1981 as a crown corporation (i.e. as a publicly owned enterprise) operating outside the state's administrative structures. After that time nothing much changed in Canada, while the international reform movement took hold in other countries. Some modernisation and rationalisation measures were introduced from the 1990s, when legislation was passed in 1994 that obliged CPC to pay taxes, subsidies were cut, the network was rationalised, and practices of franchising and contracting out were introduced. When a new Framework Agreement was passed in 1999, however, privatisation was rejected as a reform option (Campbell, 2002: 310–11). Substantive postal reform was stalled for decades (Campbell, 2002: 272–5). This reform deadlock can be explained by some peculiarities of the Canadian situation, such as the central role played by rural constituencies.

The key difference compared to other sectors that underwent change is that postal policy was insulated from wider reform agendas. First and foremost – and this goes for the USPS as well – the Canadian post office was never part of a postal and telecoms operator. Unlike most other countries in Europe and elsewhere, there was therefore no spill-over from the telecoms revolution which occurred in the 1980s and 1990s. In addition, Canada Post was initially sheltered from competitive pressures. The bigger USPS was not allowed to expand beyond the United States to its neighbouring market, and competition from private express and logistics operators only came later. In the absence of such pressures there was no means to tame the power of organised labour when the post office was corporatised, and as a result the workforce maintained many accumulated privileges from the old regime.

In view of vested interests subsequent governments from different political camps sought to maintain their political discretion in shaping postal policy, and thus deliberately abstained from introducing more formalised procedures and institutions such as an independent sector regulator (Campbell, 2002: 312). When conducting his analysis at the beginning of the new millennium, Campbell drew a gloomy picture for CPC's future, arguing that 'it is unlikely to provide sufficient revenue to modernize the postal operation and to maintain the universal service at a level in line with public standards and expectations' (Campbell, 2002: 316). The course of events since then has proven him right, given that Canada Post in late 2013 announced considerable cuts in services. CPC envisaged the phasing out of home-delivery over a five-year period and substituting the service through community post boxes, a facility that had already been used for delivery to two-thirds of the population in rural and newer suburban areas (Leonard, 2013). The first districts targeted by such measures were announced in early 2014, and the gradual phase-out started in autumn 2014 (Thanh Ha, 2014; Than Ha and Mahoney, 2014).

For a considerable time, both the United States and Canada have been paramount examples of political deadlock caused by vested interests and outdated, highly politicised governance structures. At the time of writing, Canada, like New Zealand and Australia, moved towards substantial cut-backs in service levels. By contrast, change in the United States remained stalled due to massive organised protest. Overall the scope of reforms was limited in all LMEs for a considerable period of time. An aggravating financial performance caused by a massive decline in mail volumes might drastically alter future postal policy in these large, scarcely populated, countries.

Postal reform in the Japanese CME and the SME in Singapore

> In advancing reform, we face the fact that although basic policies for reform may receive support, once individual details start to be discussed, they come up against the wall of vested interests and deep-rooted opposition [...] A typical example of this has been the privatisation of the postal services. No one has ever tried to tackle this issue as it has been the one that has met with the strongest resistance. (General Policy Speech by Prime Minister Junichiro Koizumi to the 163rd Session of the Diet, 26 September 2005)

Japan and Singapore are particularly interesting cases since these two distinct varieties of capitalism can both be considered as postal reform leaders in the Asian and international context (see also Campbell Jr and Porges, 2008; Eckert, 2009; Maruyama and Sano, 2008). In the CME Japan (Yamamura and Streeck, 2003) postal privatisation triggered no less than a political crisis, while in the SME Singapore privatisation and liberalisation went rather unnoticed.

Japan Post, one of the largest holders of personal savings worldwide, constitutes a cornerstone of the Japanese political system and its national economy. Japan Post has traditionally played an important social role by providing accessible and cheap banking and additional services for people in need, such as the delivery of necessities to the elderly (Porges and Leong, 2006: 387). The post office's nation-wide network functioned as an unofficial vote-gathering machine for the dominant Liberal Democratic Party (LDP) particularly in rural areas (for a detailed discussion see Maclachlan, 2004). Economically speaking the postal saving system constituted one of the two components alongside the banking system of the post-war Japanese financial system (Kushida and Shimizu, 2013). Japanese Post held a massive amount of household deposits and was used by the political elite for investment in infrastructure projects. Given the social, economic and political interests in maintaining the status quo, the move in 2005 by Prime Minister Junichiro Koizumi to tackle postal reform met with fervent opposition and resulted in a lengthy political battle (Maclachlan, 2006). An important anti-reform camp within the LDP opposed such change, and the reform bill was defeated in Parliament by a surprisingly wide margin (Pilling, 2005). In response, Koizumi used measures of last resort and dissolved Parliament in order to launch new elections. Supporters of reform argued that the assets captured in the postal savings were a huge loss for the Japanese economy and that there was a need to slim down the state by removing a substantial proportion of the public employees from government payrolls such as in the postal sector. Koizumi won the elections, drawing support from urban voters, competing private operators and business.

The legislative package introduced in 2005 launched gradual privatisation to be achieved by 2017 and created four business units providing postal delivery, counter services, banking and insurance under the umbrella of the Japan Postal Services Corporation. A fund to secure the financial viability of the USP was part of the deal, given that in the new context cross-subsidisation from the profitable banking and insurance business would no longer be possible (Maruyama, 2006: 380). Before that a minor reform in 2002 had already established Japan Post as a public corporation as of April 2003, and had allowed for limited competition in the mail delivery segment. The core of the 2005 reform transformed Japan Post into a limited company as of October 2007. Liberalisation and regulatory reform were a much lower priority compared to privatisation. Japan did not engage in meaningful regulatory reform, keeping regulation within the ministry. Competition was effectively limited to the area of value-added services, introducing a special authorisation for so-called 'special correspondence delivery'. In order to obtain a 'general correspondence delivery', which would allow the handling of any type of correspondence, an operator would have to meet requirements that proved unachievable (Porges and Leong, 2006: 395): delivering throughout Japan at least six days per week, setting up 100,000 collection boxes throughout the country, meeting certain service standards and charging regulated uniform rates. While liberalisation and regulatory reform were side-tracked from the outset, the momentum for privatisation was lost throughout the reform process. The 2005 move to privatise was driven by Koizumi's political leadership, lacking sustained support from the political arena and business community.

The privatisation process was brought to a halt with a change in government in 2009. The incoming Democratic Party Japan in 2010 announced that, instead of finalising privatisation, it would retain a controlling interest in Japan Post Holding Co (Melloan, 2010). In 2012 legislation was passed, eliminating the 2017 deadline for privatisation, and overturning key aspects of postal reform introduced by the Koizumi government (Dickie, 2012). This political U-turn appears less dramatic when considering that the postal savings system had remained relatively stable (as discussed by Kushida and Shimizu, 2013: 340–1). The government still owns 100 per cent of the parent holding company, and the amount of deposits and assets held by Japan Post did not change significantly between 2005 and 2010. As a result, the 'Japan Post Bank, as a single financial institution, still dwarfs the mega-banks' (Kushida and Shimizu, 2013: 341). The outcomes of postal reform in the consensus-oriented, coordinated regime of Japan were therefore very limited in scope. The reform process kicked off with a spectacular and bold political move, but in the long run failed to overcome the 'wall of vested interests and deep-rooted opposition' mentioned by Koizumi in his inaugural speech.

Postal reform in Singapore never made international headlines as did Japanese reform moves. Yet change in the state-led variant was not insignificant: From 2003 onwards Singapore engaged in privatising SingPost. In May 2003 Singapore Post Limited was listed on the main board of the Singapore Exchange. By 2014 the government's investment company, Temasek Holdings (Private) Limited, continued to be the largest shareholder owning a stake of more than 20 per cent (Wong, 2014). In 2007 the country opened up the domestic market in one single stroke. From the viewpoint of comparative capitalism such change may appear puzzling in an economy where the state traditionally plays a strong role (Peebles and Wilson, 1996: 16), and where close links between business and politics have contributed to the longevity of the dominant political elite (Jayasuriya and Rosser, 2001: 247). Such an interventionist economic policy has, however, become increasingly questionable once

Singapore engaged in a strategy of internationalisation. Privatisation reforms have thus been launched in a number of areas (Ghosh, 2000: 224; Trocki, 2006: 178). In the postal sector the preconditions for change were particularly favourable: thanks to the population density in the small island state it can be argued that there is more scope for competitors to set up their own delivery network (IDA, 2006: 33); the reduction in manpower, which was explicitly stated as an objective of reform, did not meet with major resistance in a situation close to full employment (SingPost, 2006: 36–7).

Unlike Japan, liberalisation and regulatory change constituted key elements of reform. The independence and prerogatives of the regulatory agency, the Infocomm Development Authority of Singapore, existing since 1982, were strengthened with the legislation on liberalisation. The market opening process was flanked with social guarantees in order to safeguard consumer welfare. Important exclusive rights of SingPost were maintained, such as issuing national stamps, administering the national postal code system and exclusive access to pigeonhole masterdoor keys (IDA, 2008: 22–4). Such access to the distribution infrastructure in local housing estates consistutes a key bottleneck in Singapore's delivery market. As in Japan the threshold for becoming a USP is high and too restrictive for competition to emerge (Maruyama and Sano, 2008): it requires an island-wide delivery network, reaching all addressees in Singapore and fulfilling certain quality of service requirements. In the small postal market in Singapore only three alternative operators have so far requested authorisation for services outside the universal service, namely Swiss Post International Singapore in 2007, DHL Global Mail in 2009, and the World Marketing Group in 2008.

Compared to Japan, privatisation in Singapore has led to a substantial decrease in government shares after the IPO, while Japan Post is still in public ownership. Reform also comprised full liberalisation and regulatory reform, which were absent in Japan. But as in other countries competition in Singapore's mail delivery market is a mere legal possibility rather than a reality, and the government continues to exert influence as the major shareholder.

Postal reform in emerging Asian and Latin American market economies

> You can think of India Post now as an old fashioned network trapped in the bricks and mortar of a dying mail service. Or you can think of India Post as an extraordinary human network that facilitates incredible access to virtually all Indians. Imagine the development potential of such a network with such access to people. (Mieko Nishimizu, former Vice President of the World Bank, World Bank, 2003)

Ever since New Zealand was the first country worldwide to repeal the postal monopoly, postal reform has been spreading towards Europe, Asia and other parts of the world. This international reform movement did not halt at the borders of the mature market economies, reaching emerging market economies and developing countries. Reform preconditions may diverge significantly from the experience in established market economies, as the discussion of some insightful cases in Asia and Latin America will illustrate. International organisations such as the World Bank have supported postal reform as a means of economic and industrial development (Guislain, 2004: iv). Within the United Nations system the Universal Postal Union (UPU) is providing support to member countries in implementing the Millennium Development Goals adopted in 2000. Within the Integrated Postal Reform and Development Plan (IPDP), the UPU seeks to provide strategic and policy support which allows participating countries to raise external funding for their reform projects (UPU, 2007).

In Asia several countries have engaged in privatisation, while liberalisation remains the exception (Maruyama and Sano, 2008). Besides Singapore, Malaysia is the only country in the region which has significantly diminished government shares. Following corporatisation in 1992, Pos Malaysia was sold to a private investment holding in 2001, and in 2007 it was listed on the stock markets and split into four business units dealing with mailing, courier, the network and logistics. Malaysia, alongside Indonesia and Thailand, introduced partial liberalisation, but did so at a threshold of items weighing more than 2 kg. Corporatisation in the Philippines took place in 1992, creating the Philippine Postal Corporation (PHLPost) as a government-owned and controlled corporation.

Compared to other Asian countries, postal policy in China has been rather stable. The Chinese post office was established as a State Post Bureau in 1998 and transferred into the public corporation China Post Group in 2006. The incumbent serves an important public mandate, delivering a wide range of public services (Maruyama and Sano, 2008: 366). In China the separation between regulatory and operational tasks was only introduced in 2007 and, until today, China Post is state-controlled. While countries around the world engaged in liberalisation reforms, China in 2009 tightened its regulation of the domestic express delivery sector and effectively reduced market shares of foreign and domestic express companies in order to strengthen the position of the incumbent in these profitable markets (*The Economist*, 2009). Compared to China Post, which serves the largest population in the world of more than 1.3 billion people, India Post serves the biggest territory with more than 3.3 million square km (2011 figures according to UPU, 2014). This other postal giant in the Asian world has not undergone major reform and continues to be operated as a governmental department. Carrying the burden of an enormous USO in delivering mail and other items at subsidised prices, India Post runs significant deficits year after year. These deficits are alleviated through cross-subsidies from its profitable banking and insurance operations (Campbell Jr and Porges, 2008: 424). While India Post maintains a huge network with close to 155,000 post offices across the country and secures the USO, it has consistently lost market share in the competitive segments of the market (Ranganathan, 2008).

Compared to Asia most postal markets in Latin America are competitive, to the extent that it is accurate to speak of 'destructive levels of competition' where delivery structures are being duplicated at very low volumes (Ianni, 2008: 404). While in Europe we have de jure competition, but de facto monopolies, the situation is upside-down in Latin America with a de jure monopoly combined with de facto competition where public operators are only minority players among hundreds of postal operators (Ianni, 2008: 401–2). Latin American postal markets are unstable, with a high turnover of mostly unlicensed and unregulated operators that on average hold around 65 per cent of market shares (Ansón et al., 2006: 232). This situation can be attributed to weak regulation as well as the inability of the USPs to capture significant market shares (Ianni, 2008: 404). A striking example in this respect is Paraguay where state-owned Correo only handled 5 per cent of estimated mail volumes, while the remaining 95 per cent were handled by other state-owned utilities. The share of the state-owned electricity company, operating its own bill delivery and bill payment services, was estimated at a level of 20 per cent (UPU, 2007: 42, 47). In Latin America there are few stories of successful postal reform. The first mover was Argentina, which launched privatisation in the early 1990s, but engaged in a U-turn decades later very much like Japan. In 1992 Argentina transformed the National Company for Mail and Telecommunications into a limited company. In 1997 a 30-year concession was granted to a consortium led by the Argentine services conglomerate firm Grupo Macri in exchange for an annual payment. Due to a number of factors – the economic recession and the high price of the concession fee, as well as the failure to assess the cost of the universal service obligation, to regulate illegal competition and to deal with labour (Guislain, 2004: 11) – the concession was revoked in 2003 and the post office renationalised under government leader Nestor Kirchner. It was argued that this renationalisation did not impose a financial burden on the state, in as much as thanks to modernisation and rationalisation measures during the years of private management the incumbent's financial performance had improved considerably (Guislain, 2004: 74).

Contrary to reform failure in Argentina, change in Guatemala proved more successful. Throughout the 1990s Guatemala's post office engaged in a reform programme supported by the World Bank. The incumbent was facing a threatening situation in which unlicensed operators held a market share of around 90 per cent, while it was highly overstaffed and in a weak financial position. Measures were taken to improve internal management and operation, and comprised a long-term concession with private sector participation. As a result, considerable improvements were achieved during the period 1999–2003 (discussed by Ianni, 2008: 409): the new USP Correo de Gautemala S.A. significantly increased its share of universal mail, reduced its deficit and its staff, and achieved modest profitability, while maintaining network density and price levels.

Probably the most interesting and exceptional case in the Latin American postal world is Brazil. It has been discussed as a success story (Ianni, 2008: 410–11), and certainly proves the standard recipes for postal reform wrong. Brazil engaged neither in privatisation nor in liberalisation, yet the government managed to modernise the public operator and to make it profitable. The fully state-owned Brazilian Post and Telegraph Company (*Empresa Brasileira de Correios e Telegrafos*, ECT) upholds its monopoly in letters, postcards and telegrams, while the parcel and express business are competitive. To prove the incumbent's performance the government invested in modernisation and granted more autonomy to ECT which expanded its network and successfully engaged in diversification and innovation. ECT contributes to the public treasury, while it makes a valuable contribution to the community offering logistics, value-added services and basic banking services on top of its core postal business. This good performance has to be seen in a particularly favourable context, with an urbanisation rate of above 80 per cent, exceptionally high mail volumes and a working infrastructure (Ianni, 2008: 409).

As a response to the global economic and financial crisis and the overall trend of declining mail volumes, Brazil adopted legislation in 2011 aimed at strengthening the economic position of the incumbent. This new law granted corporate-style powers to ECT allowing it to establish subsidiaries or to form partnerships with the private sector, and opened the way for international expansion. Postal workers, organised within the National Federation of Postal Workers, have viewed such change with suspicion as first steps towards privatisation. Discussions around the new bill have thus been accompanied by massive strike action, which was also motivated by demands to stop the stagnation of wages (Post & Parcel, 2011a and b).

Overall, the postal economics literature on market opening and regulation has very much focused on the industrialised and Western world (Crew and Kleindorfer, 1991; 2008a; 2013b), with rather little attention paid to emerging market economies and developing countries (Ianni, 2008). It can, however, be questioned whether the lessons drawn from the experience in mature market economies apply to the situation elsewhere, given that the underlying economics diverge significantly (Ansón et al., 2006). Thus the postal economics literature exhibits similar limitations as does the varieties of capitalism framework: both have strongly focused on Western European and Northern American countries. More recently, efforts have been made to expand the varieties of capitalism framework to emerging market economies in Asia, Latin America and Africa (Nölke and Claar, 2013; Nölke et al., 2014). The empirical findings on postal reform around the globe confirm the need to go further down this road.

10

Conclusions: the politics of reform and regulation

This book started out by asking two research questions, namely whether varieties of capitalism translate into varieties of public service reform, and how the regulatory state protects the interests of consumers and employees. Studying the politics of postal reform and regulation across varieties of capitalism, and in comparison to other sectors, the book sheds new light on key debates in the rather separate literatures on comparative capitalism and regulation. The main empirical puzzle with respect to the politics of reform has been constituted by the delay of liberal market economies in reforming their postal sectors. In the area of regulation it turned out that policy dynamics vary significantly between economic and social regulation, and that within the field of social regulation consumer interests take centre stage, while employment related issues have been a peripheral issue in sector-specific reregulation.

Varieties of public service reform

Studying the politics of postal reform in three countries and comparing them with the reform record of the same countries in other sectors, as well as with the politics of postal reform in European member states and around the globe, has generated insights into the explanatory power of the macrolevel typology. Since the varieties of capitalism literature mainly operate at the level of comparing countries, it neglects other sources of heterogeneity which can be temporal, spatial, sectoral or international in nature (Levi-Faur, 2006b: 363). Here the argument advanced in this book links to comparative capitalist research that has made use of a governance framework (Crouch, 2005; Crouch and Streeck, 1997; Deeg and Jackson, 2007; Hollingsworth and Boyer, 1997), and highlights the explanatory challenge which change and policy variation pose to macrolevel typologies (Crouch, 2009; Pierson, 2000; Streeck and Thelen, 2005a; Thelen, 1999). It also enriches our understanding of the relationship between types of capitalism and sector-specific regulatory regimes (Eckert, 2010; Thatcher, 2007c)

A major source of change in the European public service sectors was supranational law, which has imposed full market opening and regulatory reform. The level and scope of reregulation in the European telecoms, postal and electricity sectors has been discussed in detail in Chapter 4. The findings show that, despite the common legal framework, considerable leeway remains with regard to domestic policy choices. This holds particularly for the area of social regulation, where European law sets minimum standards on service provision, but leaves employment related issues to the member states. Reform trajectories in the three countries (studied in detail in Chapters 5–7), in many respects followed the patterns expected for distinct varieties of capitalism.

Reforms in the French postal sector were characterised by relative stability and were very much in line with the concept of path dependency. Thus, the postal case points to the resilience of institutional settings and confirms wider claims about the persisting predominance of state activism in France (Levy, 2005). The French postal reform record does not substantially deviate from the experience in other sectors, where change has proved difficult in all areas of public service provision. The French were more willing to embrace change in the telecoms sector than in the postal sector, yet French resistance was very strong on electricity reform.

The German experience proves validity for the relevance of coordination in this capitalist model. Reform steps have followed an incremental logic, which is why the reform trajectory is best described as negotiated change. The major trade union in the sector has played a key role throughout the reform process and has exerted effective political pressure, notably on the political left. As a result, the liberalisation process has been slowed down in several instances, and social safeguards have been introduced into the legal framework. Yet over time the pillars of postal corporatism have started to crumble with the emergence of private operators, resulting in a decline in unionisation and organisational fragmentation. Nevertheless, the scope of postal reform in Germany has been considerable, mainly driven by conservative governments, supported by the business community and, most of the time, also by the incumbent. The puzzling finding in the German case is that telecoms and postal reform occurred at the same time and with the same intensity, despite very different exogenous pressures. The momentum created by German reunification, with a need to modernise the infrastructure in both areas, has certainly contributed to this reform move, as has the expansionist strategy of Deutsche Post. By contrast, vested interests and entrenched institutions have repeatedly led to reform deadlock in the German electricity sector, resulting in a reoccurring Franco-German alliance at the European level. Germany lent support to the overall idea of market opening, but was opposed to change on key aspects of regulatory and institutional reform.

The cross-sector spill-over of reform dynamics which has been observed in the German telecoms and postal sectors has been totally absent in Britain, where the postal sector was insulated from change for a considerable period. While other public utilities were subsequently privatised and then liberalised throughout the 1970s and 1980s, the public monopoly held by the Post Office remained untouched until the late 1990s. With its dense levels of interest organisation and a strong role played by the state, the postal sector forms an outlier in the liberal model: the major trade union continues to rely on a strong organisational basis, and constitutes an anachronism in the British economy, where trade unionism was disempowered during the Thatcher era. Postal reform has ultimately been triggered by European law towards the end of the 1990s, and since then Britain has moved at double speed. Despite its organisational and policy resources, the CWU has not been involved as a major partner in the reform process, unlike its German counterpart. Its role has rather been along the line of French trade unions, engaging in opposition and contestation. The move in 2013 to privatise Royal Mail has further weakened the voices of those opposing change. Thus the variation of reform dynamics across sectors has been most pronounced in the British case. Yet in a longer-term perspective these differences have been levelled out, and today the British postal exception belongs to the past.

From a comparative capitalism perspective, it is interesting that, like the British, other LMEs such as the United States and Canada have not engaged in meaningful reform in the postal sector. Why and to what extent postal reform constitutes an outlier in the LME context has therefore been considered in some detail, contrasting the experience of LME postal reform leaders and laggards in Chapter 9. On the one hand, liberal economies such as New Zealand and Australia have constituted the vanguard of the international postal reform movement. New Zealand was among the first countries worldwide to engage in corporatisation in 1987, followed by Australia in 1989. Yet in a longer-term perspective the scope of reform remained limited, as neither of the two engaged in privatisation. The United States and Canada, by contrast, have been reform laggards. In the United States the postal exception is at least as striking as in the British context, given that the Americans took the lead in the international privatisation movement. The fact that telecommunications services were in private hands from the outset, unlike the European PTT model, may to some extent explain such deviation. Yet it is surprising that nothing much followed the transformation of the Post Office Department into the USPS, which took place as early as 1970. Similarly, Canada engaged in corporatisation in 1981, but reform was subsequently stalled for decades, and there was no spill-over from the telecoms revolution. Overall, therefore, while initial reform paths taken by these LMEs diverged significantly, the scope of change has been limited in all four countries.

At the time of writing important changes are, however, under way, mainly in response to a massive decline in mail volumes. Again it is New Zealand that has set the pace, introducing a new scheme of delivery which will involve massive cuts in service levels by 2015. Canada is the next to follow, announcing a phasing out of home delivery in wide areas of the country. At the time of writing Australia was discussing the reduction of the universal service obligation, and envisaged privatisation as a policy option. Political controversies were also taking place in the United States, where the financial situation of the USPs proved quite dramatic, yet change faced massive resistance in the political realm. Massive declines in mail volumes are thus likely to force these four LMEs, which all face particularly difficult geographic preconditions with a low level of population density and many remote areas, to engage in drastic reform measures in the near future. This may put an end to the widely accepted notion of a universal postal service, and may also have repercussions for future reform moves in the European context.

In contrast with the mixed reform record among LMEs, Chapter 9 has examined two reform leaders in the Asian context, Japan and Singapore. Adding the reform record of another CME (Japan), as well as another SME (Singapore), puts the findings gathered by the case studies on Germany and France into a broader perspective. The postal reform record in the coordinated Japanese economy is most spectacular, as it triggered not less than a fully fledged political crisis in 2005, which was overcome under the determined leadership of Koizumi, only to pave the way for a political U-turn once political majorities had changed again. As a consequence, the move towards full privatisation was politically contained half way through the process, while liberalisation had been sidelined as a policy goal from the outset. In the state-led variant Singapore, where privatisation was launched in 2003 and where liberalisation was introduced in one single stroke in 2007, there was no such political U-turn, but no massive change either. Thus in comparison to Germany and France, these two examples show that a reform process in CMEs can come to a halt in the face of powerful vested interests, while change in SMEs may simply be imposed by the political arena, especially where there is a low level of societal resistance, as in Singapore. Both findings do not contradict the expectations that can be derived from the VoC literature, but again point to reform preconditions which vary across countries, sectors and over time.

Another issue that arises when looking at postal reform in the international political economy, is about the limits of academic approaches that were developed with a strong bias towards the experience in Western European and North American countries. Such limitations have been discussed in Chapter 9 with respect to postal reform in emerging Asian and Latin American market economies. Insights from postal policy in various countries have shown that the reform preconditions and the policy goals vary significantly from those in the mature market economies. In contrast to the situation in Europe, opening up the postal markets to competition has not been on the agenda of policy makers in these countries, and there are rather few examples of privatisation. In emerging market economies postal policy mainly aims to safeguard wider general interest goals, where the postal network fulfils crucial functions in terms of territorial and socioeconomic cohesion as well as industrial policy. China and India Post are interesting examples, as both deliver a wide range of public services and reach out to a vast area and population. In order to safeguard this model, China upholds a state-controlled postal policy and has effectively sought to limit competition on profitable markets in order to sustain the financial viability of the incumbent. India struggles to finance a loss-making post office that benefits from cross-subsidies generated by its profitable banking and insurance operations, but loses out in the competitive segments of the postal and parcel markets.

The situation in Latin America is specific to the extent that most postal incumbents, although holding de jure a monopoly on their national market, are minority players among hundreds of postal operators. The preconditions as well as policy challenges in Latin American do turn the European reform recipe upside down: de jure monopoly combines with de facto competition and not the other way around; and the challenge is to ensure universal service coverage by the incumbent rather than to increase the market share of competitors. The Brazilian case, where a state-owned operator has undergone massive modernisation and effectively delivers on its public service mandate, forms an exception among the Latin American countries. But whether this state-led model of postal reform proves sustainable in the long run is open to question, since at the time of writing more liberal-minded reforms were underway in Brazil. Overall, the findings from such international comparison point to the need to widen our conceptual frameworks in order to embrace the empirical richness of comparative capitalism across the globe. Recent contributions to the varieties of capitalism literature have moved into that direction (Nölke and Claar, 2013; Nölke et al., 2014), and future research should go further down this road.

Social regulation in the public service sectors

The consequences of the transition towards the regulatory state in terms of policies and politics have been analysed and discussed at length both from a theoretical and empirical angle in the literature. I have formulated three claims which refine, and to some extent challenge the mainstream assumptions about this transition. The first claim challenged Majone's hypothesis that the positive state would progressively be replaced by the regulatory state (Majone, 1997). I argued that redistributive policies would not disappear with the transition towards the regulatory state, but rather underpin and stabilise its functioning. The empirical findings on postal reform in different countries and over time substantiate this claim. Throughout reform, redistributive modes of policymaking persist, where financial compensation is provided to fund the network of postal outlets and the provision of a universal service. Mechanisms for financial compensation to cover the cost of universal postal service provision are foreseen in the French, German and British regulatory regime. All three varieties of capitalism, including the liberal model, have provided state aid to cover the cost of counter and mail services, and of acquired employee entitlements. Private postal operators took advantage of redistributive policies in Germany by paying unsustainable wage levels that were cross-subsidised by social security benefits. European competition law sets some limits to state aid practice and requires approval for such state aid schemes, while social policy decisions are being left to the member states.

In the current context of surmounting budgetary deficits and austerity policies, governments have sought to reduce financial involvement. Particularly in the area of the USO, however, financial compensation schemes form a constituent element of social regulation. While transparent and objective mechanisms to calculate the net cost of the USO are a key concern in the regulatory economics literature and in regulatory practice (Crew and Kleindorfer, 2006), the very idea of compensation is not being questioned. Redistributive policies come on top of social regulation in the sector. Overall, the empirical findings support the observation in recent political science literature that the welfare and regulatory state are interdependent (Levi-Faur, 2013). This book thus enriches our understanding of the role of regulation in social policy (Leisering, 2011a; Mabbett, 2011) as well as of the role of redistributive policies in regulation (Haber, 2010).

The second claim was about the ways in which independent regulatory agencies will implement social, as opposed to economic, policy goals. In institutional terms, the scope of delegation of regulatory powers can be expected to be more pronounced in economic than in social regulation. Here I have built on Majone's distinction between two logics of delegation:

the agency logic, where political actors are preoccupied with control over policy outcomes, as opposed to the fiduciary logic, where political actors are preoccupied with credible commitment to a certain type of policy outcome. Applied to the fields of social and economic regulation, I have argued that the agency logic is more relevant for the former, the fiduciary logic for the latter. In the area of social regulation, political actors are likely to be hit by a 'blame boomerang' (Hood, 2002: 28) where they have sought to shift responsibility towards the nonmajoritarian arena, but are ultimately being held accountable for policy outcomes. Independent regulators, on their part, are likely to defer policy responsibility to the political arena and see themselves as enforcement agents rather than decision makers.

In the three countries studied, the transition towards depoliticised modes in postal regulation has been prescribed by European law. France, for instance, was forced to comply with a European requirement to introduce structural separation between operational and regulatory tasks, and to introduce an independent sector regulator. Regulatory reform has rationalised the policymaking process in accordance with economic principles that are transparent and reliable. This holds, in particular, for the area of rate regulation where increases in postal tariffs have been underpinned by economic evidence rather than political considerations. In all three countries, rate increases have on average become more frequent, more gradual and less politicised once tariff regulation was in the hands of an independent regulator. In their policy practice regulatory agencies have prioritised an economic rationale over social policy goals even where they disposed of a legal mandate to engage in social regulation. The German case, where the agency, in its licensing practice, was proactive in using legal prerogatives to develop a regime favouring market opening prior to full liberalisation, but reluctant to implement the social clause concerning adequate wage levels among authorised operators, is emblematic in this respect. Regulation for competition has also been a cornerstone of regulatory practice in Britain despite the regulator's prior duty to ensure the provision of the universal service. Without Postcomm's move to make the case for full liberalisation ahead of the European schedule political actors would probably not have supported such change. Thus, different politics are at play depending on whether independent agencies implement economic or social policy goals.

The third claim is about the role of organised interests in the regulatory state, and thus relates to the literature on organised capitalism and neo-corporatism (Crouch, 2006; Lash and Urry, 1987), regulated business (Coen, 2005a; Stigler, 1971), and consumer capitalism (Trumbull, 2006). I argued that depoliticisation through delegation will be to the detriment of labour interests, while business interests will prevail and consumer interests will be on the rise. The underlying argument is that the transition towards the regulatory state impacts on patterns of interest organisation, as independent regulation privileges some type of interests over others. In-depth analysis of postal reform has shown that emerging regulatory regimes incorporate consumer protection as their core business, while the social protection of employees is mostly considered to be outside the scope of independent regulators. Organised labour has lost in importance due to efforts to undermine the policy impact of trade unions, such as in Britain, a decline in union density and organisational centralisation, such as in Germany, or a lack of organisational strength of the social partners, such as in France. Organised business interests, by contrast, play a key role in the regulatory game. The historic operators, new entrants and business customers are well organised and effective in influencing the policymaking process. The regulatory process also systematically includes the interests of private customers, monitoring the performance in service provision and gathering data on consumer needs. Paradoxically, responsiveness to average consumer needs may supposedly lead to service cuts where postal delivery becomes less important as a means of communication. Consumer capitalism appears most advanced in Britain, where the sector regulator actively gathers evidence on consumer needs and is likely to push for policy innovation in this respect. Recent cuts in letter mail delivery standards in other liberal regimes such as New Zealand and Canada will give further leverage to such change.

Where independent regulation does not incorporate all types of interests equally, and where unionism is in decline, the question is whether political regulation will step in as a remedy. For the time being, European and national legal frameworks subscribe to a minimum level of service provision, yet acquired standards may be put into question in the future. In the realm of employment, statutory provisions in the form of a generally applicable minimum wage are in place in most European countries, and Germany is currently moving towards this direction. France has furthermore sought to empower postal corporatism by imposing a legal obligation on the social partners to negotiate sector-specific collective agreements, but with limited success.

In adopting a governance perspective on social regulation, in Chapter 3 I have furthermore formulated claims concerning variation across types of capitalism: close state-economy relations in the French state-led model which should facilitate political regulation; dense patterns of interest organisation in German corporatism; and a hands-off approach to the economy, combined with fragmented interest organisation, facilitating independent regulation in Britain. Chapter 5 has shown how France upheld a considerable degree of political control. Political regulation maintained a universal service obligation, and imposed the negotiation of a sector-specific collective agreement on the social partners. France opted for a lean regime of economic regulation, and delegated relatively few competencies to an independent regulator. Throughout the process, the costs of change have been cushioned by political intervention and redistributive policies.

In Germany the role of postal corporatism has been most pronounced, but its organisational pillars have started to crumble over time. Once private operators had conquered a significant share of the market, this seriously affected the established industrial relations. When the social partners were entrusted with the task of negotiating a sector-specific minimum wage, the organisational landscape was split along the lines of incumbent versus competitors' interests. These two antagonistic camps challenged one another's representativeness and legitimacy, triggering a political controversy at the highest governmental level within the grand coalition. Due to persisting political disagreement, and a reluctance to interfere with tariff autonomy, the issue was ultimately left to the judges. At the time of writing, the prospect for the German case is that a general minimum wage will be introduced which will potentially also affect wage levels in the postal sector. Such political intervention, however, will not halt the progressive decline of organisational structures and industry-wide collective bargaining, which is a more general trend in the German coordinated economy (Streeck, 2009).

In the British context independent regulation proved to be a key driver of change and, empowered by pressure from the EU, ultimately helped to overcome reform deadlock. From the outset, the independent regulator Postcomm had been entrusted with a stronger role in shaping postal policy than its counterparts in other countries, and thus was in position to prepare the grounds for full market opening. The scope of delegation has been widened further with the last round of reform. Ofcom has a say in decisions about the adequate scope and nature of the universal service, a prerogative which in all other member states remains in the political arena. Despite a shared trend fuelled by supranational law towards independent regulation, expected patterns across varieties of capitalism hold, and pose distinct policy challenges to each regime.

Challenges ahead: declining mail volumes, the Internet society and energy poverty

The postal sector is currently under massive reconstruction with an aggravating decline in mail volumes, driven by electronic substitution combined with an economic downturn. This has placed a serious threat on the financial viability of USPs in many countries. The very credentials of postal regulation, particularly in the area of universal service provision, are at stake. It is not unreasonable to pose the question whether, and to what extent, the postal sector continues to fulfil general interest goals in the face of rapid technological change. This holds at least for mature market economies, while emerging market economies continue to rely on the postal infrastructure in order to realise social and industrial policy goals. By contrast, some liberal economies in the industrialised world have already started to cut back their levels of service provision substantially. At the time of writing, policy makers in Australia and the United States have to decide whether to follow the example set by New Zealand and Canada in cutting back service. European policy makers may have to deal with similar issues in the near future.

The decline of the postal world goes hand in hand with the rise of the world of electronic communications. Controversies over issues such as access to broadband services, net equality and data protection illustrate the extent to which regulatory regimes are in flux. What declining letter mail volumes are for a shrinking postal sector, are increasing levels of consumption paired with limited resources in the expanding electricity sector. Secure and affordable supply of electricity has become increasingly important for private and industry customers around the world, and related issues of energy poverty and competitiveness are more salient than ever. All these examples pose challenges in terms of securing sufficient investment and allocating costs fairly. These challenges are not limited to the arena of public service reform, but concern other areas where regulation spreads, such as the welfare state and industrial relations, and the role of the state in the economy more generally.

References

Abromeit, H. (1988), 'British Privatisation Policy', *Parliamentary Affairs*, 41:1, 68–85.

Adams, A. (2013), 'Update to New Zealand Post's Deed of Understanding', press release, 23 October (Wellington: Ministry of Communications and Information Technology).

Aghion, P. and J. Tirole (1997), 'Formal and Real Authority in Organizations', *Journal of Political Economy*, 105:1, 1–29.

Amable, B. (2003), *The Diversity of Modern Capitalism* (Oxford: Oxford University Press).

Ambrosini, X., Boldron, F. and Roy, B. (2006), 'Universal Service Obligations in the Postal Sector. Economic Learnings from Cross-Country Comparisons', in Crew, M. A. and Kleindoerfer, P. R. (eds), *Progress toward Liberalization of the Postal and Delivery Sector* (New York: Springer), pp. 23–37.

Ambrosius, G. (2000), 'Services Publics, Leistungen der Daseinsvorsorge oder Universaldienste? Zur historischen Dimension eines zukünftigen Elements europäischer Gesellschaftspolitik', in Cox, H. (ed.), *Daseinsvorsorge und öffentliche Dienstleistungen in der Europäischen Union* (Baden-Baden: Nomos), pp. 15–43.

Anderloni, L. and Pilley, O. (2002), 'Changing Context for Postal Systems in Europe', in Ruozi, R. and Anderloni, L. (eds), *Modernisation and Privatisation of Postal Systems in Europe. New Opportunities in the Area of Financial Services* (Berlin, Heidelberg and New York: Springer), pp. 9–71.

Andres, L. Guasch, J. L. and Diop, M. et al. (2007), *Assessing the Governance of Electricity Regulatory Agencies in the Latin American and the Caribbean region: a benchmarking analysis*, in World Bank (ed.), Policy Research Working Paper, report number WPS4380 (World Bank).

Annesley, C. (2006), 'Ver.di and Trade Union Revitalisation in Germany', *Industrial Relations Journal*, 37:2, 164–79.

Ansón, J., Cuadra, R., Linhares, A. et al. (2006), 'First Steps towards New Postal Economics Models for Developing Countries: Learning from the Latin American Experience', in Crew, M. A. and Kleindoerfer, P. R. (eds), *Liberalization of the Postal and Delivery Sector* (Cheltenham, UK, and Northampton, MA: Edward Elgar), pp. 217–36.

Arnaboldi, F. and Bauer, E. (2002), 'The Experience of Floatation: the Cases of TNT – Post Group and Deutsche Post AG', in Ruozi, R. and Anderloni, L. (eds), *Modernisation and Privatisation of Postal Systems in Europe. New Opportunities in the Area of Financial Services* (Berlin, Heidelberg and New York: Springer Verlag), pp. 95–126.

Arnold, M. (2005), 'Anger over Green Light for French Postal Bank. Country's big Lenders ask Brussels to Examine Case', *The Financial Times* (2 December).

Atkinson, M. M. and Coleman, W. D. (1989), 'Strong States and Weak States: Sectoral Policy Networks in Advanced Capitalist Economies', *British Journal of Political Science*, 19:1, 47–67.

Badura, P., v. Danwitz, T., Herdegen, M. et al. (eds) (2004), *Beck'scher PostG-Kommentar* (München: C.H. Beck).

Baldwin, R., Cave, M. and Lodge, M. (2012), *Understanding Regulation. Theory, Strategy and Practice* (Oxford: Oxford University Press).

Barthel, K. (2007), 'Marktöffnung stoppen ... solange Rahmenbedingungen nicht stimmen', *Press Release* (25 May).

Barthel, K. (2008), 'Post – Kein Wettbewerb über Dumpinglöhne', *Press Release* (19 December).

Bartholomeusz, S. (2014), 'Overhaul in the Mail for Aussie Post', *The Australian* (13 May).

Bartle, I. (2002), 'When Institutions No Longer Matter: Reform of Telecommunications and Electricity in Germany, France and Britain', *Journal of Public Policy*, 22:1, 1–27.

Bartle, I. (2005), *Globalisation and EU Policy-making. The Neo-liberal Transformation of Telecommunications and Electricity* (Manchester and New York: Manchester University Press).

Bartnik, M. (2010), 'A la Poste, des médecins tirent la sonnette d'alarme', *Le Figaro* (16 June).

Bauby, P. and Varone, F. (2007), 'Europeanization of the French Electricity Policy: four paradoxes', *Journal of European Public Policy*, 14:7, 1048–60.

Beck, U. (1998), 'The Politics of Risk Society', in Franklin. J. (ed.), *The Politics of Risk Society* (Cambridge: Polity Press), pp. 9–22.

Becker, B. (2014), 'Postal Service to Close Dozens of Mail Centers', *The Hill* (7 March).

Bekkedal, T. (2011), 'Article 106 TFEU is Dead. Long Live Article 106 TFEU!', in Szyszczak, E., Davies, J., Andenæs, M. et al. (eds), *Developments in Services of General Interest* (The Hague: T. M. C. Asser Press), pp. 61–102.

Bender, G. (2001), 'Regulierungsbehörde quo vadis? Bestandaufnahme aktueller Vollzugsdefizite und Reformvorschläge', *Kommunikation & Recht*, 10, 506–15.

Bendor, J., Glazer, A. and Hammond, T. (2001), 'Theories of Delegation', *Annual Review of Political Science*, 4, 235–69.

Berger. S. (1981), *Organizing Interests in Western Europe: Pluralism, Corporatism, and the Transformation of Politics* (Cambridge: Cambridge University Press).

Bergounioux, A. (1975), *Force ouvrière* (Paris: Éditions du Seuil).

Bernhard, W., Broz, L. J. and Clark, W. R. (2002), 'The Political Economy of Monetary Institutions', *International Organization*, 56:4, 693–723.

BERR (2009), *The Future of the Universal Postal Service in the UK* (London: Department for Business Enterprise & Regulatory Reform).

Bezes, P. (2001), 'Defensive Versus Offensive Approaches to Administrative Reform in France (1988–1997): The Leadership Dilemmas of French Prime Ministers', *Governance*, 14:1, 99–132.

Bild (2007a), 'Mindestlohn? Dann gehen wir pleite!' (20 September).

Bild (2007b), 'Mindestlohn? Der kostet uns den Job!' (8 October).

Bild (2008a), 'Postchef Klaus Zumwinkel. Er liebt das Leben und scheffelt Millionen' (15 December).

Bild (2008b), 'Um 7.12 klingelt der Staatsanwalt' (15 December).

BIS (2010), *Securing the Post Office Network in the Digital Age* (London: Department for Business, Innovation and Skills).

Black, R. (1977), 'Plus ça change, plus c'est le même chose: Nine Governments in Search fro a Common Energy Policy', in Wallace, H., Wallace, W. and Webb, C. (eds), *Policy-Making in the European Communities* (New York: John Wiley & Sons), pp. 165–96.

Blanchflower, D. G. and Freeman, R. B. (1994), 'Did the Thatcher Reforms Change British Labour Market Performance?', in Barrell, R. (ed.), *The UK Labour Market. Comparative aspects and institutional development* (Cambridge: Cambridge University Press), pp. 51–92.

BNetzA (2007), *Arbeitsbedingungen im lizenzierten Bereich. Endergebnis der Auskunftsanordnung gemäß §45 PostG vom 22. Juni 2007. Stand der Auswertung: 31.12.2007* (Bonn: Bundesnetzagentur für Elektrizität, Gas, Telekommunikation, Post und Eisenbahnen).

BNetzA (2008), *Annual Report 2007* (Bonn: Federal Network Agency for Electricity, Gas, Telecommunications, Post and Railway).

BNetzA (2009a), *Auskunftsanordnung gemäß §45 Postgesetz vom 22.01.2009* (Bonn: Bundesnetzagentur für Elektrizität, Gas, Telekommunikation, Post und Eisenbahnen).

BNetzA (2009b), *Jahresbericht 2008* (Bonn: Bundesnetzagentur für Elektrizität, Gas, Telekommunikation, Post und Eisenbahnen).

BNetzA (2009c), *Tätigkeitsbericht 2008/2009 Post* (Bonn: Bundesnetzagentur für Elektrizität, Gas, Telekommunikation, Post und Eisenbahnen).

BNetzA (2013), *Tätigkeitsbericht 2012/2013 Post* (Bonn: Bundesnetzagentur für Elektrizität, Gas, Telekommunikation, Post und Eisenbahnen).

Boldron, F., Dewulf, K., Joram, D. et al. (2008), 'Accessibility of the postal retail network, social cohesion and economic development', in Crew, M. A. and Kleindorfer, P. R. (eds), *Competition and Regulation in the Postal and Delivery Sector* (Cheltenham, UK, and Northampton, MA: Edward Elgar), pp. 47–59.

Boldron, F., Joram, D., Merlin, L. et al. (2006), 'From the Size of the Box to the Costs of Universal Service Obligation: A Cross-Country Comparison', in Crew, M. A. and Kleindorfer, P. R. (eds), *Liberalization of the Postal and Delivery Sector* (Cheltenham, UK, and Northampton, MA: Edward Elgar), pp. 37–52.

Börzel, T. A. (2005), 'Europeanization: How the European Union Interacts with its Member States', in Bulmer, S. and Lequesne, C. (eds), *Member States and the European Union* (Oxford: Oxford University Press), pp. 45–69.

Börzel, T. A. (2007), 'EU Governance – Verhandlung im Schatten von Hierarchie und Wettbewerb', *Politische Vierteljahresschrift*, Sonderheft 38:2, 61–91.

Börzel, T. A. and Risse, T. (2006), 'Europeanization: The Domestic Impact of EU Politics', in Jorgensen, K. E., Pollack, M. and Rosamond, B. J. (eds), *Handbook of European Union Politics* (London: Sage), pp. 483–504.

Bougrab, J. (2004), 'Independent Administrative Authorities in France', in Caranta, R. Andenas, M. and Fairgrieve, D. (eds), *Independent Administrative Authorities* (London: British Institute of International and Comparative Law), pp. 47–63.

Bouin, B., Curien, N. and Lacroix, G. (2010), 'Price Cap Postal Regulation: the French experience', in Crew, M. A. and Kleindorfer, P. R. (eds), *Heightening Competition in the Postal and Delivery Sector* (Cheltenham, UK, and Northampton, MA: Edward Elgar), pp. 85–98.

Brachet, P. (1999), *L'Étatisme à la Française. Peut-on relégitimer le 'service public'? France en Europe* (Paris: Publisud).

Braithwaite, J. (2003), *Meta Regulation for Access to Justice*, General Aspects of Law (GALA) Seminar Series (Berkeley: University of California).

Braithwaite, J. (2008a), 'Neoliberalism or Regulatory Capitalism?', in Braithwaite, J. (ed.), *Regulatory Capitalism. How it Works, Ideas for Making it Work Better* (Cheltenham, UK, and Northampton, MA: Edward Elgar), pp. 1–31.

Braithwaite, J. (2008b), *Regulatory Capitalism. How it Works, Ideas for Making it Work Better* (Cheltenham, UK, and Northampton, MA: Edward Elgar).

Braubach, U. (1992), *Deregulierung der Postdienste* (Bamberg: Institut für Wirtschaftspolitik).

Braun, D. and Gilardi, F. (2006), *Delegation in Contemporary Democracies* (London and New York: Routledge).

Braun, D., Gilardi, F., Thatcher, M. et al. (2002), 'Debate: State Intervention and Delegation to Regulatory Agencies', *Swiss Political Science Review*, 8:1, 93–125.

Breyer, S. (1982), *Regulation and Its Reform* (Cambridge, MA and London: Harvard University Press).

Buchan, D. (2010), 'Energy Policy. Sharp Challenges and Rising Ambitions', in Wallace, H., Pollack, M. A. and Young, A. R. (eds), *Policy-Making in the European Union* (Oxford: Oxford University Press), pp. 357–80.

Bulmer, S., Dolowitz, D., Humphreys, P. et al. (2007), *Policy Transfer in European Governance. Regulating the Utilities* (London and New York: Routledge).

Burnham, P. (2001), 'New Labour and the Politics of Depoliticisation', *The British Journal of Politics & International Relations*, 3:2, 127–49.

Caisse des Dépôts (2013), *Business Review 2012* (Paris: Caisse des Dépôts Group).

Camdessus, M., Vaysset, G., le Cam, Y. et al. (2007), *Rapport de la mission sur la modernisation de la distribution du livret A et des circuits de financement du logement social* (Paris: Premier Ministre).

Cameron, P. D. (2002), *Competition in Energy Markets: Law and Regulation in the European Union* (Oxford: Oxford University Press).

Campbell Jr, J. I., Dieke, A. K. and Niederprüm, A. (2008), 'National Postal Policies in Europe on the eve of the Third Directive', in Crew, M. A.,

Campbell, J. I. and Kleindorfer, P. R. (eds), *Postal Reform* (Cheltenham, UK, and Northampton, MA: Edward Elgar), pp. 195–215.

Campbell Jr, J. I. (2013), 'A New Governance Model for US Postal Services', in Crew, M. A. and Kleindoerfer, P. R. (eds), *Reforming the Postal Sector in the Face of Electronic Competition* (Cheltenham, UK, and Northampton, MA: Edward Elgar), pp. 63–75.

Campbell Jr, J. I. and Porges, A. (2008), 'How Much Postal Reform in Japanese Postal Privatization?', in Crew, M. A., Kleindorfer, P. R. and Campbell Jr, J. I. (eds), *Handbook of Worldwide Postal Reform* (Cheltenham, UK, and Northampton, MA: Edward Elgar), pp. 373–87.

Campbell, R. M. (2001), 'Regulatory and Governance Changes in Liberalized, Commercialized Postal Environments: A Comparative Assessment', in Crew, M. A. and Kleindorfer, P. R. (eds), *Future Directions in Postal Reform* (Boston, Dordrecht and London: Kluwer Academic Publishers), pp. 83–97.

Campbell, R. M. (2002), *The Politics of Postal Transformation. Modernizing Postal Systems in the Electronic and Global World* (Montreal & Kingston, London, Ithaca: McGill Queen's University Press).

Castro, M. C. (1995), 'Deregulation of Australia's Postal Services', in Crew, M. A. and Kleindorfer, P. R. (eds), *Commercialization of Postal and Delivery Services: National and International Perspectives* (Berlin, Heidelberg and New York: Springer), pp. 27–44.

Cave, A. (2010), 'Richard Hooper: Unions say Private Sector Capital will Destroy the Royal Mail – it Won't', *Telegraph* (11 September).

CFTC (2013), 'La CFTC en audience à l'ARCEP' (11 February).

CGT-FAPT (2009), 'Spécial Poste', *Le Militant*, 73 (January–February).

CGT-FAPT (2012), 'Convention Collective des activités postales' (3 October).

CGT-FAPT (2013), 'Les administrateurs salariés de La Poste rejettent l'accord entre l'Etat et La Poste pour la période 2013–2017'.

Chevallier, J. (1984), *L'Avenir de* La Poste. *Rapport au Ministre des postes et télécommunications et de la télédiffusion, par la Commission chargée de procéder à une réflexion prospective sur* La Poste *présidée par Jacques Chevallier* (Paris: La Documentation Française).

Chevallier, J. (2003), *Le Service Publique* (Paris: Presses Universitaires de France).

Cioffi, J. W. and Höpner, M. (2006), 'The Political Paradox of Finance Capitalism: Interests, Preferences, and Center-Left Party Politics in Corporate Governance Reform', *Politics & Society*, 34:4, 463–502.

Clark, D. (2000), 'Citizens, Charters and Public Service Reform in France and Britain', *Government and Opposition*, 35:2, 152–69.

Clift, B. (2001), 'The Jospin Way', *The Political Quarterly*, 72:2, 170–9.

Clifton, J., Fuentes, D. and Comin, F. (eds) (2007), *Transforming Public Enterprise in Europe and the Americas: Networks, Integration and Transnationalisation* (Basingstoke: Palgrave Macmillan).

Coase, R. (1939), 'Rowland Hill and the Penny Post', *Economica*, 6:November, 423–35.

Coase, R. (1947), 'The Economics of Uniform Pricing Systems', *The Manchester School*, 15 (May), 139–56.

Coen, D. (2005a), 'Business-Regulatory Relations: Learning to Play Regulatory Games in European Utility Markets', *Governance: An International Journal of Policy, Administration and Institutions*, 18:3, 375–98.

Coen, D. (2005b), 'Changing Business-regulator Relations in German and UK Telecommunications and Energy Sectors', in Héritier, A. and Coen, D. (eds), *Refining Regulatory Regimes. Utilities in Europe* (Cheltenham, UK, and Northampton, MA: Edward Elgar), pp. 91–119.

Coffineau, M. (1993), *Les lois Auroux, dix ans après* (Paris: La Documentation Française).

Cohen, R. H. (2000), 'Consequences of Competition', in Hudgins, E. L. (ed.), *Mail @ the Millennium. Will the Postal Sector Go Private?* (Washington: Cato Institute), pp. 103–13.

Cole, A. (2000), 'The Service Public Under Stress', in Elgie, R. (ed.), *The Changing French Political System* (London, Portland: Frank Cass), pp. 166–84.

Cole, A. and Jones, G. (2005), 'Reshaping the State: Administrative Reform and New Public Management in France', *Governance*, 18:4, 567–88.

Coleman, J. S. (1990), *Foundations of Social Theory* (Cambridge, MA and London: Harvard University Press).

Collier, D., LaPorte, J. and Seawright, J. (2012), 'Putting Typologies to Work: Concept Formation, Measurement, and Analytic Rigor', *Political Research Quarterly*, 65:1, 217–32.

Comarow, M. (2000), 'The United States' Postal Contradiction', in Hudgins, E. L. (ed.), *Mail @ the Millennium. Will the Postal Sector Go Private?* (Washington: Cato Institute), pp. 197–209.

Comité interministériel sur l'Europe (2006), 'Communiqué du 27.11.2006'.

Commission sur le développement de La Poste (2008), *'Oui,* La Poste *a un bel avenir devant elle…'* Rapport présenté par François Ailleret, président de la commission sur le développement de La Poste.

Compass (2009), *Case Not Made. A Response to the Hooper Report on the Future of the Royal Mail* (London: Compass. Direction for the Democratic Left).

Copenhagen Economics (2010), *Main Developments in the Postal Sector (2008–2010). Final report DG Markt* (Copenhagen: Copenhagen Economics).

Cousquer, Y. (1999), 'Le service public est-il soutenable? L'exemple des postes', in Chevalier, J.-M., Ekeland, I. and Frison-Roche, M.-A. (eds), *L'idée du service public est-elle encore soutenable?* (Paris: Presses Universitaires de France), pp. 219–40.

Cremer, H., de Donder, P., Boldron, F. et al. (2008), 'Social Costs and Benefits of the Universal Service Obligation in the Postal Market', in Crew, M. A. and Kleindorfer, P. R. (eds), *Competition and Regulation in the Postal and Delivery Sector* (Cheltenham, UK, and Northampton, MA: Edward Elgar), pp. 23–31.

Crew, M. A. and Kleindoerfer, P. R. (eds) (1991), *Competition and Innovation in Postal Services* (Boston, Dordrecht and London: Kluwer Academic Publishers).

Crew, M. A. and Kleindoerfer, P. R. (2000), 'Privatizing the US Postal Service', in Hudgins, E. L. (ed.), *Mail @ the Millennium. Will the Postal Sector Go Private?* (Washington: Cato Institute), pp. 149–61.

Crew, M. A. and Kleindoerfer, P. R. (2005), 'Competition, Universal Service and the Graveyard Spiral', in Crew, M. A. and Kleindorfer, P. R. (eds), *Regulatory and Economic Challenges in the Postal and Delivery Sector* (Berlin, Heidelberg and New York: Springer), pp. 1–30.

Crew, M. A. and Kleindoerfer, P. R. (2006), 'Approaches to the USO under Entry', in Crew, M. A. and Kleindorfer, P. R. (eds), *Liberalization of the Postal and Delivery Sector* (Cheltenham, UK, and Northampton, MA: Edward Elgar), pp. 1–18.

Crew, M. A. and Kleindoerfer, P. R. (eds) (2008a), *Competition and Regulation in the Postal and Delivery Sector* (Cheltenham, UK, and Northampton, MA: Edward Elgar).

Crew, M. A. and Kleindoerfer, P. R. (2008b), 'Regulation and the USO under entry', in Crew, M. A and Kleindorfer, P.R. (eds), *Competition and Regulation in the Postal and Delivery Sector* (Cheltenham, UK, and Northampton, MA: Edward Elgar), pp. 3–17.

Crew, M. A. and Kleindoerfer, P. R. (eds) (2012), *Multi-modal Competition and the Future of Mail* (Cheltenham, UK, and Northampton, MA: Edward Elgar).

Crew, M. A. and Kleindoerfer, P. R. (2013a), 'Privatization of Postal Operators: old arguments and new realities', in Crew, M. A. and Kleindoerfer, P. R. (eds), *Reforming the Postal Sector in the Face of Electronic Competition* (Cheltenham, UK, and Northampton, MA: Edward Elgar), pp. 1–19.

Crew, M. A. and Kleindoerfer, P. R. (eds) (2013b), *Reforming the Postal Sector in the Face of Electronic Competition* (Cheltenham, UK, and Northampton, MA: Edward Elgar).

Croley, S. (2008), *Regulation and public interests. The possibility of good regulatory governance* (Princeton: Princeton University Press).

Crouch, C. (1986), 'Sharing Public Space: states and organized interests in Western Europe', in Hall, J. A. (ed.) *States in History* (Oxford, New York: Basil Blackwell), pp. 176–210.

Crouch, C. (1999), 'Employment, Industrial Relations and Social Policy: New life in an old connection', *Social Policy & Administration*, 437–57.

Crouch, C. (2005), *Capitalist Diversity and Change: Recombinant Governance and Institutional Entrepreneurs* (Oxford: Oxford University Press).

Crouch, C. (2006), 'Neo-corporatism and Democracy', in Crouch, C. and Streeck, W. (eds), *The Diversity of Democracy. Corporatism, Social Order and Political Conflict* (Cheltenham, UK, and Northampton, MA: Edward Elgar), pp. 46–79.

Crouch, C. (2009), 'Typologies of Capitalism', in Hancké, B. (ed.), *Debating Varieties of Capitalism. A Reader* (Oxford: Oxford University Press), pp. 75–94.

Crouch, C., Le Galès, P., Trigilia, C. et al. (eds) (2001), *Local Production Systems in Europe: Rise or Demise?* (Oxford: Oxford University Press).

Crouch, C., Le Galès, P., Trigilia, C.et al. (eds) (2004), *Changing Governance of Local Economies: Responses of European Local Production Systems* (Oxford: Oxford University Press).

Crouch, C. and Streeck, W. (1997), *Political Economy of Modern Capitalism: Mapping Convergence and Diversity* (London: Sage).

Crouch, C. and Streeck, W. (eds) (2006), *The Diversity of Democracy.*

Corporatism, Social Order and Political Conflict (Cheltenham, UK, and Northampton, MA: Edward Elgar).

CWU (1997), *Communication Workers Union Submission to the DTI on the Future of the Post Office* (London: Communication Workers Union).

CWU (1998), *CWU's Further Submission to the Government Review of the Post Office* (London: Communication Workers Union).

CWU (1999), *CWU & CMA. Third Submission to the Government Review of the Post Office* (London: Communication Workers Union).

CWU (2000), 'Royal Mail Pay Award. Final Agreement on the Improved Pay Restructuring/ Way Forward', *Communication Workers Union* (21 January).

CWU (2002), 'Sawyer ... Year On', *Voice* (September).

CWU (2004), 'National Agreement on Pay and Major Change between Royal Mail & Communication Workers Union', *CWU Special Issue* (January).

CWU (2008a), *Submission to Government Review of Postal Liberalisation* (London: Communication Workers Union).

CWU (2008b), *Submission to Government Review of Postal Liberalisation. Part 2* (London: Communication Workers Union).

CWU (2009), *CWU Response to the Hooper Review* (London: Communication Workers Union).

CWU (2010a), *Business Transformation 2010 and Beyond. A National Agreement Between Royal Mail & the Communication Workers' Union* (London: Communication Workers Union).

CWU (2010b), *National Industrial Relations Framework Agreement* (London: Communication Workers Union).

CWU (2012), *National Agreement between Post Office, Royal Mail Group and Communications Workers' Union in Respect of the 'Separation' of Post Office from RMG and the Resultant TUPE of Employees* (London: Communication Workers Union).

CWU (2013), 'Fight Goes on Over Unfair Competition', *Communication Workers' Union News Archive* (28 June).

Darlington, R. (1993), 'The Challenge to Workplace Unionism in the Royal Mail', *Employee Relations*, 15:5, 3–25.

Darrigrand, A. (2002), 'Modernisation du service public: l'exemple des PTT en 1990 – Leçons d'une réforme', *Politiques et management public*, 20:4, 135–45.

Daunton, M. J. (1985), *Royal Mail. The Post Office since 1840* (London: Athlone Press).

de Rothschild, A. (1984), *Histoire de* La Poste *aux Lettres et du Timbre-Poste. Depuis leurs origines jusqu'à nos jours* (Genève, Paris: Editions Slatkine).

Deeg, R. and Jackson, G. (2007), 'Towards a more Dynamic Theory of Capitalist Variety', *Socio-Economic Review*, 5:1, 149–79.

Delfau, G. (1999), La Poste, *un service public en danger. Constats et propositions* (Paris: L'Harmattan).

Department of Trade and Industry (1994), *The Future of Postal Services* (London: HMSO Cm 2614, June).

Department of Trade and Industry (1998), *A Fair Deal for Consumers – Modernizing the Framework for Utility Regulation* (London: HMSO).

Department of Trade and Industry (1999), *Post Office Reform: a World Class Service for the 21st Century*. White Paper (London: HMSO).

Department of Trade and Industry (2001a), *Social and Environmental Guidance to the Postal Services Commission Issued under Section 43(2) of the Postal Services Act 2000* (London: HMSO).

Department of Trade and Industry (2001b), *Telecommunications Liberalisation in the UK* (London: HMSO).

Deutsche Post DHL (2013), *Interim Report – January to September 2013* (Bonn: Deutsche Post DHL).

Deutsche Telekom (2014), *Anatomie der Digitalen Zukunft. Das Geschäftsjahr 2013* (Bonn: Deutsche Telekom AG).

Dickie, M. (2012), 'Japan Scraps Postal Privatisation Plans', *Financial Times* (27 April).

Dieke, K. and Wojtek, R. (2008), 'Competition, Wages and Politics in the Delivery Sector: The Case of Postal Minimum Wages in Germany', in Crew, M. A., Kleindorfer, P. R. and Campbell, J. I. (eds), *Handbook of Worldwide Postal Reform* (Cheltenham, UK, and Northampton, MA: Edward Elgar), pp. 282–97.

Dixit, A. K. (1996), *The Making of Economic Policy: a Transaction-cost Politics Perspective* (Cambridge, MA: MIT Press).

Dnes, A. (1997), 'The Future of the British Post Office', *European Journal of Law and Economics*, 4:1, 93–102.

Döhler, M. (2001), 'Institutional Choice and Bureaucratic Autonomy in Germany', *West European Politics*, 25:1, 101–24.

Dörr, M. (1994), *Die Privatisierung der Deutschen Bundespost: Postreform I und II aus verfassungsrechtlicher Sicht* (Würzburg: Julius-Maximilians-Universität Würzburg).

DPWN (1999), *Annual Report 1998. Growth in Global Markets* (Bonn: Deutsche Post World Net).

DPWN (2001), *Annual Report 2000* (Bonn: Deutsche Post World Net).

DPWN (2003), *Company report 2002. Solutions tailored to our customers' needs* (Bonn: Deutsche Post World Net).

Dreyfus, M. (1995), *Histoire de la CGT* (Paris: Éditions Complexe).

Dudley, P., Agar, S., Mautino, L. et al. (2009), 'Competition Through Downstream Access in the UK Postal Sector: the first four years', in Crew, M. A. and Kleindorfer, P. R. (eds), *Progress in the Competitive Agenda in the Postal and Delivery Sector* (Cheltenham, UK, and Northampton, MA: Edward Elgar), pp. 52–66.

Duesterberg, T. J. (2000), 'The Post Office and the Digital Switch: Observations on an Outmoded Industry', in Hudgins, E. L. (ed.). *Mail @ the Millennium. Will the Postal Service Go Private?* (Washington: CATO Institute), pp. 135–48.

Dyson, K. (1983), 'The Cultural, Ideological and Structural Context', in Dyson, K. and Wilks, S. (eds), *Industrial Crisis: A Comparative Study of the State and Industry* (New York: St. Martin's Press), pp. 26–66.

Eberlein, B. (2001), 'To Regulate or not to Regulate Electricity. Explaining the German Sonderweg in the EU Context', *Journal of Network Industries*, 2:3, 353–84.

Eberlein, B. (2008), 'The Making of the European Energy Market: The Interplay of Governance and Government', *Journal of Public Policy*, 28:1, 73–92.

Eberlein, B. (2012), 'Inching Towards a Common Energy Policy: Entrepreneurship, Incrementalism, and Windows of Opportunity', in Richardson, J. (ed.), *Constructing a Policy-Making State? Policy Dynamics in the EU* (Oxford: Oxford University Press), pp. 147–69.

Eccles, R. (2008), 'United Kingdom Postal Services Regulation', in Crew, M. A., Kleindorfer, P. R. and Campbell Jr., J. I. (eds), *Handbook of Worldwide Postal Reform* (Cheltenham, UK, and Northampton, MA: Edward Elgar), pp. 341–54.

Eccles, R. (2011), 'State Funding and Cost Sharing of the USO under the 2008 EU Postal Services Directive', in Crew, M. A. and Kleindorfer, P. R. (eds), *Reinventing the Postal Sector in an Electronic Age* (Cheltenham, UK, and Northampton, MA: Edward Elgar), pp. 152–62.

Eccles, R. (2013), 'The UK Postal Services Act 2011', in Crew, M. A. and Kleindorfer, P. R. (eds), *Reforming the Postal Sector in the Face of Electronic Competition* (Cheltenham, UK, and Northampton, MA: Edward Elgar), pp. 20–35.

Eckert, S. (2009), 'Postal Reform Around The Globe: Comparing the Asian and European experience', *Policy and Society*, 27:3, 261–72.

Eckert, S. (2010), 'Between Commitment and Control: Varieties of Delegation in the European Postal Sector', *Journal of European Public Policy* 17:8, 1231–52.

Economic Reconstruction Group (1977), *Final Report of the Nationalised Industry Policy Group chaired by the Hon. Nicholas Ridley* (London: The Conservative Research Department).

The Economist (2009), 'Logistics in China. Return to Sender: A New Law Restores State Control to Yet Another Area of China's Economy' (30 April).

ECORYS (2005), *Development of Competition in the European Postal Sector. Study for European Commission Internal Market DG. Annex II Country information sheets* (Rotterdam: ECORYS Research and Consulting).

ECORYS (2008), *Main Developments in the Postal Sector (2006–2008). Final Report for the European Commission, DG Internal Market and Services* (Rotterdam: ECORYS Nederland BV).

Egan, M. (2010), 'The Single Market', in Cini, M. (ed.), *European Union Politics* (Oxford: Oxford University Press), pp. 258–74.

Eikeland, P. O. (2011), 'The Third Internal Energy Market Package: New Power Relations among Member States, EU Institutions and Non-state Actors?', *Journal of Common Market Studies*, 49:2, 243–63.

Eising, R. (2002), 'Policy Learning in Embedded Negotiations: explaining EU electricity liberalization', *International Organization*, 56:1, 85–120.

Eising, R. and Jabko, N. (2001), 'Moving Targets: national interests and EU electricity liberalization', *Comparative Political Studies*, 34:7, 742–67.

Elsenbast, W. and Smit, H. (2000), *Gesamtwirtschaftliche Auswirkungen der Marktöffnung auf dem deutschen Postmarkt. Studie im Auftrag des Bundesministeriums für Wirtschaft und Technologie* Wissenschaftliches Institut für Kommunikationsdienste. Diskussionsbeitrag (Bad Honnef: Wissenschaftliches Institut für Kommunikationsdienste).

EP (2007), 'Postal Services: open to competition by 2011, but subject to safeguards', *Europarl.europa.eu press release* (11 July).

EP (2008), 'Postal Services Liberalisation: MEPs back market opening by 2011', *Europarl.europa.eu press release* (31 January).

EP (2014), 'Ensure Open Access for Internet Service Suppliers and ban Roaming Fees, say MEPs', *Europarl.europa.eu press release* (3 April).

Epstein, D. and O'Halloran, S. (1999), *Delegating Powers. A Transaction Cost Politics Approach to Policy Making under Separate Powers* (Cambridge: Cambridge University Press).

Epstein, G. A. (ed.) (2005), *Financialization and the World Economy* (Cheltenham, UK, and Northampton, MA: Edward Elgar).

Estrosi, C. (2009), 'Pour la Poste, le statu quo serait mortel', *Press Release no 856 Ministry of Economicy, Industry and Employment* (6 October).

EurActiv (2009), 'Telecoms Package Passes Final Hurdle' (25 November).

European Commission (1995), *European Parliament Committee Economic and Monetary Affairs and Industrial Policy. 5 January 1995 hearing with Commissioner-designate Mr. Martin Bangemann. Summary record. SP (95) 82* (Luxembourg: Office for Official Publications of the European Communities).

European Commission (1996), *Communication from the Commission. Services of General Interest in Europe.* COM (96) 443 final (Luxembourg: Office for Official Publications of the European Communities).

European Commission (1997), *Effects on Employment of the Liberalization on the Telecommunications sector* (Luxembourg: Office for Official Publications of the European Communities).

European Commission (1999), *Towards a New Framework for Electronic Communication Infrastructure and Associated Services: The 1999 Tele-communications Review*, COM (1999) 539 (Luxembourg: Office for Official Publications of the European Communities).

European Commission (2000), *Communication from the Commission. Services of General Interest in Europe.* COM (2000) 580 (Luxembourg: Office for Official Publications of the European Communities).

European Commission (2002), *Report from the Commission to the European Parliament and the Council on the application of the Postal Directive* (97/67/EC Directive). COM (2002) 632 final (Luxembourg: Office for Official Publications of the European Communities).

European Commission (2003), *Green Paper on Services of General Interest in Europe.* COM (2003) 270 (Luxembourg: Office for Official Publications of the European Communities).

European Commission (2004), *White Paper on Services of General Interest in Europe.* COM (2004) 374 (Luxembourg: Office for Official Publications of the European Communities).

European Commission (2011a), *Communication from the Commission. A Quality Framework for Services of General Interest in Europe.* COM (2011) 900 final (Luxembourg: Office for Official Publications of the European Communities).

European Commission (2011b), *Communication. Universal Service in e-Communications: Report on the Outcome of the Public Consultation and the Third Periodic Review of the Scope in Accordance with Article 15 of Directive 2002/22/EC*. COM (2011) 795 final (Luxembourg: Office for Official Publications of the European Communities).

European Commission (2012a), *Communication from the Commission on the Application of the European Union State Aid Rules to Compensation Granted for the Provision of Services of General Economic Interest* (2012/C 8/02) (Luxembourg: Office for Official Publications of the European Communities).

European Commission (2012b), *Communication from the Commission. European Union framework for State Aid in the Form of Public Service Compensation* (2012/C 8/03) (Luxembourg: Office for Official Publications of the European Communities).

European Commission (2012c), *Communication from the Commission. Making the Internal Energy Market Work. Country Report France* (Luxembourg: Office for Official Publications of the European Communities).

European Commission (2012d), *Communication from the Commission. Making the Internal Energy Market Work. Country Report Germany* (Luxembourg: Office for Official Publications of the European Communities).

European Commission (2013), *Communication on the Telecommunications Single Market*. COM (2013) 634 final (Brussels: Commission of the European Communities).

European Commission (2014a), *Communication. A Policy Framework for Climate and Energy in the Period from 2020 to 2030*. COM (2014) 15 final (Luxembourg: Office for Official Publications of the European Communities).

European Commission (2014b), *Communication. Energy Prices and Costs in Europe*. COM (2014) 21 (Luxembourg: Office for Official Publications of the European Communities).

European Social Dialogue Committee for the Postal Sector (2007), *Final Report of the Social Observatory of the Postal Sector Project* (Brussels).

Eurostat (2008), *EU Postal Survey* (Brussels: European Communities).

Eurostat (2012), *Postal Service Statistics – Universal Service Providers. Main Figures* (Luxembourg: Publications Office of the European Union).

Faucher-King, F., Le Galès, P. and Elliott, G. (2010), *New Labour Experiment: Change and Reform under Blair and Brown* (Palo Alto, CA: Stanford University Press).

FAZ (1996), 'Postgewerkschaft befürchtet Stellenabbau', *Frankfurter Allgemeine Zeitung* (8 May).

FAZ (1997), 'Schalter zu: Postler-Protest gegen Bonn', *Frankfurter Allgemeine Zeitung* (16 February).

FAZ (2001), 'Briefmonopol wird verlängert', *Frankfurter Allgemeine Zeitung* (9 February).

FAZ (2004), 'Unionsländer wollen Briefmonopol kippen', *Frankfurter Allgemeine Zeitung* (13 December).

FAZ (2005), 'Kein vorzeitiges Ende des Briefmonopols', *Frankfurter Allgemeine Zeitung* (18 February).

FAZ (2007a), 'Studie über Löhne im Briefmarkt. Kein flächendeckendes Lohn-Dumping', *Frankfurter Allgemeine Zeitung* (21 May).

FAZ (2007b), 'Wirtschaftsministerium gegen Post-Mindestlohn', *Frankfurter Allgemeine Zeitung* (8 September).

FAZ (2007c), 'Zumwinkels Gedankenspiele. Spekulationen um Samstagszustellung der Post', *Frankfurter Allgemeine Zeitung* (9 March).

FAZ (2008), 'Streit um Mindestlohn. Verdi half angeblich Postverband', *Frankfurter Allgemeine Zeitung* (7 April).

Federal Audit Court (2004), *Bemerkungen 2004 zur Haushalts- und Wirtschaftsführung des Bundes* (Bonn: Bundesrechnungshof).

Federal Ministry of Economics and Technology (2002), *Das Postwesen im Umbruch – Ziele und Perspektiven der deutschen Postpolitik* (Berlin: Bundesministerium für Wirtschaft und Technologie).

Federal Ministry for Post and Telecommunications (1995), *Eckpunkte eines künftigen Regulierungsrahmens im Telekommunikationsbereich* (Bonn: Bundesministerium für Post und Telekommunikation).

Financial Times (2007), 'EU postal workers in liberalisation protests' (6 June).

Fioretos, O. (2011a), 'Capitalist Diversity in Open Economies', in Fioretos, O., *Creative Reconstructions: Multilateralism and European Varieties of Capitalism after 1950* (Ithaca and London: Cornell University Press), pp. 1–15.

Fioretos, O. (2011b), *Creative Reconstructions. Multilateralism and European Varieties of Capitalism after 1950* (Ithaca and London: Cornell University Press).

Flinders, M. and Buller, J. (2006), 'Depoliticisation: Principles, Tactics and Tools', *British Politics*, 1:3, 293–318.

Fokus (2010), 'Deutsche Post. Briefzustellung am Samstag in Gefahr' (12 June).

Foster, C. D. (1992a), 'The Dangers of Mixing Social with Economic Regulation', *Privatization, Public Ownership and the Regulation of Natural Monopoly* (Oxford and Cambridge, MA: Blackwell), pp. 291–332.

Foster, C. D. (1992b), *Privatization, Public Ownerhip and the Regulation of Natural Monopoly* (Oxford and Cambridge, MA: Blackwell).

Freeman, G. P. (1986), 'National Styles and Policy Sectors: Explaining Structured Variation', *Journal of Public Policy*, 5:4, 467–96.

Fried, N. (2007), 'Die Koalition und der Mindestlohn. Nach der Einigung ist vor dem Streit', *Sueddeutsche* (5 December).

Froelke, D. R. (2000), 'Labor Market Outcomes of Postal Reorganization', in Hudgins, E. L. (ed.) *Mail @ the Millennium. Will the Postal Sector Go Private?* (Washington: Cato Institute), pp. 75–101.

Gall, G. (2003), *The Meaning of Militancy? Postal Workers and Industrial Relations* (Aldershot, Burlington: Ashgate).

Gassner, K. (2001), 'Contrasts in Germany: Decentralised versus sector-specific regulation', in Henry, C., Matheu, M. and Jeunemaître, A. (eds), *Regulation of Network Utilities. The European Experience* (Oxford: Oxford University Press), pp. 230–52.

Geppert, M., Piepenbrock, H.-J., Schütz, R. et al. (eds) (2006), *Beck'scher TKG-Kommentar* (München: C.H. Beck).

Geradin, D. (ed.) (2002), *The Liberalization of Postal Services in the European Union* (The Hague and Dordrecht: Kluwer Law International).

Ghosh, R. (2000), 'Privatisation in Singapore: A Holistic View', in Ghosh, B. N. (ed.), *Privatisation: The ASEAN Connection* (Huntington, NY: Nova Science), pp. 207–31.

Gilardi, F. (2005), 'The Formal Independence of Regulators: A Comparison of 17 Countries and 7 Sectors', *Swiss Political Science Review*, 11:1, 139–67.

Glazer, A. (1989), 'Politics and the Choice of Durability', *American Economic Review*, 79:5, 1207–13.

Goldschmitt, W. (2007), 'Gelber Riese. Zahl der Postfilialen sinkt', *Frankfurter Rundschau* (10 January).

Goldstein, A. (1996), 'Privatisations et contrôle des entreprises en France', *Revue économique*, 47:6, 1309–32.

Goldthorpe, J. H. (ed.) (1984), *Order and Conflict in Contemporary Capitalism* (New York: Clarendon Press).

Gospel, H. and Edwards, T. (2012), 'Strategic transformation and muddling through: industrial relations and industrial training in the UK', *Journal of European Public Policy*, 19:8, 1229–48.

Grabitz, I. (2006), 'Post plant Umbau bei DHL', *Welt* (12 March).

Graham, A. (1997), 'The UK 1979–95: Myths and Realities of Conservative Capitalism', in Crouch, C. and Streeck, W. (eds), *Political Economy of Modern Capitalism. Mapping Convergence and Diversity* (London: Sage), pp. 117–32.

Gramlich, L. (1990), 'Öffentliche Unternehmungen im Verfassungsstaat des Grundgesetzes. Anmerkungen zur Privatisierungsdebatte', *Betriebs-Berater (BB). Zeitschrift für Recht und Wirtschaft*, 45:22, 1493–501 .

Gramlich, L. (1998), 'Ende gut, alles gut? – Anmerkungen zum neuen Postgesetz', *NJW*, 866–73.

Grande, E. (1989), *Vom Monopol zum Wettbewerb? Die neokonservative Reform der Telekommunikation in Großbritannien und der Bundesrepublik Deutschland* (Wiesbaden: Deutscher Universitätsverlag).

Granzow, A. (2009), 'Monika Wulf-Mathies. Die "rote" Cheflobbyistin', *Handelsblatt* (26 April).

Guardian (2013), 'Royal Mail Privatisation: The Coalition goes where Thatcher Feared to Tread. Business Minister Michael Fallon says it will happen by April 2014' (28 April).

Guislain, P. (ed.) (2004), *The Postal Sector in Developing and Transition Countries. Contributions to a Reform Agenda* (Washington: The World Bank Group. Global Information and Communication Technologies Department, Policy Division).

Gumbrell-McCormick, R. and Hyman, R. (2006), 'Embedded Collectivism? Workplace Representation in France and Germany', *Industrial Relations Journal*, 37:5, 473–91.

Guyomarch, A. (1999), '"Public Service", "Public Management" and the "Modernization" of French Public Administration', *Public Administration*, 77:1, 171–93.

Haber, H. (2010), 'Regulating-for-Welfare: A Comparative Study of "Regulatory Welfare Regimes" in the Israeli, British and Swedish Electricity Sectors', *Law & Policy*, no. doi: 10.1111/j.1467–9930.2010.00332.x.

Hall, P. A. (1986), *Governing the Economy: The Politics of State Intervention in Britain and France* (New York: Oxford University Press).

Hall, P. A. and Soskice, D. (2001a), 'An Introduction to Varieties of Capitalism', in Hall, P. A. and Soskice, D. (eds), *Varieties of Capitalism* (Oxford: Oxford University Press), pp. 1–68.

Hall, P. A. and Soskice, D. (eds) (2001b), *Varieties of Capitalism* (Oxford: Oxford University Press).

Hamburger Abendblatt (2005), 'Postbank kauft 850 Post-Filialen' (21 December).

Hancké, B. (2009), *Debating Varieties of Capitalism. A Reader* (Oxford: Oxford University Press).

Hancké, B., Rhodes, M. and Thatcher, M. (eds) (2007a), *Beyond Varieties of Capitalism. Conflict, Contradictions, and Complementarities in the European Economy* (Oxford: Oxford University Press).

Hancké, B., Rhodes, M. and Thatcher, M. (2007b), 'Introduction: Beyond Varieties of Capitalism', in Hancké, B., Rhodes, M. and Thatcher, M. (eds), *Beyond Varieties of Capitalism. Conflict, Contradictions, and Complementarities in the European Economy* (Oxford: Oxford University Press), pp. 3–38.

Hancké, B., Rhodes, M. and Thatcher, M. (2009), 'Beyond Varieties of Capitalism', in Hancké, B. (ed.) *Debating Varieties of Capitalism. A Reader* (Oxford: Oxford University Press), pp. 273–300.

Hassel, A. (2006), *Wage Setting, Social Pacts and the Euro. A New Role for the State?* (Amsterdam: Amsterdam University Press).

Hay, C. and Rosamond, B. (2002), 'Globalization, European integration and the discursive construction of economic imperatives', *Journal of European Public Policy*, 9:2, 147–67.

Hayward, J. (1986), *The State and the Market Economy. Industrial Patriotism and Economic Intervention in France* (Brighton: Harvester Press).

Hennemann, G. (2005), 'Mehr Filialen, kleineres Angebot', *Sueddeutsche Zeitung* (26 June).

Héritier, A. (1987), *Policy Analyse – Eine Einführung* (Frankfurt/ New York: Campus Verlag).

Héritier, A. (2001), 'Market Integration and Social Cohesion: the politics of public services in European regulation', *Journal of European Public Policy*, 8:5, 825–52.

Héritier, A. (2003), 'New Modes of Governance in Europe: Increasing Political Capacity and Policy Effectiveness?', in Börzel, T. A. and Cichowski, R. A. (eds), *The State of the European Union. Law, Politics, and Society* (Oxford: Oxford University Press), pp. 105–26.

Héritier, A. and Coen, D. (eds) (2005), *Refining Regulatory Regimes. Utilities in Europe* (Cheltenham, UK, and Northampton, MA: Edward Elgar).

Héritier, A., Kerwer, D., Knill, C. et al. (2001), *Differential Europe: The European Union Impact on National Policymaking* (Lanham: Rowman & Littlefield).

Héritier, A. and Lehmkuhl, D. (2008), 'The Shadow of Hierarchy and New Modes of Governance', *Journal of Public Policy*, 28:1, 1–17.

Héritier, A. and Schmidt, S. K. (2000), 'After Liberalization: Public Interest Services and Employment in the Utilities', in Scharpf, F. W. and Schmidt, V. A.

(eds), *Welfare and Work in the Open Economy. Volume II. Diverse Responses to Common Challenges* (Oxford: Oxford University Press), pp. 554–69.

Héritier, A. and Soriano, L. M. (2002), 'Differentiating and Linking Politics and Adjudication – The Example of European Electricity Policy', *European Law Journal*, 8:3, 363–83.

Hillyard, M. (2000), *Postal Services Bill (Bill 54 of 1999/2000)*, House of Commons Library Research Paper (London).

Hirst, N. (2014), 'Net Neutrality divides MEPs', *European Voice* (20 February).

HM Government (2010), *The Coalition: Our Programme for Government* (London: Cabinet Office).

HMSO (2011), *Postal Services Act* (London).

Hoffmann, A. and Schneider, J. (2007), 'Unionsfraktion blockiert Post-Mindestlohn "Politisches Gammelfleisch"', *Sueddeutsche* (18 September).

Hollingsworth, J. R. and Boyer, R. (eds) (1997), *Contemporary Capitalism: The Embeddedness of Institutions* (Cambridge: Cambridge University Press).

Hollingsworth, J. R., Schmitter, P. C. and Streeck, W. (eds) (1994a), *Governing Capitalist Economies. Performance and Control of Economic Sectors* (New York, Oxford: Oxford University Press).

Hollingsworth, J. R. and Streeck, W. (1994b), 'Countries and Sectors. Concluding Remarks on Performance, Convergence, and Competitiveness', in Hollingsworth, J. R., Schmitter, P. C. and Streeck, W. (eds), *Governing Capitalist Economies. Performance and Control of Economic Sectors* (New York, Oxford: Oxford University Press), pp. 270–300.

Hollingsworth, J. R., Schmitter, P. C. and Streeck, W. (1994c), 'Capitalism, Sectors, Institutions and Performance', in Hollingsworth, R. J., Schmitter, P. C. and Streeck, W. (eds), *Governing Capitalist Economies. Performance and Control of Economic Sectors* (New York, Oxford: Oxford University Press), pp. 3–16.

Hood, C. (2002), 'The Risk Game and the Blame Game', *Government and Opposition*, 37:1, 15–37.

Hooper, R. (2010), *Saving the Royal Mail's Universal Postal Service in the Digital Age. An Update of the 2008 Independent Review of the Postal Services Sector* (London: HMSO Cm 7973, September).

Hooper, R., Hutton, D. D. and Smith, I. R. (2008), *Modernise or Decline. Policies to Maintain the Universal Postal Service in the United Kingdom. An Independent Review of the UK Postal Services Sector* (London: HMSO Cm 7529, 16 December).

Horn, M. J. (1995), *The Political Economy of Public Administration: institutional choice in the public sector* (Cambridge: Cambridge University Press).

House of Commons (2005), *Public Accounts. Fourteenth Report: Energywatch and Postwatch* (London: House of Commons, Committee of Public Accounts).

Howell, C. (1992), *Regulating Labor. The State and Industrial Relations Reform in Postwar France* (Princeton: Princeton University Press).

Howell, C. (1998), 'Virtual Trade Unionism in France', in Chapman, H., Kesselman, M. and Schain, M. (eds), *A Century of Organized Labor in France: A Union Movement for the Twenty-first Century?* (New York: St. Martin's), pp. 205–12.

Howell, C. (2006), 'The State and the Recontruction of Industrial Relations Institutions after Fordism: Britain and France Compared', in Levy, J. D. (ed.) *The State after Statism* (Cambridge, MA and London: Harvard University Press), pp. 139–84.

Howell, C. (2009), 'The Transformation of French Industrial Relations: Labor Representation and the State in a Post-Dirigiste Era', *Politics & Society*, 37:2, 229–56.

Hudgins, E. L. (2000a), 'The Coming Revolution in Mail Delivery', in Hudgins, E. L. (ed.), *Mail @ the Millennium. Will the Postal Sector Go Private?* (Washington: Cato Institute), pp. 1–16.

Hudgins, E. L. (ed.) (2000b), *Mail @ the Millenium. Will the Postal Service Go Private?* (Washington: Cato Institute).

Hulverscheidt, C. (2007), 'SPD will Briefmonopol erhalten', *Sueddeutsche* (30 January).

Humphreys, P. and Padgett, S. (2006), 'Globalization, the European Union, and Domestic Governance in Telecoms and Electricity', *Governance: An International Journal of Policy, Administration, and Institutions*, 19:3, 383–406.

Hutter, B. M. (2001), *Regulation and Risk: Occupational Health and Safety on the Railways* (Oxford: Oxford University Press).

Ianni, J. B. (2008), 'Postal Reform in Developing Countries: Challenges and Choices', in Crew, M. A, Kleindorfer, P. R. and Campbell, J. I. (eds), *Handbook of Worldwide Postal Reform* (Cheltenham, UK, and Northampton, MA: Edward Elgar), pp. 400–15.

IDA (2006), *Public Consultation on Further Liberalisation of the Postal Services Sector in Singapore* (Singapore: Info-Communications Development Authority of Singapore).

IDA (2008), *Postal Competition Code 2008 and Postal Services Operation Code 2008* (Singapore: Info-Communications Development Authority of Singapore).

input consulting (2006), *Liberalisierung und Prekarisierung – Beschäftigungsbedingungen bei den neuen Briefdienstleistern in Deutschland* (Stuttgart: input consulting – Beratungsgesellschaft für Innovationstransfer Post & Telekommunikation).

Intergovernmental Committee Established by the Messina Conference (1956), *Rapport des chefs de délégation aux ministres des affaires étrangères* (Brussels: Secrétariat).

Interview (ARCEP), Autorité de Régulation des Communications Éléctroniques et des Postes, member of Executive Board and head of postal units, Paris (16 April 2007, 23 April 2008, 8 October 2010, 22 September 2011).

Interview (BIS), Department for Business Innovation & Skills, London (22 March 2013).

Interview (BKartA), Bundeskartellamt, unit dealing with postal sector, Bonn (1 March 2007).

Interview (BNetzA 1), Bundesnetzagentur, Bonn (2 March 2007).

Interview (BNetzA 2), Bundesnetzagentur, Bonn (27 May 2008).

Interview (CF), Consumer Focus, London (26 March 2013).

Interview (CFDT), French Democratic Confederation of Labour, Secretary General and Federal Secretary, Paris (17 April 2007).
Interview (CFTC), French Confederation of Christian Workers, President and National Secretary Postal Sector, Paris (18 April 2007).
Interview (CGT-PTT), National Confederation of Workers in the Postal and Telecommunications Sector, Paris (18 April 2007 and 11 October 2010).
Interview (Council), Council of the European Union, General Secretariat, administrator postal services, Brussels (25 and 26 October 2007).
Interview (CWU 1), Communications Workers Union, head of research department and policy adviser, London (26 March 2013).
Interview (CWU 2), Communications Workers Union, policy adviser, London (26 March 2013).
Interview (EP), European Parliament, rapporteur second and third postal directive, Brussels (18 December 2007).
Interview (FFPI), The Free and Fair Postal Initiative, secretary general, Brussels (25 October 2007).
Interview (FO-COM), Labour Force trade union for the Communications sector, member of La Poste's Administrative Council, Paris (23 April 2008).
Interview (MP 1), German Bundestag, deputee for the CDU 1990–2002, chief negotiator postal reforms, Offenbach (30 November 2007).
Interview (MP 2), German Bundestag, deputee for the SPD since 1994, spokesperson and rapporteur for postal policy, member of the Federal Network Agency Advisory Committee, Berlin (22 January 2008).
Interview (Ofcom), The Office of Communications, London (22 March 2013).
Interview (PostEurop), Association of European Public Postal Operators, secretary general and chairman of European affairs committee, Brussels (26 October 2007).
Interview (POSTRS), Postal Redress Scheme, London (25 March 2013).
Interview (SUD-PTT), Solidarity, Unity, Democracy trade union for posts and telecommunications, Federal Secretary, Paris (18 April 2007, 11 October 2010).
Interview (ver.di), United Trade Union for Services, vice president and spokesperson postal sector, Berlin (24 January).
ITA Consulting and WIK-Consult (2009a), *The Evolution of the European Postal Market since 1997* (Bad Honnef, Hamburg: Wissenschaftliches Institut für Infrastruktur und Kommunikationsdienste and Intelligence, Transactions and Advice Consulting GmbH).
ITA Consulting and WIK-Consult (2009b), *The Evolution of the European Postal Market since 1997. Annex: Country Fiches* (Bad Honnef, Hamburg: Wissenschaftliches Institut für Infrastruktur und Kommunikationsdienste and Intelligence, Transactions and Advice Consulting GmbH).
Iversen, T. (1999), *Contested Economic Institutions: The Politics of Macro-economics and Wage Bargaining in Advanced Economies* (Cambridge: Cambridge University Press).
Jabko, N. (2006), *Playing the Market. A Political Strategy for Uniting Europe* (Ithaca and London: Cornell University Press).
Jackson, G. and Deeg, R. (2012), 'The long-term Trajectories of Institutional

Change in European Capitalism', *Journal of European Public Policy*, 19:8, 1109–25.

Jamison, M. A. (2011), 'Liberalization and Regulation of Telecoms, Electricity, and Gas in the United States', in Finger, M. and Künneke, R. W. (eds), *International Handbook of Network Industries. The Liberalization of Infrastructure* (Cheltenham, UK, and Northampton, MA: Edward Elgar), pp. 366–83.

Jayasuriya, K. and Rosser, A. (2001), 'Economic Crisis and the Political Economy of Economic Liberalisation in South-East Asia', in Rodan, G. (ed.) *The Political Economy of South-East Asia. Conflicts, Crises and Change* (Oxford: Oxford University Press), pp. 233–58.

Jenkins, S. (2014), 'There was Only One Loser in this Royal Mail Privatisation: the taxpayer', *The Guardian* (1 April).

Jordana, J. (ed.) (2002), *Governing Telecommunications and the New Information Society in Europe* (Cheltenham, UK, and Northampton, MA: Edward Elgar).

Kanning, T. (2008), 'Schließungen. Post ohne Filialen', *Frankfurter Allgemeine Zeitung* (21 May).

Kantrowitz, J. (1978), 'L'influence américaine sur Force ouvrière: mythe ou réalité?', *Revue française de science politique*, 28:4, 717–39.

Katz, E. (2013), 'Senate Postal Reform Bill Delayed 'Indefinitely'', *Government Executive* (4 November).

Katz, E. (2014), 'Republicans, White House Finally Agree on Something: Postal Reform', *Government Executive* (8 April).

Katzenstein, P. J. (ed.) (1978a), *Between Power and Plenty: Foreign Economic Policies of Advanced Industrial States* (Madison: University of Wisconsin Press).

Katzenstein, P. J. (1978b), 'Conclusion: Domestic Structures and Strategies of Foreign Economic Policy', in Katzenstein, P. J. (ed.) *Between Power and Plenty: Foreign Economic Policies of Advanced Industrial States* (Madison: University of Wisconsin Press), pp. 295–336.

Kelemen, R. D. (2006), 'Suing for Europe: Adversarial Legalism and European Governance', *Comparative Political Studies*, 39:1, 101–27.

Keller, B. (2005), 'Union Formation through Merger: The Case of Ver.di in Germany', *British Journal of Industrial Relations*, 43:2, 209–32.

Kietzmann, M. and Stadler, R. (2001), 'Affäre. Klaus und die Detektive. Im Kampf um den Briefmarkt ließ der Chefjurist der Deutschen Post eine staatliche Behörde ausspionieren', *Focus* (30 July).

Knauth, P. and Dommermuth, F. (1996), *Reorganisation of the Postal Sector in Germany* in Stumpf, U. and Plum, M. (eds), Diffusion of New Regulatory Approaches in the Postal Sector. Papers presented at the 4th Königswinter Seminar. Königswinter, 23–25 October 1996 (Bad Honnef: Wissenschaftliches Institut für Kommunikationsdienste GmbH).

Knotts, M. (2014), 'No sell-off but Australia Post Delivery Reduction to be felt by City Dwellers', *The Sidney Morning Herald* (8 June).

Kranz, B. (2009), 'Sieben Hamburger Post-Filialen betroffen. Die Deutsche Post zieht ihr Sparprogramm durch: Bundesweit sollen bis 2011 alle 475 eigenen Postfilialen geschlossen werden.', *Hamburger Abendblatt* (15 August).

Krippner, G. R. (2005), 'The Financialization of the American Economy', *Socio-Economic Review*, 3:2, 173–208.

Kumar, D. K. (2014), 'Staples, USPS End Program to Set up Mini-Post Offices in Stores', *Reuters* (15 July).

Kushida, K. E. and Shimizu, K. (2013), 'Syncretism: the politics of Japan's financial reforms', *Socio-Economic Review*, 11:2, 337–69.

L'État et La Poste (2008), *Contrat de Service Public 2008–2012* (Paris: La Poste).

L'État et La Poste (2013), *Contrat d'Entreprise 2013–2017. Contrat relatif aux missions de service public confiées au Groupe* La Poste (Paris: La Poste).

La Banque Postale (2006), 'La Banque Postale défend le Livret A et les missions qui lui sont attachées', *Press Release* (13 December).

La Poste (1995), *Contrat de Plan entre l'Etat et* La Poste *1995–1997* (Paris: Groupe La Poste).

La Poste (1998), *Contrat d'objectifs et de progrès portant contrat de plan entre l'Etat et* La Poste *1998–2001* (Paris: Groupe La Poste).

La Poste (2003), *Performances et Convergences. Les engagements de* La Poste *et de l'État pour moderniser l'entreprise et conforter ses missions de service public. Le contrat de plan 2003–2007* (Paris: Groupe La Poste).

La Poste (2006), *Activity Report 2005* (Paris: Groupe La Poste).

La Poste (2008), *Performance et confiance* (Paris: La Poste).

La Poste (2011), *Rapport d'activité et de développement responsable 2010* (Paris: Groupe La Poste).

La Poste (2012), *Un projet pour l'emploi et les salaires. Communiqué de presse* (15 February).

La Poste (2013), *La Poste présente son projet stratégique 2013–2018. Dossier de Presse* (4 July).

Laborie, L. (2006), 'A Missing Link? Telecommunications Networks and European Integration, 1945–1970', in Van Der Vleuten, E. and Kaijser, A. (eds), *Networking Europe: Transnational Infrastructures and the Shaping of Europe, 1850–2000* (Sagamore Beach: Science History Publications), pp. 187–215.

Labour Party (1997), *General Election Manifesto* (London: Labour Party).

Lane, C. (2003), 'The Emergence of German Transnational Companies: A Theoretical Analysis and Empirical Study of the Globalization Process', in Morgan, G., Kristensen P. H. and Whitley, R. (eds), *The Multinational Firm. Organizing Across Institutional and National Divides* (Oxford: Oxford University Press), pp. 69–96.

Lange, P., Wallerstein, M. and Golden, M. (1995), 'The End of Corporatism? Wage Setting in the Nordic and Germanic Countries', in Jacoby, S. M. (ed.) *The Workers of Nations. Industrial Relations in a Global Economy* (Oxford: Oxford University Press), pp. 76–100.

Larcher, G. (1999), *Les principales évolutions de* La Poste *et du secteur postal au cours des vingt derniers mois (novembre 1997–juin 1999). Rapport d'information* (Paris: Le Sénat).

Larcher, G. (2003), La Poste*: le temps de la dernière chance. Rapport d'information n°344 (2002–2003)* (Paris: Le Sénat).

Lash, S. (1985), 'The End of Neo-corporatism?: The Breakdown of Centralised Bargaining in Sweden', *British Journal of Industrial Relations*, 23:2, 215–39.

Lash, S. and Urry, J. (1987), *The End of Organized Capitalism* (Cambridge: Polity Press).

Lawson, N. (2009), *Modernisation by Consent. A Royal Mail for Everyone* (London: Compass. Direction for the Democratic Left).

Le Figaro (2008), 'La Poste: grève nationale mardi' (22 September).

Le Galès, P. (2004), 'Contrôle et surveillance, la restructuration de l'État en Grande-Bretagne', in P. Lascoumes and P. Le Galès (eds), *Gouverner par les instruments* (Paris: Presses de Sciences Po), pp. 237–72.

Le Monde (2005), 'Le meilleur pour la France?' (7 September).

Le Monde (2006), '15 à 30 % de postiers en grève contre la libéralisation prévue en 2009' (14 November).

Le Monde (2007), 'Journée d'action européenne contre la libéralisation des services postaux' (6 June).

Le Monde (2008a), '49% des Français opposés au projet' (25 September).

Le Monde (2008b), 'Cacophonie à droite sur la réforme de La Poste' (2 November).

Le Monde (2008c), 'Changement de statut de La Poste: la CGT entend 'créer les conditions pour que le projet ne voie jamais le jour'' (8 July).

Le Monde (2008d), 'L'idée d'un référendum sur La Poste fait débat' (13 September).

Le Monde (2008e), 'La Poste: "2 millions" de personnes ont participé à la votation citoyenne' (5 October).

Le Monde (2008f), 'La Poste veut changer de statut pour devenir une société anonyme' (4 July).

Le Monde (2008g), 'Les syndicats de La Poste appellent à la grève contre la privatisation' (2 September).

Le Monde (2008h), 'Quand La Poste rassemble la gauche' (8 October).

Le Monde (2009a), 'La Poste plaide pour ouvrir son capital en 2011' (7 September).

Le Monde (2009b), 'La réforme du statut de La Poste est reportée' (5 May).

Le Monde (2009c), 'Les syndicats menacent d'une nouvelle mobilisation' (2 February).

Le Point (2012), 'Pupunat, cofondateur du Parti de Gauche, se met "en congé" de cette formation' (21 August).

Lehmbruch, G. (1989), 'Marktreformstrategien bei alternierender Parteiregierung: Eine vergleichende institutionelle Analyse', in Ellwein, T., Hesse, J. J., Mayntz, R. et al. (eds), *Jahrbuch zur Staats- und Verwaltungswissenschaft* (Baden-Baden: Nomos), pp. 15–45.

Leisering, L. (ed.) (2011a), *The New Regulatory State: Regulating Pensions in Germany and the UK* (Basingstoke: Palgrave Macmillan).

Leisering, L. (2011b), 'Transformations of the State: Comparing the New Regulatory State to the Post-War Provider State', in Leisering, L. (ed.) *The New Regulatory State: Regulating Pensions in Germany and the UK* (Basingstoke: Palgrave Macmillan), pp. 254–74.

Leisering, L. and Mabbett, D. (2011), 'Towards a New Regulatory State in Old-Age Security? Exploring the Issues', in Leisering, L. (ed.), *The New*

Regulatory State: Regulating Pensions in Germany and the UK (Basingstoke: Palgrave Macmillan), pp. 1–28.

Leonard, D. (2013), 'The Unstoppable Postal-Service Retreat Starts in Canada', *Bloomberg Businessweek* (11 December).

Les Echos (2006), 'La Poste: trop d'Europe pourrait tuer l'Europe!' (10 November).

Leuffen, D., Rittberger, B. and Schimmelfennig, F. (2013), 'The Single Market', *Differentiated Integration. Explaining Variation in the European Union* (Basingstoke: Palgrave Macmillan), pp. 111–41.

Levi-Faur, D. (1999), 'The Governance of International Telecommunications Competition: Cross-International Study of International Policy Regimes', *Competition and Change*, 4:1, 1–28.

Levi-Faur, D. (2005), 'The Global Diffusion of Regulatory Capitalism', *The Annals of the American Academy of Political and Social Science*, 598:1, 12–32.

Levi-Faur, D. (2006a), 'Varieties of Regulatory Capitalism: Getting the Most Out of the Comparative Method', *Governance*, 19:3, 367–82.

Levi-Faur, D. (2006b), 'Varieties of Regulatory Capitalism: Sectors and Nations in the Making of a New Global Order', *Governance*, 19:3, 363–6.

Levi-Faur, D. (2011), 'Regulation and regulatory governance', in Levi-Faur, D. (ed.), *Handbook on the Politics of Regulation* (Cheltenham, UK, and Northampton, MA: Edward Elgar), pp. 3–21.

Levi-Faur, D. (2013), 'The Welfare State: A Regulatory Perspective', *Jerusalem Papers in Regulation & Governance*, 55 (August).

Levi-Faur, D. and Jordana, J. (2005), 'Globalizing Regulatory Capitalism', *The Annals of the American Academy of Political and Social Science* 598:1, 6–9.

Levy, D. M. and Field, M. D. (2011), 'The United States postal service business model: lessons from the American railroad industry?', in Crew, M. A. and Kleindorfer, P. R. (eds), *Reinventing the Postal Sector in an Electronic Age* (Cheltenham, UK, and Northampton, MA: Edward Elgar), pp. 306–218.

Levy, J. (2005), 'Redeploying the State: Liberalization and Social Policy in France', in Streeck, W. and Thelen, K. (eds), *Beyond Continuity. Institutional Change in Advanced Political Economies* (Oxford: Oxford University Press), pp. 103–27.

Levy, J. (2006), *The State after Statism* (Cambridge, MA and London: Harvard University Press).

Levy, J. D. (2002), 'France. Directing Adjustment?', in Scharpf, F. W. and Schmidt, V. A. (eds), *Welfare and Work in the Open Economy* (Oxford: Oxford University Press), pp. 308–50.

Levy, J. D. (2008), 'From the Dirigiste State to the Social Anaesthesia State: French Economic Policy in the Longue Durée', *Modern & Contemporary France*, 16:4, 417–35.

Lijphart, A. and Crepaz, M. M. L. (1991), 'Corporatism and Consensus Democracy in Eighteen Countries: Conceptual and Empirical Linkages', *British Journal of Political Science*, 21:2, 235–46.

Lodge, M. (2008), 'Regulation, the Regulatory State and European Politics', *West European Politics*, 31:1, 280–301.

Lodge, M., Cave, M. and Baldwin, R. (2012), *Oxford Handbook of Regulation* (Oxford: Oxford University Press).

London Economics (1994), *The Future of Postal Services: a Critique of the Government's Green Paper* (London: London Economics).

Lord Sawyer, I. Borkett and N. Underhill (2001), 'Independent Review of Industrial Relations between Royal Mail and the Communication Workers Union' (London, unpublished).

Lowi, T. (1964), 'American Business, Public Policy, Case-Studies, and Political Theory', *World Politics*, 16:4, 677–715.

Lütz, S. (2004), 'Convergence Within National Diversity – the Regulatory State in Finance', *Journal of Public Policy*, 24:2, 169–97.

Lumio, M. and Fickinger, S. (2007), *Postal Services in Europe* (Luxembourg: Publications Office of the Europan Union).

Mabbett, D. (2011), 'The Regulatory Rescue of the Welfare State', in Levi-Faur, D. (ed.), *Handbook on the Politics of Regulation* (Cheltenham, UK, and Northampton, MA: Edward Elgar), pp. 215–26.

Mabbett, D. and Schelkle, W. (2007), 'Bringing Macroeconomics Back into the Political Economy of Reform: the Lisbon Agenda and the 'Fiscal Philosophy' of EMU', *Journal of Common Market Studies*, 45:1, 81–103.

Machatschke, M. (2003), 'Der temperierte Manager', *Manager Magazin* (December).

MacIntyre, D. (2000), *Mandelson and the Making of New Labour* (London: HarperCollins).

Maclachlan, P. L. (2004), 'Post Office Politics in Modern Japan: The Postmasters, Iron Trangles, and the Limits of Reform', *Journal of Japanese Studies*, 30:2, 281–313.

Maclachlan, P. L. (2006), 'Storming the Castle: The Battle for Postal Reform in Japan', *Social Science Japan Journal*, 9:1, 1–18.

Mahoney, J. and Thelen, K. (2010), 'A Theory of Gradual Institutional Change', in Mahoney, J. and Thelen, K. (eds), *Explaining Institutional Change. Ambiguity, Agency and Power* (Cambridge: Cambridge University Press), pp. 1–37.

Mai, C. (2007), 'Deutschland führt Europa: Der Kampf um die Postdienste. Testfall für den Wettbewerb', *Financial Times Deutschland* (5 January).

Majone, G. (1993), 'The European Community Between Social Policy and Social Regulation', *Journal of Common Market Studies*, 31:2, 153–70.

Majone, G. (1994), 'The Rise of the Regulatory State in Europe', *West European Politics*, 17:3, 77–101.

Majone, G. (1996a), *Regulating Europe* (London and New York: Routledge).

Majone, G. (1996b), 'Regulation and its Modes', in Majone, G. (ed.), *Regulating Europe* (London: Routledge), pp. 9–27.

Majone, G. (1997), 'From the Positive to the Regulatory State: Causes and Consequences of Changes in the Mode of Governance', *Journal of Public Policy*, 17:2, 139–67.

Majone, G. (2001), 'Two Logics of Delegation: Agency and Fiduciary Relations in EU Governance', *European Union Politics*, 2:1, 103–22.

Martimort, D. (1999), 'The Life Cycle of Regulatory Agencies: Dynamic Capture and Transaction Cost', *The Review of Economic Studies*, 66:4, 920–47.

Maruyama, S. (2006), 'Competition Structure and Future Postal Reform in

Japan: In Comparison with International Liberalisation', in Crew, M. A. and Kleindorfer, P. R. (eds), *Progress toward Liberalization of the Postal and Delivery Sector* (New York: Springer), pp. 369–84.

Maruyama, S. and Sano, S. (2008), 'The diverse characteristics of postal reforms in Asia: privatization, corporatization and liberalization', in Crew, M. A., Kleindorfer, P. R. and Campbell Jr, J. I. (eds), *Handbook of Worldwide Postal Reform* (Cheltenham, UK, and Northampton, MA: Edward Elgar), pp. 355–72.

Matláry, J. H. (1997), *Energy Policy in the European Union* (Basingstoke: Macmillan Press).

Mayntz, R. (2005), 'Governance Theory als Fortentwicklung der Steuerungstheorie?', in Schuppert, G. F. (ed.), *Governance-Forschung. Vergewisserung über Stand und Entwicklungslinien* (Baden-Baden: Nomos), pp. 11–20.

McCubbins, M., Noll, R. and Weingast, B. (1987), 'Administrative Procedures as Instruments Of Political Control', *Journal of Law, Economics & Organization*, 3:2, 243–77.

McCubbins, M. D. and Schwartz, T. (1984), 'Congressional Oversight Overlooked: Police Patrols and Fire Alarm', *American Journal of Political Science*, 28:1, 165–79.

McGowan, F. (2002), 'British Postal Reform in the context of European Changes – Lagging Behind, Catching Up or leading the Way?', in Geradin, D. (ed.), *The Liberalization of Postal Services in the European Union* (The Hague and Dordrecht: Kluwer Law International), pp. 333–52.

McKinsey & Company (2012), 'Leading in the 21st cenury: An interview with Moya Greene' (September).

Meck, G. (2007), 'Die hohe Kunst des Lobbying', *Frankfurter Allgemeine Zeitung* (30 August).

Meck, G. and Siedenbiedel, C. (2007), 'Deutsche Post. Die Entzauberung des Klaus Zumwinkel', *Frankfurter Allgemeine Zeitung* (23 September).

Melloan, G. (2010), 'Killing Postal Reform Won't Help Japan. The Hatoyama Government is Cloaking Fiscal Profligacy in Populist Cant', *Wall Street Journal* (28 March).

Melody, W. H. (2011), 'Liberalization in the Telecom Sector', in Finger, M. and Künneke, R. W. (eds), *International Handbook of Network Industries. The Liberalization of Infrastructure* (Cheltenham, UK, and Northampton, MA: Edward Elgar), pp. 103–22.

Menz, G. (2005), *Varieties of Capitalism and Europeanization. National Response Strategies to the Single European Market* (Oxford: Oxford University Press).

Michel, A. (2005), 'Une banque est née: La Poste', *Le Monde* (1 December).

Michel, A. (2007), 'Pour apaiser le climat social, La Poste engage des négociations salariales anticipées', *Le Monde* (23 January).

Michel, A. (2008a), 'La Poste veut changer de statut pour devenir une société anonyme', *Le Monde* (4 July).

Michel, A. (2008b), 'Pour la première fois, La Poste va verser un dividende à l'État', *Le Monde* (27 March).

Michel, A. (2009), 'Les syndicats de La Poste font entendre leur colère avant une réforme à risque', *Le Monde* (22 September).

Michel, A. (2013a), 'Jean-Paul Bailly va quitter La Poste prématurément', *Le Monde* (3 July).

Michel, A. (2013b), 'M. Wahl pourrait être nommé PDG de La Poste le 25 septembre', *Le Monde* (5 September).

Milward, R. (2011), 'The institutional economic history of infrastructure industries, 1830–1990: iedology, technology, geopolitics?', in Finger, M. and Künneke, R. W. (eds), *International Handbook of Network Industries. The Liberalization of Infrastructure* (Cheltenham, UK, and Northampton, MA: Edward Elgar), pp. 87–99.

Ministère de la Fonction Publique et des Réformes Administratives (1990), 'Circulaire du 23 Février 1989 Relative au Renouveau du Service Public [The Circular of 23 February 1989 concerning the Renewal of the Public Service]', *Renouveau du Service Public: Sélections des Textes Officiels [Public Service Renewal: Selection of Official Documents]* (Paris: Journaux Officiels), pp. 3–18.

Moe, T. M. (1990), 'Political Institutions. The Neglected Side of the Story', *Journal of Law, Economics and Organization*, 6:Special Issue, 213–53.

Moe, T. M. (1995), 'The Politics of Structural Choice: Toward a Theory of Public Bureaucracy', in Williamson, O. E. (ed.), *Organization Theory: from Chester Barnard to the Present and Beyond* (Oxford: Oxford University Press), pp. 116–53.

Monopolies and Mergers Commission (1980), *The Inner London Letter Post. A Report on the Letter Post Service in the Area comprising the Numbered London Postal Districts* in HMSO (ed.) (London).

Monopolies and Mergers Commission (1984), *The Post Office Letter Post Service. A Report on the Letter Post Service of the Post Office in the Head Post Office areas of Glasgow, Belfast and Cardiff and in the numbered London Postal Districts* (London: HMSO).

Morgan, G., Whitley, R. and Moen, E. (eds) (2005), *Changing Capitalisms? Internationalization, Institutional Change, and Systems of Economic Organization* (Oxford: Oxford University Press).

Moss, B. H. (1988), 'Industrial Law Reform in an Era of Retreat: The Auroux Laws in France', *Work, Employment & Society*, 2:3, 317–34.

Möstl, M. (1999), *Grundrechtsbindung öffentlicher Wirtschaftstätigkeit. Insbesondere die Bindung der Nachfolgeunternehmen der Deutschen Bundespost an Art. 10 GG nach der Postreform II* (München: Beck'sche Verlagsbuchhandlung).

Mouriaux, R. (2010), *Le Syndicalisme en France* (Paris: Presses Universitaires de France).

Musgrave, R. A. and Musgrave, P. B. (1973), *Public Finance in Theory and Practice* (New York: McGraw-Hill).

NAO (2014), 'The Privatisation of Royal Mail', *National Audit Office* (1 April).

National Audit Office (2006), *Re-opening the Post: Postcomm and the Quality of Mail Services. Report by the Controller and Auditor General* HC 944 Session 2005–2006 (London: The Stationery Office).

National Audit Office (2009), *Department for Business, Enterprise and*

Regulatory Reform Oversight of the Post Office Network Change Programme HC 558 Session 2008–2009 (London: The Stationery Office).

National Commission of Audit (2014), *Towards Responsible Government. The Report of the National Commission of Audit. Phase One* (Canberra: Commonwealth of Australia, Australian Government).

National Competition Council (NCC) (1998), *Review of the Australian Postal Corporation Act* (Melbourne: National Competition Council).

National Federation of SubPostmasters (2012), *Ofcom – Review of Postal Users' Needs. Response from the National Federation of SubPostmasters* (West Sussex: National Federation of SubPostmasters).

Neate, R. (2013), 'Goldman Sachs and UBS to lead privatisation of Royal Mail. Government announces selection of Goldman Sachs and UBS to advise on Royal Mail's sale and collect majority of fees', *The Guardian* (29 May).

New Zealand Post (2013a), 'New Zealand Post seeks flexibility for the future', *New Zealand Post media release* (29 January).

New Zealand Post (2013b), *Review of Deed of Understanding between New Zealand Post Limited and the Government of New Zealand dated 17 February 1998. Proposal by New Zealand Post to Minister for Communications and Information Technology* (Wellington: New Zealand Post).

Newell, H. (2008), *Representativeness of the European social partner organizations: Post and courier services sector – United Kingdom* in Eurofound (ed.), Representativeness of the European social partner organizations: Post and courier services sector (Cologne: Institute for Economic and Social Research).

Nienhaus, L. and Siedenbiedel, C. (2009), 'Viele Briefe verspätet. Mit der Deutschen Bummel-Post', *Frankfurter Allgemeine Zeitung* (30 August).

Nixon, R. (2013), 'Postal service is still losing money, but not quite as much', *The New York Times* (9 August).

Nölke, A. and Claar, S. (2013), 'Varieties of capitalism in emerging economies', *Transformation*, 81/82, 33–54.

Nölke, A., May, C. and Claar, S. (eds) (2014), *Die großen Schwellenländer. Ursachen und Folgen ihres Aufstiegs in der Weltwirtschaft* (Wiesbaden: Springer).

North, G. (1995), *Die Post. Ihre Geschichte in Wort und Bild* (Heidelberg: R.v. Decker's Verlag).

Novácek, J. and Kopecký, V. (1989), *Geschichte der Post* (Hanau: Dausien).

OECD (2005), *Designing Independent and Accountable Regulatory Authorities for High Quality Regulation* (Paris: Organisation for Economic Co-operation and Development).

Ofcom (2013a), *The Affordability of Universal Postal Services. Report on Findings* (London: Office of Communications).

Ofcom (2013b), *Review of Postal Users' Needs. An Assessment of The Reasonable Needs of Users in Relation to the Market for the Provision of Postal Services in the United Kingdom* (London: Office of Communications).

Offe, C. (1985a), 'The Attribution of Public Status to Interest Groups', in Keane, J. (ed.), *Disorganized Capitalism: Contemporary Transformations of Work and Politics* (Oxford: Polity), pp. 221–58.

Offe, C. (1985b), 'Legitimation Through Majority Rule?', in Keane, J. (ed.), *Disorganized Capitalism: Contemporary Transformations of Work and Politics* (Oxford: Polity), pp. 259–99.

Ogus, A. (2004), 'W(h)iter the Economic Theory of Regulation? What Economic Theory of Regulation?', in Jordana, J. and Levi-Faur, D. (eds), *The Politics of Regulation. Institutions and Regulatory Reforms for the Age of Governance* (Cheltenham, UK, and Northampton, MA: Edward Elgar), pp. 31–44.

Ogus, A. I. (1994), *Regulation: Legal Form and Economic Theory* (Oxford: Clarendon Press).

Okholm, H. B. and Möller, A. (2012), 'Liberalization and Postal Workers', in Crew, M. A. and Kleindorfer, P. R. (eds), *Multi-modal Comptetion and the Future of Mail* (Cheltenham, UK, and Northampton, MA: Edward Elgar), pp. 247–64.

Olson, M. (1965), *The Logic of Collectice Action* (Cambridge, MA and London: Harvard University Press).

OPEL (2006), *Rapport sur les autorités administratives indépendantes par M. Patrice Gélard, Sénateur* (Paris: Office Parlementaire d'Évaluation de la Législation, Assemblée Nationale).

Oxera (2007), *Funding universal service obligations in the postal sector* (Oxford, Brussels, London: Oxera Consultancy).

Panzar, J. C. (2012), 'Towards a 21st Century Postal Service', in Crew, M. A. and Kleindorfer, P. R. (eds), *Multi-modal Comptetion and the Future of Mail* (Cheltenham, UK, and Northampton, MA: Edward Elgar), pp. 139–49.

Parti Socialiste (2012), 'Rencontre avec l'intersyndicale de La Poste: François Hollande apporte des garanties aux partenaires sociaux', *Press Release Presidential Elections 2012* (27 March 2012).

Patel, K. K. (2013), 'Provincialising European Union: Co-operation and Integration in Europe in a Historical Perspective', *Contemporary European History*, 22:4, 649–73.

Paterson, C. (2008), 'Postal Reform in Australia', in Crew, M. A., Kleindorfer, P. R. and Campbell, J. I. (eds), *Handbook of Worldwide Postal Reform* (Cheltenham, UK, and Northampton, MA: Edward Elgar), pp. 388–99.

Peebles, G. and Wilson, P. (1996), *The Singapore Economy* (Cheltenham, UK, and Northampton, MA,: Edward Elgar).

Pernot, J.-M. (2010), *Syndicats: lendemains de crise?* (Paris: Gallimard).

Peston, R. (2008), *Who runs Britain?* (London: Hodder & Stoughton).

Petel, Y. (1996), 'The New Regulatory Framework in France: Assessments and Prospects', in Stumpf, U. and Plum, M. (eds), *Diffusion of New Regulatory Approaches in the Postal Sector* (Königswinter: Wissenschaftliches Institut für Kommunikationsdienste), pp. 33–42.

Pierson, P. (1994), *Dismantling the Welfare State? Reagan, Thatcher, and the Politics of Retrenchment* (Cambridge: Cambridge University Press).

Pierson, P. (2000), 'Increasing Returns, Path Dependence, and the Study of Politics', *American Political Science Review*, 94:2, 251–67.

Pierson, P. (ed.) (2001), *The New Politics of the Welfare State* (Oxford: Oxford University Press).

Pietralunga, C. (2013), 'Philippe Wahl, nouveau patron de La Poste', *Le Monde* (1 August).

Pilling, D. (2005), 'Koizumi calls snap poll over reform vote', *Financial Times* (8 August).

PIU (2000), *Counter Revolution: Modernising the Post Office Network* (London: Cabinet Office, Performance and Innovation Unit).

Plagemann, J. (1996), 'Der rechtlich-institutionelle Rahmen des Postmarktes in der Bundesrepublic Deutschland', in Berger, H. and Knauth, P. (eds), *Liberalisierung und Regulierung der Postmärkte* (Munich and Vienna: R. Oldenbourg Verlag), pp. 51–90.

Polanyi, K. (1957), *The Great Transformation. The Political and Economic Origins of Our Time* (Boston: Beacon Press).

Pollack, M. A. (2002), 'Learning from the Americanists (Again): Theory and Method in the Study of Delegation', *West European Politics*, 25:1, 200–19.

Porges, A. and Leong, J. M. (2006), 'The Privatization of Japan Post. Ensuring both a Viable Post and a Level Playing Field', *Progress Toward Liberalization of the Postal and Delivery Sector* (New York: Springer), pp. 385–400.

Post Office (2013), *The Post Office Network Report 2012* (London: The Post Office).

Post & Parcel (2011a), 'Brazil's Postal Reforms Becomes Law, as Strikes Continue' (20 September).

Post & Parcel (2011b), 'Postal Reform Law Gains Approval in Brazil's Congress' (22 August).

Postal Heritage Trust (2005), 'The history of the Post Office: Key dates', *The British Postal Museum & Archive.*

Postbank (2013), *Sustainability Report* (Bonn: Deutsche Post AG).

Postcomm (2001), *Post Offices, Customers and Communities: Postcomm's First Annual Report on the Network of Post Offices: 2000–2001* (London: Postal Services Commission).

Postcomm (2005), *Giving Customers Choice: A Fully Open Postal Services Market. A Decision Document* (London: Postal Services Commission).

Postcomm (2009), *Postcomm's Ninth Annual Report on the Network of Post Offices in the UK 2008/2009* (London: Postal Services Commission).

Postcomm (2011), *The Building Blocks for a Sustainable Postal Service Universal Service – Discussion Paper on Affordability* (London: Postal Services Commission).

Prévot, H. (1989), *Rapport de Synthèse* (Paris: PTE Ministry).

PricewaterhouseCoopers (1997), *Employment Trends in the European Postal Sector* (Sint-Stevens-Woluwe: PricewaterhouseCoopers Enterprise Advisory).

PricewaterhouseCoopers (2006), *The Impact on Universal Service of the Full Market Accomplishment of the Postal Internal Market in 2009* (Sint-Stevens-Woluwe: PricewaterhouseCoopers Enterprise Advisory).

Priestman, M. (2003), 'Sawyer's one year review', *The Business* (28 June).

Prime Minister (1991), *The Citizen's Charter. Raising the Standard* (London: HMSO).

Prosser, T. (2000), 'Public Service Law: Privatization's Unexpected Offspring', *Law and Contemporary Problems*, 63:4, 63–82.

Prosser, T. (2005), *The Limits of Competition Law. Markets and Public Services* (Oxford: Oxford University Press).

Prosser, T. (2006), 'Regulation and Social Solidarity', *Journal of Law and Society*, 33:3, 364–87.

Prosser, T. (2010), 'Models of Economic and Social Regulation', in Oliver, D., Prosser, T. and Rawlings, R. (eds), *The Regulatory State: Constitutional Implications* (Oxford: Oxford University Press), pp. 34–49.

Protecting Postal Services (PPS) (1994), *Freedom to Deliver. Commercial Freedom for the Post Office in the Public Sector*, Post Office Review (London: Centurion Press).

Ramboll (2002), *Employment Trends in the Postal Sector. Final Report to DG Internal Market* (Aarhus: PLS Ramboll Management).

Ranganathan, V. (2008), 'India Post: An Agenda for Restructuring and Commercialization', in Crew, M. A., Kleindorfer, P. R. and Campbell, J. I. (eds), *Handbook of Worldwide Postal Reform* (Cheltenham, UK, and Northampton, MA: Edward Elgar), pp. 416–25.

RegTP (2004), *Annual Report 2003* (Bonn: Regulierungsbehörde für Telekommunikation und Post. Press and Public Relations Section).

Reiss Rubinstein, D. (2009), 'Agency Accountability Strategies After Liberalization: Universal Service in the United Kingdom, France, and Sweden', *Law & Policy*, 31:1, 111–41.

Reynaud, J.-D., Dassa, S., Dassa, J. et al. (1971), 'Les évènements de mai et juin 1968 et le système français de relations professionnelles', *Sociologie du Travail*, 1, 73–97.

Ricard, P. (2007a), 'Bruxelles donne neuf mois à Paris pour ouvrir à la concurrence la distribution du Livret A', *Le Monde* (10 May).

Ricard, P. (2007b), 'Pas de compromis sur la libéralisation des postes', *Le Monde* (6 June).

Ricard, P. and Michel, A. (2007), 'Bercy s'oppose à Bruxelles sur le Livret A', *Le Monde* (10 May).

Richardson, J. (2012), 'New Governance or Old Governance? A Policy Style Perspective', in Levi-Faur, D. (ed.), *Oxford Handbook of Governance* (Oxford: Oxford University Press), pp. 311–24.

Risse, T., Cowles, M. G. and Caporaso J. (eds) (2001), *Transforming Europe. Europeanization and Domestic Change* (Ithaca and London: Cornell University Press).

Rocard, M. (1988), 'Discours de politique générale' (29 June).

Rodrigues, S. (2002), 'The French Postal Sector: Old Mission, New Challenges', in Geradin, D. (ed.), *The Liberalization of Postal Services in the European Union* (The Hague: Kluwer Law International), pp. 237–58.

Rodriguez, F. (2013), 'The Postal Economy in the UK and Rutgers CRRI Conferences since 1990: a review of developments and economic themes', in Crew, M. A. and Kleindoerfer, P. R. (eds), *Reforming the Postal Sector in the Face of Electronic Competition* (Cheltenham, UK, and Northampton, MA: Edward Elgar), pp. 375–92.

Röhm, U. and Voigt, W. (2007), *Das Lohndumping-Kartell. Großverlage bekämpfen den Post-Mindestlohn* (Hamburg: VSA Verlag).

Säcker, F. J. (2007), *Soziale Schutzstandards im Postregulierungsrecht. Rechtsgutachten erstattet der Bundesnetzagentur für Elektrizität, Gas, Telekommunikation, Post und Eisenbahn* (Berlin: Institut für Deutsches und Europäisches Wirtschafts- Wettbewerbs- und Regulierungsrecht der Freien Universität Berlin).

Sandholtz, W. (1992), *High-Tech Europe: The Politics of International Cooperation* (Berkeley: University of California Press).

Sandholtz, W. (1998), 'The Emergence of a Supranational Telecommunications Regime', in Sandholtz, W. and Stone Sweet, A. (eds), *European Integration and Supranational Governance* (Oxford: Oxford University Press), pp. 134–63.

Sandholtz, W. and Zysmans, J. (1989), '1992: Recasting the European Bargain', *World Politics*, 42:1, 95–128.

Sauter, W. (1998), 'Universal Service Obligations and the Emergence of Citzen's Rights in European Telecommunications Liberalization', in Freedland, M. and Sciarra, S. (eds), *Public Services and Citzenship in European Law. Public and Labour Law Perspectives* (Oxford: Clarendon Press), pp. 117–43.

Savary, G. (2005), *L'Europe, va-t-elle démanteler les services publics?* (La Tour d'Aigues: Éditions de l'Aube).

Sbragia, A. (2000), 'Governance, The State, and the Market: What is going on?', *Governance*, 13:2, 243–50.

Schaub, C. (2013), 'Wahl, un banquier pour faire le tri. Le successeur de Jean-Paul Bailly va devoir adapter la Poste à la baisse du courrier', *La Libération* (2 August).

Schelkle, W. (2006), 'The theory and practice of economic governance in EMU revisited: What have we learnt about commitment and credibility?', *Journal of Common Market Studies*, 44:4, 669–85.

Scheurle, K.-D. and Mayen, T. (eds) (2002), *Telekommunikationsgesetz (TKG)* (München: C. H. Beck).

Schmid, B. (2008), 'Razzia bei Post-Chef Zumwinkel – Haftbefehl vorbereitet', *Der Spiegel* (14 February).

Schmidt, S. K. (1998), *Liberalisierung in Europa. Die Rolle der Europäischen Kommission* (Frankfurt/Main and New York: Campus).

Schmidt, S. K. (2005), 'Reform in the Shadow of Community Law: Highly regualted economic sectors', *German Politics*, 14:2, 157–73.

Schmidt, V. (2002), *The Futures of European Capitalism* (Oxford: Oxford University Press).

Schmidt, V. (2005), 'The Europeanization of National Economies?', in Lequesne, C. and Bulmer, S. (eds), *The Member States of the European Union* (Oxford: Oxford University Press), pp. 260–87.

Schmidt, V. (2008), 'European Political Economy: Labour Out, State Back In, Firm to the Fore', *West European Politics*, 31:1–2, 302–20.

Schmitter, P. (1991), 'From National Corporatism to Transnational Pluralism: Organized Interests in the Single European Market', *Politics & Society*, 19:2, 133–64.

Schmitter, P. and Streeck, W. (1985), *Private Interest Government: Beyond Market and State* (London: Sage).

Schmitter, P. C. (1974), 'Still the Century of Corporatism?', *The Review of Politics*, 36:1, 85–131.

Schmitter, P. C. and Lehmbruch, G. (eds) (1979), *Trends toward Corporatist Intermediation* (London: Sage).

Schneider, Dang-Nguyen, V.G. and Werle, R. (1994), 'Corporate Actor Networks in European Policy-Making: Harmonizing Telecommunications Policy', *Journal of Common Market Studies*, 32:4, 473–95.

Schneider, V. (2001), 'Institutional Reform in Telecommunications: The European Union in Transnational Policy Diffusion', in Green Cowles, M., Caporaso, J. and Risse, T. (eds), *Transforming Europe. Europeanization and Domestic Change* (Ithaca and London: Cornell University Press), pp. 60–78.

Schneider, V. (2002), 'The Institutional Transformation of Telecommunications between Europeanization and Globalization', in Jordana, J. (ed.), *Governing Telecommunications and the New Information Society in Europe* (Cheltenham, UK, and Northampton, MA: Edward Elgar), pp. 27–46.

Schneider, V. and Werle, R. (1990), 'International Regime or Corporate Actor? The European Community in Telecommunications Policy', in Dyson, K. and Humphreys, P. (eds), *The Political Economy of Telecommunications* (London and New York: Routledge), pp. 77–106.

Schneider, V. and Werle, R. (2007), 'Telecommunications Policy', in Graziano, P. V. and Maarten, P. (eds), *Europeanization. New Research Agendas.* (Basingstoke: Palgrave Macmillan), pp. 266–80.

Schrader-Frechette, K. S. (1991), *Risk and Rationality: Philosophical Foundations for Populist Reforms* (Berkeley: University of California Press).

Schwarz-Schilling, C. (2001), 'The Regulatory Framework for the Postal Markets in Germany', in Crew, M. A. and Kleindoerfer, P. R. (eds), *Future Directions in Postal Reform* (Boston, Dordrecht and London: Kluwer Academic Publishers), pp. 181–93.

Schweitzer, H. (2001), *Daseinsvorsorge, 'service public', Universaldienst. Art. 86 Abs. 2 EG-Vertrag und die Liberalisierung in den Sektoren Telekommunikation, Energie und Post* (Baden-Baden: Nomos).

Selznick, P. (1985), 'Focusing Organizational Research on Regulation', in Noll, R. G. (ed.), *Regulatory Policy and the Social Sciences* (Berkeley and Los Angeles: University of California Press), pp. 363–7.

Shonfield, A. (1965), *Modern Capitalism: The Changing Balance of Public and Private Power* (Oxford: Oxford University Press).

Siedenbiedel, C. (2007), 'Post schafft neue Kleinstfilialen in Geschäften', *Frankfurter Allgemeine Zeitung* (20 June).

Simpson, S. (2009), 'Supranationalization through Institutionalization and its Limits in European Telecommunications', *Information, Communication & Society*, 12:8, 1224–41.

SingPost (2006), *Submission to the Info-communications Development Authority of Singapore IDA. Consultation Paper on further Liberalisation of the Postal Services Sector in Singapore* (Singapore: Singapore Post Limited).

Smith, A. D. (1986), 'State-Making and Nation-Building', in Hall, J. A. (ed.), *States in History* (New York: Basil Blackwell), pp. 228–63.

Smith, M. P. (2001), 'In Pursuit of Selective Liberalization: Single Market Competition and its Limits', *Journal of European Public Policy*, 8:4, 519–40.

Smith, M. P. (2005a), 'Delayed Delivery: Postal Services Liberalization in Comparative Context', in Smith, M. P., *States of Liberalization. Redefining the Public Sector in Integrated Europe* (Albany, NY: State University of New York Press), pp. 107–44.

Smith, M. P. (2005b), *States of Liberalization. Redefining the Public Sector in Integrated Europe* (Albany, NY: State University of New York Press).

Soriano, L. M. (2005), 'Public Services. The Role of the European Court of Justice in correcting the market', in Héritier, A. and Coen, D. (eds), *Refining Regulatory Regimes. Utilities in Europe* (Cheltenham, UK, and Northampton, MA: Edward Elgar), pp. 183–211.

Spiegel (2007a), 'Niederlage für die Post. Bundesregierung schafft Briefmonopol ab' (24 April).

Spiegel (2007b), 'Pin Group geht beim Kartellamt gegen Mindestlohn vor' (6 December).

Spiegel (2007c), 'Postmarkt. Briefträger verdienen mehr als Mindestlohn' (21 May 2007).

Spiegel (2007d), 'Streit um Mindestlohn. Post streicht Springer-Verlag die Werbeanzeigen' (14 October).

Spiegel (2008a), 'Bundesregierung wehrt sich gegen Mindestlohn-Stopp' (18 December).

Spiegel (2008b), 'Verdacht auf Bestechlichkeit. Ver.di will neue Post-Gewerkschaft anzeigen' (10 March).

Spiegel (2014), 'Beschluss im Bundestag: Deutschland bekommt den Mindestlohn' (3 July).

Starr, P. (1990), 'The New Life of the Liberal State: Privatization and the Restructuring of State-Society Relations', in Suleiman, E. N. and Waterbury, J. (eds), *The Political Economy of Public Sector Reform and Privatization* (Boulder, San Francisco and Oxford: Westview Press), pp. 22–54.

Steele, I. (1991), 'Comments', in Crew, M. A. and Kleindoerfer, P. R. (eds), *Competition and Innovation in Postal Services* (Boston, Dordrecht and London: Kluwer Academic Publishers), pp. 283–5.

Stewart, H. (2011), 'From New Coke to Consignia: brands consigned to the dustbin of history. BlackBerry is not the first firm to suffer a serious brand meltdown. Here are some other memorable examples', *The Guardian* (16 October).

Stigler, G. J. (1971), 'The Theory of Economic Regulation', *The Bell Journal of Economics and Management Science*, 2:1, 3–21.

Storn, A. (2007), 'Verlogener Streit um die Post. Ein Zwischenruf', *Die Zeit* (8 February).

Streeck, W. (2006), 'The Study of Organized Interests: Before "The Century" and after', in Crouch, C. and Streeck, W. (eds), *The Diversity of Democracy. Corporatism, Social Order and Political Conflict* (Cheltenham, UK, and Northampton, MA: Edward Elgar), pp. 3–45.

Streeck, W. (2009), *Re-Forming Capitalism. Institutional Change in the German Political Economy* (Oxford: Oxford University Press).

Streeck, W. and Thelen, K. (eds) (2005a), *Beyond Continuity: Institutional Change in Advanced Political Economies* (Oxford: Oxford University Press).

Streeck, W. and Thelen, K. (2005b), 'Introduction: Institutional Change in Advanced Political Economies', in Streeck, W. and Thelen, K. (eds), *Beyond Continuity: Institutional Change in Advanced Political Economies* (Oxford: Oxford University Press), pp. 1–39.

SUD-PTT (2013), 'Un nouveau patron, et après?', Press Release published by the Tradion Union Solidary, Unitary and Democratic (August).

Sueddeutsche (2007a), 'Deutsche Post. Neuer Wirbel um Briefmonopol' (22 March).

Sueddeutsche (2007b), 'Eilverfahren beim Kartellamt. Pin will Post-Mindestlohn stoppen' (6 December).

Tellier, H. (2010), 'Convention collective des activités postales: un enjey de taille pour toute la profession', *La Fédération. CGT-FAPT*, 514 (September), 5–7.

De Villepin, D. (2005), 'Discours de politique générale', *Portail du Gouvernement* (8 June).

Thanh Ha, T. (2014) 'Canada Post rolls out first wave of door-to-door delivery cuts', *The Globe and Mail* (20 October).

Thanh Ha, T. and Mahoney, J. (2014), 'Canada Post reveals first postal codes to lose home mail delivery', *The Globe and Mail* (20 February).

Thatcher, M. (1999), *The Politics of Telecommunications. National Institutions, Convergence and Change in Britain and France* (Oxford: Oxford University Press).

Thatcher, M. (2001), 'The Commission and National Governments as Partners: EC Regulatory Expansion in Telecommunications 1979–2000', *Journal of European Public Policy*, 8:4, 558–84.

Thatcher, M. (2002), 'Delegation to Independent Regulatory Agencies: Pressures, Functions and Contextual Mediation', *West European Politics*, 25:1, 127–47.

Thatcher, M. (2004a), 'Varieties of Capitalism in an Internationalised World. Domestic Institutional Change in European Telecommunications', *Comparative Political Studies*, 37:7, 751–80.

Thatcher, M. (2004b), 'Winners and Losers in Europeanization: Reforming the National Regulation of Telecommunications', *West European Politics*, 27:2, 102–27.

Thatcher, M. (2007a), *Internationalisation and Economic Institutions. Comparing European Experiences* (Oxford: Oxford University Press).

Thatcher, M. (2007b), 'Liberalising the Letter: The Reform of Postal Services', *Internationalisation and Economic Institutions. Comparing European Experiences* (Oxford: Oxford University Press), pp. 235–50.

Thatcher, M. (2007c), 'Reforming National Regulatory Institutions: the EU and Cross-National Variety in European Network Industries', in Hancké, B., Rhodes, M. and Thatcher, M. (eds), *Beyond Varieties of Capitalism. Conflict, Contradictions, and Complementarities in the European Economy* (Oxford: Oxford University Press), pp. 147–72.

Thatcher, M. (2007d), 'Regulatory Agencies, the State and Markets: A Franco-British Comparison', *Journal of European Public Policy*, 14:7, 1028–47.

Thatcher, M. (2011), 'The Creation of European Regulatory Agencies and its Limits: a Comparative Analysis of European Delegation', *Journal of European Public Policy*, 18:6, 790–809.

Thatcher, M. and Coen, D. (2008), 'Reshaping European Regulatory Space: An Evolutionary Analysis', *West European Politics*, 31:4, 806–36.

Thatcher, M. and Stone Sweet, A. (2002), 'Theory and Practice of Delegation to Non-Majoritarian Institutions', *West European Politics*, 25:1, 1–22.

Thelen, K. (1999), 'Historical Institutionalism in Comparative Politics', *Annual Review of Political Science*, 2, 369–404.

Thibault, B. (2002), *Qu'est-ce que la CGT* (Paris: L'Archipel).

TNT (2006), 'Momentum Grows for Major Postal Operators Backing EU Liberalisation plan' (17 October).

Todd, P. (1980), 'The Employment Act 1980: Anti-Union Law Today, or Merely a Gateway to Harsher Measures Tomorrow?', *British Journal of Law and Society*, 7:2, 275–86.

Toime, E. (1991), 'Competitive Strategy for New Zealand Post', in Crew, M. A. and Kleindoerfer, P. R. (eds), *Competition and Innovation in Postal Services* (Boston, Dordrecht and London: Kluwer Academic Publishers), pp. 275–82.

Towers, B. (1989), 'Running the Gauntlet: British Trade Unions under Thatcher, 1979–1988', *Industrial and Labor Relations Review*, 42:2, 163–88.

Trade and Industry Committee (1994), *The Post Office. Third Report with Proceedings, Evidence and Memoranda, HC 170 1994/95* (London: House of Commons).

Trade and Industry Committee (1998), *The Post Office, Third Report with Proceedings, Evidence and Appendices, HC 380 1997/98* (London: House of Commons).

Traxler, F., Blaschke, S. and Kittel, B. (2001), *National Labour Relations in Internationalized Markets. A Comparative Study of Institutions, Change and Performance* (Oxford: Oxford University Press).

Trocki, C. A. (2006), *Singapore. Wealth, Power and the Culture of Control* (London and New York: Routledge).

Trumbull, G. (2006), *Consumer Capitalism. Politics, Product Markets, and Firm Strategy in France and Germany* (Ithaca and London: Cornell University Press).

UCW (1993), *Protecting Postal Services – Potential Threats. Post Office Unions' Submission on the Future of the Post Office* (London: Union of Communication Workers).

UCW (1994), *Stand by your Post* (London: Union of Communication Workers).

UPU (2007), *Promoting Investment in the Postal Sector as a Means of Achieving the Millennium Development Goals. Guide for Member Countries* (Berne: Universal Postal Union International Bureau).

UPU (2014), *Postal Statistics. Global or Regional Estimates* (Berne: Universal Postal Union International Bureau).

Ver.di (2007), 'Postdienste. Bundesnetzagentur muss Postdienstleister kontrollieren', *Press Release Vereinte Dienstleistungsgewerkschaft* (17 August).

Verdin, M. (2002), 'Consignia: nine letters that spelled fiasco', *BBC News* (31 May).

Vezinat, N. (2008), 'La poste entre service public et marché', *La Vie des Idées* (22 September).

Villepin, D. de (2005), 'Discours de politique générale', *Portail du Gouvernement* (8 June)

Viscusi, K. W. (1983), *Risk by Choice: Regulating Health and Safety in the Workplace* (Cambridge, MA and London: Harvard University Press).

Visser, J. (2006), 'Union membership statistics in 24 countries', *Monthly Labor Review* (January), 38–49.

Vogel, S., Stettes, O., Beese, B. et al. (2008), 'Germany', in Eurofound (ed.), *Representativeness of the European Social Partner Organizations: Post and courier Services Sector* (Cologne: Institute for Economic and Social Research).

Vogel, S. K. (1996), *Freer Markets, More Rules. Regulatory Reform in Advanced Industrial Countries* (Ithaca and London: Cornell University Press).

Wachter, M. L., Hirsch, B. T. and Gillula, J. W. (2001), 'Difficulties of Deregulation When Wage Costs are the Major Costs', in Crew, M. A. and Kleindorfer, P. R. (eds), *Future Directions in Postal Reform* (Boston, Dordrecht and London: Kluwer Academic Publishers), pp. 3–24.

Wachter, M. L. and Perloff, J. M. (1991), 'A Comparative Analysis of Wage Premiums and Industrial Relations in the British Post Office and the United States Postal Service', in Crew, M. A. and Kleindorfer, P. R. (eds), *Competition and Innovation in Postal Services* (Boston, Dordrecht and London: Kluwer Academic Publishers), pp. 115–37.

Walsh, T. (2012), 'Royal Mail 1986–2010' (London, unpublished).

Walsh, T. (2013), 'Economic Regulation and the UK Postal Sector, 2000–2011', in Crew, M. A. and Kleindoerfer, P. R. (eds), *Reforming the Postal Sector in the Face of Electronic Competition* (Cheltenham, UK, and Northampton, MA: Edward Elgar), pp. 322–35.

Wanner, C., Marschall, B. and Ehrlich, P. (2007), 'Berliner Brieffreunde', *Financial Times Deutschland* (21 January).

Weiss, L. (2003a), 'Introduction: Bringing Domestic Institutions Back in', in Weiss, L. (ed.), *States in the Global Economy. Bringing Domestic Institutions Back In* (Cambridge: Cambridge University Press), pp. 1–33.

Weiss, L. (ed.) (2003b), *States in the Global Economy: Bringing Domestic Institutions Back In* (Cambridge: Cambridge University Press).

Welt (2000), 'Streit um Postmonopol entbrannt' (12 May).

Wendel, T. H. (2000), 'Chefregulierer Scheurle erklärt seinen Rücktritt', *Berliner Zeitung* (24 November).

WIK-Consult (2004), *Main developments in the European Postal Sector. Study for the European Commission DG Internal Market* (Bad Honnef: Wissenschaftliches Institut für Kommunikationsdienste).

WIK-Consult (2007), *Arbeitsbedingungen im Briefmarkt* WIK Diskussionsbeiträge no. 295 (Bad Honnef, Bonn: Wissenschaftliches Institut für Infrastruktur und Kommunikationsdienste (WIK)).

WIK-Consult (2009a), *Nachfrage von Postdienstleistungen von Geschäftskunden* (Bad Honnef: Wissenschaftliches Institut für Kommunikationsdienste).

WIK-Consult (2009b), *The Role of Regulators in a More Competitive Postal Market* (Bad Honnef: Wissenschaftliches Institut für Kommunikationsdienste).

WIK-Consult (2013a), *Main Developments in the Postal Sector (2010–2013). Country Reports. Study for the European Commission, Directorate General for Internal Market and Services* (Bad Honnef: Wissenschaftliches Institut für Kommunikationsdienste).

WIK-Consult (2013b), *Main Developments in the Postal Sector (2010–2013). Study for the European Commission, Directorate General for Internal Market and Services* (Bad Honnef: Wissenschaftliches Institut für Kommunikationsdienste).

Willman, P., Coen, D., Currie, D. et al. (2003), 'The Evolution of Regulatory Relationships: Regulatory Institutions and Firm Behavior in Privatized Industries', *Industrial and Corporate Change*, 12:1, 69–89.

Windisch, R. (1987), *Privatisierung natürlicher Monopole im Bereich von Bahn, Post und Telekommunikation* (Tübingen: Mohr Siebeck Verlag).

Wintour, P. and Webb, T. (2009), 'Peter Mandelson Abandons Plan for Part-Privatisation of Royal Mail', *The Guardian* (1 July).

Wirtschaftswoche (2007a), 'Kurth kritisiert Deutsche Post' (27 February).

Wirtschaftswoche (2007b), 'Post kontra Springer' (8 September).

Wissmann, M. ed. (2003), *Telecommunications Law. A Practitioner's Guide in German and English with new EU-Framework* (Heidelberg: Verlag Recht und Wirtschaft GmbH).

Wong, C. H. (2014), 'Alibaba to Buy Stake in Singapore Post', *The Wall Street Journal* (28 May).

Wonka, A. and Rittberger, B. (2010), 'Credibility, Complexity and Uncertainty: Explaining the Institutional Independence of 29 EU Agencies', *West European Politics*, 33:4, 730–52.

World Bank (2003), 'India: Challenges and Opportunities for India Post in a New Environment. Press Release No:2003/139/SAR'.

Yamamura, K. and Streeck, W. (eds) (2003), *The End of Diversity? Prospects for German and Japanese Capitalism* (Ithaca and London: Cornell University Press).

Young, A. R. (2010), 'The Single Market. Deregulation, Reregulation and Integration', in Wallace, H., Pollack, M. A. and Young, A. R. (eds), *Policy-Making in the European Union* (Oxford: Oxford University Press), pp. 107–31.

Zeit (1997), 'Aufruhr im Amt. Die Postler laufen gegen die Öffnung des Briefmarktes Sturm' (21 February).

Index

Note: page numbers in italic refer to figures and tables